Calvin
in
Context

† † † †

David C. Steinmetz

New York   Oxford
OXFORD UNIVERSITY PRESS
1995

Oxford University Press

Oxford   New York
Athens   Auckland   Bangkok
Calcutta   Cape Town   Dar es Salaam   Delhi
Florence   Hong Kong   Istanbul   Karachi
Kuala Lumpur   Madras   Madrid   Melbourne
Mexico City   Nairobi   Paris   Singapore
Taipei   Tokyo   Toronto

and associated companies in
Berlin   Ibadan

Published by Oxford University Press, Inc.
198 Madison Avenue, New York, New York 10016

Oxford is a registered trademark of Oxford University Press, Inc.

Library of Congress Cataloging-in-Publication Data
Steinmetz, David Curtis.
Calvin in context / David Steinmetz.
p.   cm.   Includes bibliographical references and index.
ISBN 0-19-509164-7 (cloth). — ISBN 0-19-509165-5 (pbk.)
1. Calvin, Jean, 1509–1564.   2. Calvinism—History.
3. Reformation—History.   4. Reformed Church—Doctrines—
History—16th century.   I. Title.
BX9418.S698   1995
230'.42'092—dc20   94-39937

3 5 7 9 8 6 4 2

Printed in the United States of America
on acid-free paper

For Claire and Matthew

PREFACE

This book began with a request from the editors of *Interpretation* to write an essay on John Calvin's exposition of the prophet Isaiah. Although I taught a regularly scheduled seminar on Calvin, I had never written about him and was at the time deeply involved in Luther studies. Nevertheless, I welcomed the invitation to write on Calvin as a pleasant diversion from Luther research. After all, I reasoned, we sometimes see old issues in a clearer light if we take a vacation from them and occupy our minds with something new. So I plunged into Calvin studies like a tourist on an unexpected holiday, secure in the knowledge that, however far I wandered from familiar sights and sounds, I could in the end return safely home.

But Calvin studies began to exercise their own fascination for me and I turned back to them with increasing frequency. What especially engaged my imagination was Calvin's biblical exegesis. It is now common for Calvin scholars to assert that Calvin cannot be understood from the *Institutes* alone. All of his writings—his letters, treatises, and commentaries as well as successive editions of his *Institutes*—contribute to a right understanding of the man and his thought, and none can be omitted without real loss.

The commentaries in particular are important, not only because the sixteenth century witnessed an unprecedented explosion of biblical studies, but also because they provide an opportunity for comparative study that is difficult to achieve in any other way. After all, not every striking insight in Calvin's writings is original with him and not every opinion he expresses is a hard-won and deeply felt conviction. Like any Christian theologian of the sixteenth century, Calvin spends a good deal of his time repeating theological and exegetical commonplaces, none of which are seriously disputed by his theological critics. To be sure, Calvin phrases traditional ideas elegantly, briefly, and clearly—at times one might even say, luminously. But an elegantly phrased commonplace is still a commonplace. By reading what Calvin and his contemporaries read, by comparing one commentator with another, we are better able to distinguish Calvin's original insights from the ordinary traditions he repeats.

Calvin in Context attempts to illuminate Calvin's thought by placing it in the context of the theological and exegetical traditions—ancient, medieval, and contemporary—that formed it and gave it its particular texture. The range of issues it addresses is almost as wide as the Reformation itself. The book deals with such questions as the knowledge of God, the nature and extent of God's power, the influence of scholasticism, the role of law, the relation of the two testaments, the problem of iconoclasm, the quest for a more adequate exegetical methodology, the definition of sexual morality, the character of prophetic vision, the nature of the believing self, the authority of early Christian writers, the doctrines of justification and predestination, the sacraments of baptism and the eucharist, the place of monastic ideology, and the role of the state and the civil magistrate. Along the way, it attempts to clarify the substance of Calvin's quarrels with Lutherans, Catholics, Anabaptists, and assorted radicals from Ochino to Sozzini.

Although composed as a series of discrete essays, the book can serve as a general introduction to Calvin's thought. What sets it off from standard introductions to Calvin is the range of primary sources it engages and the method it develops. The context it provides for understanding Calvin is not a generalized picture of the later Middle Ages and Renaissance drawn from secondary literature, but a context provided by the writings of Calvin's own contemporaries and the rich sources on which they drew. No search for the historical Calvin will be successful if it abstracts him from the company of his contemporaries and leaves him alone and vulnerable in the company of historians.

Such a book could not have been written without access to the large collection of sixteenth-century biblical commentaries and theological treatises in the Herzog August Bibliothek in Wolfenbüttel, Germany. I am especially grateful to the National Endowment for the Humanities, the Forschungsbereich of the Herzog August Bibliothek, and the Duke University Research Council for generous grants that enabled me to spend the summers of 1986, 1988, 1990, and 1992 in the reading room of the Zeughaus in Wolfenbüttel surrounded by piles of rare and priceless books. Anyone who has spent time in the Herzog August Bibliothek knows how much scholars who work there owe to the remarkable former director, Professor Paul Raabe, and his knowledgeable staff. I am particularly indebted to Dr. Sabine Solf, the head of research, whose encouragement and flexibility made my stays in Wolfenbüttel more productive than I had any reason to hope they could have been.

Many of the essays in this book were first given as papers at the American Society of Church History, the Society of Biblical Literature, the Society for Reformation Research, the Verein für Reformationsgeschichte, the

Calvin Studies Society, and the Renaissance Society of America. Others were offered as lectures at Princeton Theological Seminary, Eden Theological Seminary, Concordia Theological Seminary (Ft. Wayne), Gettysburg Lutheran Theological Seminary, Waterloo Lutheran Theological Seminary, Hendrix College, Wheaton College, and the universities of Bonn, Geneva, and Arizona. I am grateful to my hosts on those occasions and to the audiences whose questions helped me think through issues that were incompletely formulated or confusingly stated. I am also grateful to Professors Susan E. Schreiner of the University of Chicago and Richard A. Muller of Calvin Theological Seminary, who read through the completed manuscript and offered helpful criticism. The mistakes that remain are, of course, all mine.

Durham, N.C.   D. C. S.
December 1994

ACKNOWLEDGMENTS

I am grateful to the following publishers for permission to make use of all or part of previously published essays. In every case the essays have been revised and updated.

"The Baptism of John and the Baptism of Jesus in Huldrych Zwingli, Balthasar Hubmaier, and Late Medieval Theology," in *Continuity and Discontinuity in Church History*. Festschrift for George H. Williams, ed. F. F. Church and T. George (Leiden: E.J. Brill, 1979): 169–81.

"John Calvin on Isaiah 6: A Problem in the History of Exegesis," *Interpretation* 36 (1982): 156–70.

"Calvin and Melanchthon on Romans 13:1–7," *Ex Auditu* 2 (1986): 74–81.

"Calvin and the Absolute Power of God," *Journal of Medieval and Renaissance Studies* 18 (1988): 65–79.

"Calvin and Abraham: The Interpretation of Romans 4 in the Sixteenth Century," *Church History* 57 (1988): 443–55.

"The Reformation and the Ten Commandments," *Interpretation* 43 (July, 1989): 256–66.

"Calvin and the Patristic Exegesis of Paul," in *The Bible in the Sixteenth Century*. Duke Monographs in Medieval and Renaissance Studies 11. (Durham, N.C. and London: Duke University Press, 1990): 100–118.

"Calvin and His Lutheran Critics," *The Lutheran Quarterly* 4(2) (Summer 1990): 179–94.

"Calvin and the Divided Self of Romans 7," in *Augustine, the Harvest, and Theology (1300–1650)*, ed. Kenneth G. Hagen (Leiden: E.J. Brill, 1990): 300–313.

"Calvin and the Natural Knowledge of God," in *Via Augustini: Augustine in the Later Middle Ages, Renaissance and Reformation*, ed. H. A. Oberman et al. (Leiden: E.J. Brill, 1991): 142–56.

"Calvin among the Thomists," in *Biblical Hermeneutics in Historical Perspective*, ed. M. S. Burrows and P. Rorem (Grand Rapids: Wm. B. Eerdmans, 1991): 198–214.

"Calvin and the Monastic Ideal," in *Anticlericalism in Late Medieval and Early Modern Europe*, ed. Peter A. Dykema and H. A. Oberman (Leiden: E.J. Brill, 1992): 605–16.

CONTENTS

ABBREVIATIONS

BoA   [Bonner Ausgabe] Luthers Werke in Auswahl, 6 vols. (Bonn and Berlin, 1912–)

CCh   Corpus Christianorum (Turnholt: Brepols)

CO   Ioannis Calvini Opera Quae Supersunt Omnia, 59 vols., ed. Wilhelm Baum, Eduard Cunitz, and Eduard Reuss (Brunswick and Berlin, 1863–1900)

CR   Corpus Reformatorum (Halle, Berlin, Brunswick, Leipzig, and Zurich, 1834–)

CSEL   Corpus Scriptorum Ecclesiasticorum Latinorum (Vienna, 1866–)

Denz.   Heinrich Denziger, *Enchiridion Symbolorum*, ed. 32 (Barcinone: Herder, 1963)

LCC   Library of Christian Classics (Philadelphia, 1953–)

OS   Ioannis Calvini Opera Selecta, 5 vols., ed. Peter Barth and Wilhelm Niesel (Munich, 1926–1936)

PG   Patrologia Graeca, ed. J. P. Migne (Paris, 1857–1912)

PL   Patrologia Latina, ed. J. P. Migne (Paris, 1844–1890)

SS   Huldrich Zwinglis Werke, 8 vols., ed. M. Schuler and J. Schulthess (Zurich, 1828–1842)

WA   D. Martin Luthers Werke: Kritische Gesamtausgabe (Weimar, 1883–)

ZW   Huldreich Zwinglis Sämtliche Werke, ed. E. Egli et al., Corpus Reformatorum, vols. 88– (Berlin, Leipzig, Zurich, 1905–)

TRANSLATIONS

Translations of Calvin, unless otherwise noted, are taken from:

Calvin's Commentaries, 47 vols. (Edinburgh, 1843–1859).

Calvin's Commentaries, ed. D. W. Torrance and T. F. Torrance. (Grand Rapids, Mich.: Wm. B. Eerdmans, 1959–   ).

Calvin's Tracts, 3 vols. (Edinburgh, 1844–1851).

Calvin: Institutes of the Christian Religion, 2 vols., ed. J. T. McNeill and F. L. Battles, LCC 20–21 (Philadelphia: Westminster Press, 1960). Abbreviated as *Inst*.

Institution of the Christian Religion, trans. F. L. Battles (Atlanta: John Knox Press, 1975).

Letters of John Calvin, 4 vols., ed. Henry Beveridge and Jules Bonnet (Philadelphia, 1858).

Calvin
in
Context

1

Introduction to Calvin

John Calvin was not a man who inspired immediate confidence in those who first met him.[1] In an age of dynamic and colorful personalities—from Martin Luther to Teresa of Avila—Calvin cut a curiously diminutive figure. He was a slight man, even in his youth, shy and bookish, never robust, plagued in his later years by a series of chronic illnesses that forced him at times to dictate his commentaries and treatises while propped up in bed. He was never more content than when he was left alone and spent some of his happiest years as pastor to a congregation of French refugees in the German city of Strasbourg. Yet there is no Protestant leader in the sixteenth century, with the obvious exception of Martin Luther, who left a more profound mark on Western culture than he did. For more than four hundred years Calvin has influenced the way successive generations of Europeans and Americans have thought about religion, structured their political institutions, looked at paintings, written poetry and music, theorized about economic relations, or struggled to uncover the laws which govern the physical universe.

Nowhere has Calvin's influence been more pervasive than in the English-speaking world. During Calvin's own lifetime his *Institutes of the Christian Religion* was translated into English by Thomas Norton and went through eleven editions by 1632. There were eighteen editions of Calvin's catechism by 1628. Even Arthur Golding's translation of Calvin's sermons on Job appeared in five editions between 1574 and 1584. The *Institutes* was retranslated into English in the nineteenth century by John Allen and Henry

Beveridge, and in the twentieth century by Ford Lewis Battles. The Calvin
Translation Society of Edinburgh published translations of all of Calvin's
commentaries in the mid-nineteenth century, while the New Testament
commentaries were redone in the mid-twentieth. The Old Testament commentaries are currently being retranslated in the Rutherford House edition.

Even more important than the translation and publication of Calvin's
works in English has been the role played in the English-speaking world
by Calvinist churchmen, theologians, politicians, and writers. Although it
is never possible to separate with great accuracy Calvin's influence on English
culture from the influence of his friends and allies—such as Martin Bucer,
Peter Martyr Vermigli, and Heinrich Bullinger—and while Calvinism has
remained a dynamic and changing movement to which later generations
have made original contributions undreamed of by Calvin himself, still it
is true that Calvin's direct influence on English life and thought has been
substantial. William Whittingham, later Dean of Durham, and John Knox,
later reformer of Scotland, studied in Geneva and led the English-speaking
congregation there. Although Edmund Grindal, who eventually became
the Archbishop of Canterbury under Elizabeth I, took refuge in Strasbourg
and John Jewel, destined to become Bishop of Salisbury, fled to Zurich,
Grindal became one of the most outspokenly Calvinist divines ever to hold
the see of Canterbury, while Jewel echoed the arguments of Calvin in
his *Apologie of the Church of England*. Even Archbishop William Whitgift,
whose distaste for Puritanism was legendary, remained a staunch Calvinist
in his views on predestination, as the Lambeth Articles of 1595 amply
demonstrate.

Calvin was, understandably enough, more interested in political devel-
opments in France than in England. Bullinger in Zurich had more English
contacts than Calvin and there is, in any event, nothing in Calvin's collected
letters to rival the more massive correspondence of the Zurich reformers
with Jewel, Pilkington, Parkhurst, Sandys, and Cox. Calvin did, however,
correspond with the young English king, Edward VI; with the Lord Protector, the Duke of Somerset, to whom he dedicated his commentary on
Timothy; with Somerset's daughter, Lady Anne Seymour; and with William Cecil, Elizabeth's chief minister. Several letters also passed between
Calvin and Archbishop Thomas Cranmer, approving, among other matters,
Cranmer's proposal for a synod to deal with the question of Protestant unity.

But the principal influence of Calvin on English thought came later, after
the reign of Edward VI. The return of the Marian exiles to England created
a climate favorable to the translation of Calvin's works into English. This
new infusion of Calvinist literature merged with the earlier streams of
Reformed theology introduced by Bucer at Cambridge and Peter Martyr
at Oxford. While the Puritan party in England was particularly susceptible

to influences from Geneva and Zurich, it would be a serious error of historical judgment to equate Puritanism with Calvinism. Calvinism was a more pervasive religious and intellectual movement than Puritanism, though Puritanism can be regarded as a special type of Calvinism. In England Calvinism touched anti-Puritans as well as Puritans, Anglicans as well as Dissenters, High Churchmen as well as Low.

This broadly based English Calvinist heritage was exported to the New World, where it found a home both in New England and in the colony of Virginia. Alexander Whitaker, the "Apostle of Virginia," carried Anglicanism in its Low Church, Calvinist form to the settlements along the James River, while John Robinson, a defender of the theological decisions of the Calvinist Synod of Dort, directed the founding of the Plymouth Plantation. This English Calvinist strain was strengthened by the Dutch Calvinists of New York and New Jersey, the German Reformed of Pennsylvania and Maryland, and the Scotch-Irish Presbyterians who settled in the mid-Atlantic and southern colonies. While not all settlers in the New World were Protestant and not all Protestants were Calvinist, nevertheless there was from the very beginning a strongly Calvinist influence on American thought and institutions. Calvinists founded universities, pioneered the New England town meeting, insisted on the separation of powers in the federal government, played a prominent role in the movement for the abolition of slavery, and even promoted such characteristic institutions of frontier revivalism as "the anxious bench" and the "camp-meeting." Calvinist and anti-Calvinist themes have recurred in American literature from the poetry of Michael Wigglesworth and Anne Bradstreet to the novels of Peter De Vries and John Updike.

In short, although Calvinism is not the only ingredient in American intellectual and religious history, it is such an important ingredient that no one can claim to understand American history and culture without some appreciation of its Calvinist heritage. Because Calvinism is deeply woven into the fabric of American cultural history, the study of the thought of John Calvin can never be for Americans a purely detached examination of an interesting aspect of European religious history in the sixteenth century. The pervasive influence of Calvinism in American life makes the study of Calvinism, to some extent at least, an exercise in self-understanding.

Calvin did not intend to devote his life to the study of theology. Indeed, Calvin belongs to that venerable company of lawyers, to which Thomas More, Theodore Beza, and Caspar Olevianus also belonged, who found themselves overtaken by events and were plunged from the study and practice of law into the middle of religious controversies. Calvin was born on July 10, 1509, in the north of France in the episcopal city of Noyon. His family name in French was Cauvin and Calvin's father, Gérard Cauvin, was a notary who had responsibility for conducting the legal affairs of the cathedral chapter in Noyon. Because Calvin was quick in his studies, he was taken into the home of the Montmor family for private tutoring and was sent at the age of fourteen with the Montmor children to Paris in order to study for the priesthood at the Collège de la Marche.[2] His education was to be financed by the income from certain benefices arranged through the patronage of the Bishop of Noyon.

Before Calvin could study theology, however, he had to earn a degree in the liberal arts and, before he could study for his B.A., he had to pass a series of preparatory linguistic and logical studies, designed to enable beginning students to understand advanced Latin lectures on philosophy proper. Because Mathurin Cordier, who usually taught the advanced class, was dissatisfied with the way the elementary class had been taught and so decided to take the beginning class himself, Calvin had the great fortune to be rigorously trained in Latin and rhetoric by one of the finest teachers at the university. It was a stroke of luck for which Calvin never forgot to be grateful.

Within a brief period of time, probably no more than a year, Calvin was judged ready to begin work in earnest for his degree in the liberal arts. He enrolled in the Collège de Montaigu, an institution very different in its ethos and discipline from the somewhat more loosely governed Collège de la Marche. Calvin must have felt on entering the Collège de Montaigu very much like Nicholas Nickleby when he first laid eyes on Dotheboys Hall in Yorkshire. Rabelais called it "that verminous college" where boys were subjected to "enormous cruelty and villainy."[3] It had been the college of Erasmus when he was a student in Paris, though at that time under the direction of the reformer, Standonck, who had embued it with the spirit of the Brethren of the Common Life. It was under Noel Beda when Calvin matriculated, a reactionary theologian who had made a certain reputation by attacking proponents of the New Learning such as Erasmus and Lefèvre d'Etaples. It even had its own Mr. Squeers, a certain M. Tempête, who lived up to the puns on his stormy name by beating malefactors for their offenses with a ferocious enthusiasm.

Calvin spent five years at Montaigu, where he studied philosophy with the Spaniard Antonio Coronel. Some historians have surmised that Calvin may have heard lectures on theology by the Scottish theologian and historian John Major.[4] Attempts have been made to draw a parallel between the influence of Gabriel Biel on Martin Luther and the supposed influence of Major on Calvin. However, there is no evidence that Calvin ever attended Major's lectures. He was, after all, in Paris to earn his arts degree and, while he planned to enter the priesthood, it is unlikely he would have attended lectures on theological subjects as an undergraduate. At any rate, Calvin took no degree in Paris beyond the M.A.

About 1528, or possibly earlier, Calvin's father suddenly changed the plans for his son and sent him instructions to withdraw from Paris and enroll at Orléans as a candidate for a degree in civil law. Calvin obeyed and spent the year studying law under the distinguished jurist Pierre de l'Estoile, and Greek under the Alsatian humanist Melchior Wolmar. Wolmar was not only a brilliant classical scholar, who had placed first at Paris in a class of one hundred; he was also a convinced Lutheran.

Theodore Beza in his *Life of Calvin* has left this picture of Calvin as a law student in Orléans:

> Some persons, still alive, who were then on familiar terms with him, say, that, at that period, his custom was, after supping very frugally, to continue his studies until midnight, and on getting up in the morning, to spend some time meditating, and, as it were, digesting what he had read in bed, and that while so engaged, he was very unwilling to be interrupted. By these prolonged vigils he no doubt acquired solid learning, and an excellent memory; but it is probable he also contracted that weakness of stomach, which afterwards brought on various diseases, and ultimately led to his untimely death.[5]

Calvin continued his legal studies at Bourges, where the Italian jurist, Andreas Alciati, had been persuaded to accept a chair by the offer of a magnificent stipend. Alciati claimed to have written his first legal book at the age of fifteen, a study of the Greek words in the *Digesta*. Whether that claim was true or not, Alciati's flamboyant lecture style and his application of the methods of the textual critic to the study and interpretation of the law made him an important figure in the world of French jurisprudence. Although Calvin did not altogether approve of Alciati's extravagant rhetoric or of his attacks on the legal faculty at Orléans, he did learn an approach to the explication of a legal text that could, with certain modifications, be employed in the exposition of Scripture.

In 1531 Calvin's father became seriously ill and Calvin returned as quickly as he could to Noyon. He arrived to find that both his father and his brother, Charles, were under a sentence of excommunication. Gérard had quarreled with the cathedral chapter and Charles had, as a consequence, handled two of the officials of the chapter less gently than their dignity demanded. When Gérard died on May 26, 1531, it was only with some difficulty that Charles persuaded the chapter to allow his father to be buried in consecrated ground.

While Calvin mourned his father's death, he also experienced it as a liberation from the obligation to practice law. He returned to Paris to the Collège de France, where he studied Greek with Danès and Hebrew with Vatable. He was now free to put his legal books on the shelf and to devote himself to humanist studies. In 1532 he published at his own expense, possibly with money inherited from his father, a commentary on Seneca's *De Clementia*. In a letter to François Daniel, an old friend from student days at Orléans, Calvin shows himself to be actively promoting his book through acquaintances at Paris, Orléans, and Bourges in the hope of recouping some of the costs of publication:

> Well, at length the die is cast. My Commentaries on the Books of Seneca "De Clementia," have been printed, but at my own expense, and have drawn from me more money than you can well suppose. At present I am using every endeavour to collect some of it back. I have stirred up some of the professors of this city to make use of them in lecturing. In the University of Bourges I have induced a friend to do this from the pulpit by a public lecture. You can also help me not a little, if you will not take it amiss; you will do so on the score of our old friendship; especially as, without any damage to your reputation, you may do me this service, which will also tend perhaps to the public good. Should you determine to oblige me by this benefit, I will send you a hundred copies, or as many as you please. Meanwhile, accept this copy for yourself, while you are not to suppose that by your acceptance of it, I hold you engaged to do what I ask. It is my wish that all may be free and unconstrained between us.[6]

Calvin's commentary on Seneca has been the subject of occasional controversy among historians. Some historians have regarded the commentary as an indirect appeal to the French king, Francis I, to show clemency toward his subjects who had embraced Protestant beliefs. Other historians have treated it as a work of pure scholarship, utterly lacking in contemporary relevance and therefore inadvertently providing important evidence that Calvin had not yet been converted to the Protestant cause. The dispute is very difficult to resolve because historians are still uncertain of the exact date of Calvin's conversion.

Emile Doumergue, Karl Holl, Peter Barth and T. H. L. Parker favor a comparatively early date for Calvin's conversion, perhaps as early as 1527, certainly no later than the end of 1529 or the beginning of 1530.[7] They point in this connection to the possible influence of the Lutheran scholar Wolmar, or of German students at Orléans and Bourges. Parker, who has written most recently on this subject, is convinced that Calvin's conversion must be traced back to the years when Calvin was still a law student. John T. McNeill, Ford Lewis Battles, Heiko Oberman, and Alexandre Ganoczy argue for a later date.[8] It seems inconceivable to them that Calvin, who was so scrupulous in other matters, would have retained Roman Catholic chaplaincies after his break with Rome. Since Calvin did not resign his benefices in Noyon until 1534, his conversion cannot be dated any earlier than 1533 and very possibly should be dated later.

On All Saints' Day, 1533, Calvin first came to the attention of the French authorities. Calvin's friend, Nicholas Cop, the rector of the University of Paris, delivered a sermon which attacked the views of the Paris theologians. The Paris theological faculty, still smarting from the humiliation of a rebuke administered by a Royal Commission of which Cop had been chairman, responded angrily and demanded the arrest of Cop as theologically heterodox. Calvin, too, was believed to have had a role in the composition of the sermon and his room at the Collège Fortet, where he was lecturing, was searched. But Calvin, like Cop, managed to give the police the slip and walked out of the city of Paris disguised as a common laborer.

During the next few months Calvin's movements are difficult to trace. He returned briefly to Paris, where he was granted an audience with the king's sister, Marguerite d'Angoulême, who had established herself as a patron of French reformist movements. He found sanctuary for a time in the home of a rich friend, Louis du Tillet, curé of the village of Claix and canon in the cathedral of Angoulême. Du Tillet had an excellent library and it may, indeed, have been in du Tillet's library that Calvin began to write the first pages of his *Institutes of the Christian Religion*. In May 1534, he resigned his benefices in Noyon. At about the same time he interviewed Lefèvre d'Étaples in Nérac, the capital of Marguerite d'Angoulême, an interview which Beza later described as a great success.

Calvin may have passed through Paris on his way south from Noyon. At any rate, we do know that he spent some weeks in Orléans, where he wrote his first Protestant treatise, *Psychopannychia*. The essay was an attack on the Anabaptist notion that the souls of the just sleep after death until the general resurrection. In point of fact, this idea, which Calvin found so objectionable, was also held in a fairly sophisticated form by Martin Luther.[9]

Calvin might have been able to have lived quietly in France for a few more years had it not been for the Affair of the Placards. In October 1534, posters attacking the Catholic doctrine of the Mass appeared overnight in several of the important cities in France, including Paris. These denunciations were violent and uncompromising, and one placard was even found in the king's bedchamber. This demonstration of the strength of the Protestant movement in France alarmed the French court. Unfortunately for the authors of the placards, the Protestant attack on the Mass coincided with a new treaty between the pope and Francis I. Francis decided to prove his loyalty to the papacy by arresting and executing the Protestants responsible for the placards. Over two hundred were arrested and twenty were executed, including Etienne de la Forge, a Parisian merchant with whom Calvin had once taken furnished lodgings.

Calvin and his friend, du Tillet, were justifiably alarmed by this turn of events and decided to flee for their lives to Basel, where Nicholas Cop had flown the year before. Their escape almost ended in disaster, when a treacherous servant stole one of their horses and all of their money. Luckily, another servant had a small sum of money, which he was willing to lend to Calvin to cover the expenses for the rest of the journey to Switzerland.

In Basel, Calvin completed the first edition of his *Institutes of the Christian Religion* (1536). It was a comparatively short book with six chapters: (1) law, (2) faith, (3) prayer, (4) the sacraments, (5) the five false sacraments, and (6) a concluding omnibus section on Christian liberty, ecclesiastical power, and civil government. An *institutio* is a manual that introduces the basic principles of a subject to beginners who are learning for the first time the terminology and structure of a new discipline. Calvin's *Institutio*, however, had a dual purpose. It was designed not only to "transmit certain rudiments by which those who are touched with any zeal for religion might be shaped to true godliness" but also to explain the theological views of Protestants to the French king and to defend the essentially peaceful character of their political intentions.[10]

In 1536 Calvin and du Tillet left Basel for the ducal court at Ferrara, where Princess Renée of France, daughter of Louis XII and sister-in-law of Francis I, was linked in a desperately unhappy marriage to Duke Hercules II, son of the infamous Lucrezia Borgia. Renée welcomed the scholarly refugees to her court and there is some reason to believe that she offered Calvin a position as secretary. But Calvin, somewhat ungratefully, found Italy not at all to his taste. "I only went to Italy," he later claimed, "that I might have the pleasure of leaving it."[11] When members of Renée's entourage were arrested in April 1536, on a charge of heresy, Calvin, already restless, concluded that it was time to find some other, more congenial city of refuge.

Calvin returned to Paris by way of Basel, where, after arranging for the sale of some land which he had inherited, he was joined by his brother, Antoine, and his half-sister Marie. The Cauvin family planned to relocate in the free imperial city of Strasbourg. Unfortunately, the movement of troops on the roads between Paris and Strasbourg made the direct route to Alsace hazardous for a party of civilians. To avoid the danger, Calvin chose a detour through the south up the valley of the Rhone to the French-speaking city of Geneva.

Calvin intended to spend no more than one night in Geneva, even though his friend, du Tillet, was already living there. Someone, however, told William Farel, the leader of the reform movement in Geneva, that Calvin was in the city for the night. Without waiting for an invitation, Farel strode over to the house where Calvin was staying and announced to him that it was his duty to remain in Geneva. The Genevan church had need of him.

In the preface to his commentary on the Psalms, Calvin has left his own record of this astonishing conversation:

William Farel forced me to stay in Geneva not so much by advice or urging as by command, which had the power of God's hand laid violently upon me from heaven. Since the wars had closed the direct road to Strasbourg, I had meant to pass through Geneva quickly and had determined not to be delayed there more than one night. A short time before, by the work of the same good man and of Peter Viret, the papacy had been banished from the city; but things were still unsettled and the place was divided into evil and harmful factions. One man, who has since shamefully gone back to the papists, took immediate action to make me known. Then Farel, who was working with incredible zeal to promote the gospel, bent all his efforts to keep me in the city. And when he realized that I was determined to study in privacy in some obscure place, and saw that he gained nothing by entreaty, he descended to cursing, and said that God would surely curse my peace if I held back from giving help at a time of such great need. Terrified by his words, and conscious of my own timidity and cowardice, I gave up my journey and attempted to apply whatever gift I had in defense of my faith.[12]

Geneva at the time of Calvin's first visit was not a part of Switzerland, but a free republic which had repudiated the authority of the Prince-Bishop of Geneva, on the one hand, and of the Dukes of Savoy, on the other. In their struggle to remain independent, the Genevese were supported by the largest and strongest of the Swiss cantons, the canton of Bern, which had declared itself for the Reformation as early as 1528. When Charles, the Duke of Savoy, laid siege to Geneva in 1535, he was beaten off with the joint assistance of the king of France and the canton of Bern. The Bernese had hoped that their support of Geneva in the war with Savoy would be rewarded with a greater say in the internal affairs of the city. As it turned out, they had to be satisfied with the lesser role of a somewhat distant but still influential protector. But while the Genevese were jealous of their political independence, they nevertheless voted on May 25, 1536, to accept the Reformation and to align themselves religiously with Bern and the Protestant cantons.

The Reformation, therefore, was still a fresh experiment for the people of Geneva and had only a tenuous hold on their loyalties when Farel intercepted Calvin and recruited him for the Geneva church. Calvin was a lawyer by training and, though he had had considerable experience as a teacher in Paris and Orléans, he had had none whatever as a pastor. At first Calvin seems to have been appointed a "reader in Holy Scripture," an office which obligated him to lecture or preach on the Bible, but which carried with it no additional pastoral duties. During the course of the next year, however, there is evidence that Calvin was elected pastor and given the principal oversight of one of the city churches.

Calvin and Farel set about organizing the life of Geneva. They presented to the city council a *Confession of Faith* on November 10, 1536, and a modest plan of discipline called the *Articles concerning the Organization of the Church and of Worship at Geneva* on January 16, 1537.[13] The articles proposed a monthly celebration of holy communion (Calvin would have preferred a weekly celebration), a method for the excommunication of impenitent offenders, congregational singing of psalms during worship, a program of catechetical instruction for children, and a comprehensive revision of the laws concerning marriage. The city council accepted most of the proposals in the *Articles*, adding only its own Sunday blue laws and restricting the celebration of the eucharist to once a quarter.

Passing a confession of faith and a plan of discipline was one thing; persuading the ordinary citizens of Geneva to conform to them was quite another. Genevans who were unenthusiastic about the reform program of Calvin and Farel on religious grounds began to inquire into Calvin's motivations on political grounds as well. After all, both Farel and Calvin were French, not Genevese. Some of Calvin's enemies wondered out loud whether he had been sent to Geneva as an agent of the French government in order to undermine the independence of the Genevan republic.

Calvin's reputation in Geneva was further tarnished by a public quarrel in 1537 with Pierre Caroli, an off-again on-again supporter of the Reformation who was then a Protestant minister in Lausanne. The argument began over the question of the propriety of prayers for the dead and ended in mutual recrimination. Caroli labeled Calvin an Arian—that is, someone who regarded Jesus Christ as a creature who was less than fully divine. Calvin did nothing to make the charge seem implausible when he refused to subscribe to the Athanasian Creed, a refusal that embarrassed his strongest supporters. While Calvin's christology was orthodox, his distaste for the Athanasian Creed and his reluctance to use nonbiblical language in theological formulations lent credence to Caroli's charge that he was theologically heterodox. In Easter week, 1538, tensions exploded into riots, and Calvin and Farel were ordered by the Council of Two Hundred to leave Geneva within three days. The two ejected ministers appealed first to Bern and then to the synod meeting in Zurich, but, when all attempts to have them reinstated miscarried, they sought temporary shelter in Basel.

If the truth were known, the Germans and Swiss thought that Calvin had brought many of his calamities on himself by adopting a too rigid stance in dealing with the opposition in Geneva. Still they did not wish to see a man of such unusual learning and talent wasted in Basel, where there was little for him to do. Bucer and Wolfgang Capito seized the opportunity to invite Calvin to Strasbourg to become the new minister of the French-speaking church, which numbered at that time four or five hundred members. After some initial hesitation, Calvin accepted. It was a decision he never regreted.

Calvin's hesitation to accept a fresh appointment as pastor of a church is understandable. His ministry in Geneva was widely regarded as a failure. When Calvin remonstrated with his old friend, Louis du Tillet, who had defected from Geneva and returned to the Roman Catholic Church, du Tillet replied in a letter of his own with some searching questions about Calvin's vocation. How could Calvin still believe, after his shattering experiences in Geneva, that God's blessing rested on his ministry among the schismatic Protestants? Perhaps the obstinate Genevese were the chosen instruments of God to recall Calvin to the church of his ancestors. Calvin felt the full force of du Tillet's argument, but responded that he was satisfied that the evangelicals were the church of Christ and that he had been called to a valid ministry among them.[14]

Calvin's first months in Strasbourg were clouded by a series of unexpected deaths: first, Farel's nephew; then blind Courauld, pastor of Orbe and a former colleague from Geneva; and, finally, his kinsman, the French reformer Pierre Robert Olivétan. To compound his distress, Caroli appeared in Strasbourg, having reconverted to Protestantism after a brief interlude as a Roman Catholic. Caroli managed to persuade the ministers of Strasbourg with a very self-serving account of his earlier quarrel with Calvin that he was more sinned against than sinner. Farel welcomed the prodigal back to the Protestant fold, but Calvin remained aloof. The ministers of Strasbourg disapproved of Calvin's attitude toward Caroli and urged him to subscribe to a series of articles which Bucer had edited. This action on the part of the Strasbourg clergy led to a stormy session in which Calvin demonstrated that he had inherited the fiery temper of the Cauvin family. Although in the end Caroli was given conditional and unenthusiastic approval, he did not stay in Strasbourg but wandered off, eventually returning one final time to the Roman Catholic fold.

Aside from the Caroli affair, Calvin's years in Strasbourg were happy and productive. In 1539 he published a second edition of his *Institutes*, now twice the size of the first edition, and in 1540 a commentary on Paul's letter to the Romans.[15] In the preface to his commentary on Romans, Calvin discusses his own exegetical method. While he confesses that he has learned an immense amount from reading the commentaries of Melanchthon and Bucer, he finds that he must develop an exegetical method somewhat different from theirs. For example, Bucer discusses at length all the theological problems which he encounters in the text. The unhappy result of this method is that Bucer's comments are frequently much too long and stand as a barrier between the student of Scripture and the biblical text. Melanchthon, on the other hand, only discusses the important themes or *topoi* in each chapter, thereby omitting the discussion of many lesser—but to Calvin still important—details.

Calvin attempts to resolve the dilemma posed by the antithetical methods of Bucer and Melanchthon by commenting on each verse of a chapter (contra Melanchthon) and by making those comments as brief as the nature of the text will allow (contra Bucer). All lengthy discussions of theological topics are reserved for the pages of the *Institutes*, where they do not distract the reader from the immediate task of exegesis and can therefore serve as a kind of general introduction to the structure and meaning of Scripture as a whole. Calvin called his exegetical method "lucid brevity" and it is one of his principal contributions to the intellectual heritage of the Reformation. In his "Letter to the Reader," which accompanies the revised editions of the *Institutes*, Calvin describes the reciprocal relationship that he envisaged between his biblical commentaries and his major systematic work:

> Moreover, it has been my purpose in this labor to prepare and instruct candidates in the sacred theology for the reading of the divine Word, in order that they may be able both to have easy access to it and to advance in it without stumbling. For I believe I have so embraced the sum of religion in all its parts, and have arranged it in such an order, that if anyone rightly grasps it, it will not be difficult for him to determine what he ought especially to seek in Scripture, and to what end he ought to relate its contents. If, after this road has, as it were, been paved, I shall publish any interpretation of Scripture, I shall always condense them, because I have no need to undertake long doctrinal discussions, and to digress into commonplaces. In this way the godly reader will be spared great annoyance and boredom, provided he approach Scripture armed with a knowledge of the present work, as a necessary tool. But because the program of this instruction is clearly mirrored in all my commentaries, I prefer to let the book itself declare its purpose rather than to describe it in words.[16]

Calvin did not spend all of his time in Strasbourg writing and preaching. As a citizen of Strasbourg, he was selected to accompany the representatives of the city to Worms (1540) and Regensburg (1541), where, under the sponsorship of the Holy Roman Emperor Charles V, Protestant and Roman Catholic delegates attempted to resolve the theological issues which divided them. While Calvin did not take much part in the proceedings (he was, after all, at thirty-one a fairly junior member of the delegation), he nevertheless was grateful for the opportunity to meet Melanchthon and the prominent Lutherans from northern Germany. The colloquy was not a great success, though Protestants and Roman Catholics were able to agree briefly on a compromise formula concerning the doctrine of justification by faith. No satisfactory compromise was possible on the doctrine of transubstantiation and Calvin was unimpressed with the efforts of Bucer and Melanchthon to paper over the fundamental disagreement with an ambiguous formulation that only postponed the inevitable. Writing to Farel on May 12, 1541 Calvin observed:

> So far as I could understand, if we could be content with only a half Christ we might easily come to understand one another. Philip and Bucer have drawn up ambiguous and insincere formulas concerning transubstantiation, to try whether they could satisfy the opposite party by yielding nothing. I could not agree to this device, although they have, as they conceive, reasonable grounds for doing so, for they hope that in a short time it would so happen that they would begin to see more clearly if the matter of doctrine shall be left an open question for the present; therefore they rather wish to skip over it, and do not dread that equivocation in matters of conscience, than which nothing can possibly be more hurtful. I can promise, however, both to yourself and to all the pious, that both are animated with the best intentions, and have no other object in view than promoting the kingdom of Christ. Nor can you desire anything on the part of either of them which they do not faithfully and steadily perform, except that in their method of proceeding they accommodate themselves too much to the time.[17]

During this period Calvin met and married Idelette de Bure. As the widow of a refugee in Strasbourg, Idelette had no dowry to offer Calvin, only a ready-made family in the form of a son and daughter by her previous husband. Farel, who took an interest in such matters, wrote to Christophe Fabri, the pastor of Thonon, that Calvin had married an "upright and honest," "even pretty" woman.[18]

Idelette brought out the gentle side of Calvin's disposition. He was sick with worry when, as a delegate of the Protestants to the colloquy at Regensburg, he was required to be out of Strasbourg at the very moment the plague struck Alsace. His relief on his return at finding Idelette and the children unharmed was palpable. Calvin took enormous pride in her good sense, her courage, and her warm and communicable piety. Idelette gave Calvin a son on July 28, 1542, named Jacques after his uncle, but the child did not live.[19] In spite of Calvin's devotion and care for Idelette during her extended period of declining health, she died on March 29, 1549. Calvin was desolate when a few days later he wrote to his friend Pierre Viret:

> I have been bereaved of the best companion of my life, of one who, had it been so ordered, would not only have been the willing sharer of my indigence, but even of my death. During her life she was the faithful helper of my ministry. From her I never experienced the slightest hindrance. She was never troublesome to me throughout the entire course of her illness; she was more anxious about her children than herself.[20]

In March 1539, Jacopo Cardinal Sadoleto, Bishop of Carpentras in southern France, sent a letter to Geneva, recalling it to the traditional faith of its ancestors. The letter was an eloquent appeal for reconciliation and reunion, which accused the Protestant reformers of arrogantly introducing into the Christian faith heretical innovations that had no foundation in the Christian past. The Geneva authorities recognized the force of Sadoleto's arguments and their own inability to write a persuasive response. After lengthy consultations with Bern that stretched over several months and a vain attempt to persuade Pierre Viret to answer Sadoleto, the Genevese reluctantly concluded that Simon Sulzer should be sent from Bern to Strasbourg to ask Calvin to reply to Sadoleto on their behalf. In spite of some initial hesitation to embrace this unexpected and not wholly welcome invitation (it was difficult, after all, not to take modest pleasure in the public embarrassment of old enemies), Calvin decided that the matter was too important to be clouded by personal resentments and agreed to speak for the inarticulate and theologically tongue-tied citizens of Geneva.

The *Response to Sadoleto* was a polemical masterpiece that turned Sadoleto's arguments back on himself and discomfited him with the very charges he had leveled against the Protestants.[21] Calvin's allies in Geneva were delighted and even his enemies were impressed. By the summer of 1540 most Genevese were convinced that it had been a disastrous mistake to drive Calvin and Farel from the city in 1538. On September 21, 1540, the council reversed its earlier decision against Calvin and instructed Ami Perrin to find a way to recall him to Geneva.

Calvin was taken aback when he learned of Geneva's desire to reinstate him in his old position. He was very happy in Strasbourg and had no inclination to return to a city that had humiliated him with its stubborn ingratitude. As early as May 19, 1540, Calvin had written to Viret:

> I read that passage of your letter, certainly not without a smile, where you show so much concern about my health, and recommend Geneva on that ground! Why could you not have said at the cross? For it would have been far preferable to perish once for all than to be tormented again in that place of torture.[22]

Nevertheless, by the summer of 1541 Calvin agreed to return. Strasbourg gave Geneva permission to "borrow" Calvin for six months. As it turned out, the loan was permanent. Calvin never returned to Strasbourg, but spent the remaining years of his life as a minister in Geneva. He was given an annual stipend of 500 florins (not princely but adequate), a furnished house on the rue de Chanoines, two casks of wine, and twelve strikes of corn. Calvin entered the city on Tuesday, September 13, 1541. The Register of the Company of Pastors contains the following note:

M. Iehan Calvin, minister of the gospel. The same has arrived from Strasbourg, and has delivered letters from Strasbourg and from the pastors there, as well as from Basel; these have been read. Afterwards he made, at some length, his excuses for his delay in coming. That done, he asked that the church be set in order, and a memorandum was drawn up to this effect, and that council-lors should be elected to consider this. And as for him, he offered himself to be always the servant of Geneva.[23]

Calvin moved swiftly to implement a program of reform in the city of Geneva. The *Ecclesiastical Ordinances* which he proposed were studied and amended by the Little Council, the Council of Two Hundred, and the General Council. The Council, for example, rejected monthly communion in favor of quarterly. Nevertheless, in spite of some emendations, the *Ordinances* with their fourfold ministry of pastors, teachers, elders, and deacons were adopted as law on November 20, 1541.

There were to be twelve lay elders, elected from the Little Council, the Sixty, and the Two Hundred, and drawn from various sections of the city. Together with the ministers, the elders formed the *Consistoire* or consistory court, responsible for the enforcement of discipline. The *Consistoire* met every Thursday to hear cases summoned before it by an officer of the council. It could even excommunicate the stubbornly impenitent, but only after making three attempts to persuade the offenders to abandon their unacceptable behavior. In any event, its powers were ecclesiastical rather than civil and it was expected to report to the council on the more prickly cases that required punishment.

Poor relief and charity were in the hands of lay deacons. Deacons were divided into two groups: administrative officers, who acted as trustees and guarded the funds, and executive officers, who actually managed the hospital for the care of the sick and distributed goods to the poor.

Doctors or teachers were expected to teach the truth and to refute all errors, whether Catholic, Anabaptist, or Lutheran. Geneva needed two professors to teach Old and New Testaments and a schoolmaster with his assistants to instruct children in the preparatory humane disciplines. Whereas education should be provided for both boys and girls, it should be provided in separate schools.

Pastors had the threefold task of preaching the Word, administering the sacraments, and participating in the administration of discipline through the *Consistoire*. New pastors were elected by the company of pastors and confirmed in their office by the council. While pastors were to meet weekly for Bible study and quarterly for the mutual correction of faults, they enjoyed no exemption from civil law or the legal obligations of ordinary citizens. Sunday services should be held in three churches, Saint Pierre, la Madeleine, and Saint Gervais. All three parishes should offer mid-day catechism classes for the young and weekday sermons on Monday, Wednesday, and Friday. These duties required the services of five ministers and three assistants.

Calvin himself agreed to preach twice on Sunday and once on Monday, Wednesday, and Friday. Somewhat later he restricted his weekday preaching to every second week, though by that time sermons were delivered on Tuesday and Thursday as well. He preached on the New Testament on Sundays, on the Old Testament on weekdays, and occasionally on the Psalms on Sunday afternoons. He preached on Acts from 1549 to 1554, on various letters of Paul from 1554 to 1558, and on the Gospels from 1559 to 1564. On weekdays he preached on Jeremiah and Lamentations, Daniel and the minor prophets, Ezekiel, Job, Deuteronomy, Isaiah, Genesis, Judges, first and second Samuel, and Kings. In addition to these sermons, Calvin was writing commentaries on biblical books and lecturing in the Academy. Like Martin Luther, Calvin did not write or preach on the book of Revelation, though there are nevertheless twenty-six references to Revelation in his 1559 edition of the *Institutes*.[24]

The years in Geneva were filled with theological controversy. Calvin disputed in writing, and sometimes in person, with Andreas Osiander, Jerome Bolsec, Michael Servetus, Menno Simons, Joachim Westphal, Tilemann Hesshusen, Albert Pighius, Laelius Socinus, Sebastian Castellio, and a host of nameless figures whom he somewhat imprecisely categorized as Epicureans, Libertines, Anabaptists, Nicodemites, Sorbonnists, and Sophists. His recurring disputes with theological opponents, together with the daily exegetical work to which he had committed himself, clarified his thinking over time and enriched the successive editions of his *Institutes*. The Latin edition of 1536, which had been revised in Strasbourg in 1539, was revised and expanded three more times in Geneva (1543, 1550, 1559). It was translated into French in 1541 and 1560. During Calvin's own lifetime the *Institutes* also appeared in Spanish (1540), Italian (1557), Dutch (1560), and English (1561). In the preface to the 1559 Latin edition, Calvin describes this process of revision and pronounces himself satisfied with the final edition:

> In the first edition of this work of ours I did not in the least expect that success which, out of his infinite goodness, the Lord has given. Thus, for the most part I treated the subject summarily, as is usually done in small works. But when I realized that it was received by almost all godly men with a favor for which I never would have ventured to wish, much less to hope, I deeply felt that I was much more favored than I deserved. Consequently I thought that I should be showing extreme ingratitude not to try at least, to the best of my slender ability, to respond to this warm appreciation for me, an appreciation that demanded my further diligence. Not only did I attempt this in

the second edition, but each time the work has been reprinted since then, it has been enriched with some additions. Although I did not regret the labor spent, I was never satisfied until the work had been arranged in the order now set forth. Now I trust I have provided something that all of you will approve.[25]

Although Calvin was one of the two theological professors in Geneva, he did not lecture on systematic theology. The *Institutes* was not first written as a set of classroom exercises. Calvin appears to have held the chair in Old Testament and to have lectured on the Hebrew text of the Bible. Many, though not all, of his commentaries on the Old Testament took their origin as lectures to students; sometimes they were even based on the student lecture notes of Charles de Jonviller and his friends. Calvin's principal occupation was the interpretation of the Bible. Dogmatic theology grew out of exegesis and remained subordinate to it.

Even though Calvin was reconciled to spending his life in Geneva, he had not forgotten his responsibilities for the Protestant churches in his homeland. On the accession of Henry II in 1547, French Protestants were subjected to programmatic persecution. Henry established a special court, the so-called *Chambre ardente*, which carried on a reign of terror among French Protestants similar to the persecution of Protestants by Mary Tudor in England. Calvin saw to it that the persecuted congregations in France were provided with a steady stream of literature from the presses of Geneva. Whenever possible, he assisted them to find ministers as well. Between 1555 and 1562 over one hundred ministers were sent to France under the sponsorship of the Venerable Company of Pastors.

Calvin maintained an active correspondence with leaders in the French church, both lay and clerical. He knew in advance of the Conspiracy of Amboise against the Cardinal of Lorraine and his brother, the Duc de Guise, conservative advisors of the Queen Mother, Catherine de Medici, who promoted the continuation of the anti-Protestant policies of Henry II after his death. When the conspiracy to arrest the Guises failed, as Calvin feared it would, he even supported the Huguenots in their civil war against the Catholic monarchy, though he was opposed to armed rebellion in their case and severely critical of the peace terms which they ultimately accepted.

Calvin's health, which was always delicate, failed rapidly in 1564. In a letter to the physicians of Montpellier, Calvin complained of gout, kidney stones, ulcerated hemorrhoids, chronic indigestion, and quartan fever. He was also suffering, it now appears, from pulmonary tuberculosis, which left him faint and unable to catch his breath. Finally, on April 28, 1564, he summoned the ministers of Geneva to his home for a farewell address. The address is a curious combination of piety and truculence, rehearsing old wrongs and warning against innovations:

When I first came to this church, I found almost nothing in it. There was preaching and that was all. They would look out for idols it is true, and they burned them. But there was no reformation. Everything was in disorder. . . . I have lived here amid continual bickerings. I have been from derision saluted of an evening before my door with forty or fifty shots of an arquebuse. . . . They set the dogs at my heels, crying, Here! here! and these snapped at my gown and legs. . . . though I am nothing, yet know I well that I have prevented three thousand tumults that would have broken out in Geneva. But take courage and fortify yourselves, for God will make use of this church and will maintain it, and assures you that he will protect it.[26]

To Farel, who was older than he was, and who had first called him to the work in Geneva, Calvin wrote:

Farewell, my most excellent and upright brother; and since it is the will of God that you should survive me in the world, live mindful of our intimacy, which, as it was useful to the church of God, so the fruits of it await us in heaven. I am unwilling that you should fatigue yourself for my sake. I draw my breath with difficulty, and every moment I am in expectation of breathing my last. It is enough that I live and die for Christ, who is to all his followers a gain both in life and death. Again I bid you and your brethren Farewell.[27]

Calvin died on May 27, 1564, between 8 and 9 in the evening. His body lay in state briefly and was buried in an unmarked grave in the common cemetery on Sunday, May 28. As he himself had foreseen, his mind was lucid to the end.

NOTES

1. This brief sketch of Calvin's life is based on the standard biographies, the earliest of which were written by Theodore Beza (CO 21.21–50; 119–72) and Nicholas Colladon (CO 21.51–118). Indispensable for the serious student is the seven-volume biography by Emile Doumergue, *Jean Calvin, Les hommes et les choses de son temps* (Lausanne, 1899–1927). Three recent studies are T. H. L. Parker, *John Calvin* (Berkhamsted, Herts: Lion Publishing, 1977); William J. Bouwsma, *John Calvin: A Sixteenth-Century Portrait* (New York: Oxford University Press, 1988); Alister E. McGrath, *A Life of John Calvin, A Study in the Shaping of Western Culture* (Oxford: Basil Blackwell, 1990). The best general introduction to Calvin remains François Wendel, *Calvin: Origins and Development of His Religious Thought* (Durham, N.C.: Labyrinth Press, 1963, 1987). See also Wulfert de Greef, *The Writings of John Calvin, An Introductory Guide*, trans. Lyle D. Bierma (Grand Rapids, Mich.: Baker Books, 1993).

2. The information that Calvin studied at La Marche before enrolling at the Collège de Montaigu rests on information provided by Calvin's biographer,

Colladon. Alister McGrath is convinced that this view is mistaken and that Calvin studied Latin at Paris with Cordier while unattached to any college. If McGrath is correct, Calvin's first college at Paris was Montaigu. On this problem see McGrath, *Life of John Calvin*, pp. 21–27.

3. For this quotation see Parker, *John Calvin*, pp. 8–9.

4. See, for example, Karl Reuter, *Das Grundverständnis der Theologie Calvins* (Neukirchen, 1963). Reuter argued that through John Major the young Calvin was influenced by Duns Scotus and Gregory of Rimini. The most recent attempt to pursue the question of Major's possible influence on Calvin is Thomas F. Torrance, *The Hermeneutics of John Calvin* (Edinburgh: Scottish Academic Press, 1988). Heiko A. Oberman, *Initia Calvini: The Matrix of Calvin's Reformation* (Amsterdam: Koninklijke Nederlandse Akademie van Wetenschappen, 1991), pp. 10–19, accepts the influence of Scotus, though not Gregory of Rimini or John Major.

5. The English translation is taken from *Selected Works of John Calvin, Tracts and Letters 1*, ed. Henry Beveridge and Jules Bonnet (Grand Rapids, Mich.: Baker Book House, 1983), p. xxiii.

6. The English translation is taken from *Selected Works of John Calvin, Tracts and Letters 4*, ed. Henry Beveridge and Jules Bonnet (Grand Rapids, Mich.: Baker Book House, 1983), pp. 31–32. For the Latin text, see CO 10a.19–20.

7. In this connection see Appendix 2 in T. H. L. Parker, *Calvin*, pp. 192–96.

8. On Calvin's conversion see the long and nuanced discussion by Alexandre Ganoczy, *The Young Calvin* (Philadelphia: Westminster Press, 1987), pp. 76–91, 241–312.

9. Oberman wants to make two points: (1) that Luther speaks of the sleep, but not the death of the soul; and (2) that Calvin denies the natural immortality of the soul, since it is immortal solely by God's power (*Initia Calvini*, pp. 30–33). For a thorough discussion of the issue of soul sleep in the Reformation, see Willem Balke, *Calvin and the Anabaptist Radicals* (Grand Rapids, Mich.: Wm. B. Eerdmans, 1981), pp. 31–34, 304–308.

10. OS 1.21–36.

11. Theodore Beza, *Vita Calvini*, CO 21.125: "Caeterum ex Italia, in cuius fines se ingressum esse dicere solebat, ut inde exiret, in Galliam regressus."

12. English translation by Joseph Haroutunian, *Calvin: Commentaries*, LCC 23 (Philadelphia: Westminster Press, 1958), p. 53. The autobiographical fragment is found in CO 31.23–26.

13. OS 1.369–77, 418–26.

14. CO 10a.269–72.

15. For a critical edition of Calvin's commentary on Romans, see T. H. L. Parker, ed., *Iohannis Calvini Commentarius in Epistolam Pauli ad Romanos* (Leiden: E.J. Brill, 1981).

16. The English translation is from the McNeill-Battles edition of the 1559 *Institutes*, John T. McNeill and Ford Lewis Battles, *Calvin: Institutes of the Christian Religion*, 2 vols., LCC 20–21 (Philadelphia: Westminster Press, 1960). The 1539 edition contained the additional sentence: "The Commentaries on the Letter to the Romans will furnish an example."

17. CO 11.217.

18. CO 11.78.

19. On the basis of letters found in CO 11.719, 12.322, and 12.580, Bouwsma is convinced that Calvin was the father of at least three children by Idelette, two sons and a daughter, *John Calvin*, p. 23. The references, however, are far from clear and could be understood to refer to Calvin's stepson and stepdaughter. In 1562, in his *Responsio Balduini Convicia,* Calvin mentions only one son who died. CO 9.576: "Dederat mihi Deus filiolum: abstulit. Hoc quoque recenset inter probra liberis me carere. Atqui mihi filiorum sunt myriades in toto orbe christiano."

20. CO 10b.430–31.

21. OS 1.457–489. See my essay, "Luther and Calvin on Church and Tradition," in David C. Steinmetz, *Luther in Context* (Bloomington: Indiana University Press, 1986), pp. 85–97.

22. CO 11.36.

23. CO 21.282.

24. On Calvin's preaching in Geneva, see especially T. H. L. Parker, *Calvin's Preaching* (Louisville, Ky.: Westminster/John Knox Press, 1992).

25. *Inst.*, "Johannes Calvinus Lectori: Praefatio Altera."

26. CO 9.891–94.

27. CO 20.302–3.

2

Calvin and the Natural Knowledge of God

The problem of the natural knowledge of God in Calvin's theology was sharply posed in the 1930s in a famous debate between Karl Barth and Emil Brunner. In his little book, *Natur und Gnade*, Brunner argued for what he called a "Christian natural theology."[1] By the use of this somewhat ambiguous phrase, Brunner meant to suggest that the image of God had not been completely destroyed by human sin and disobedience. Remnants of the image were still present in human nature and formed a point of contact for the gospel. Furthermore, the revelation of God in nature was not lost to Christians, who, by using the spectacles of Scripture, could once again know God in and through his works. In all these contentions Brunner claimed Calvin as his ally and mentor.

> Calvin considers this remnant of the *imago Dei* to be of great importance. One might almost say that it is one of the pillars supporting his theology, for he identifies it with nothing less than the entire human, rational nature, the immortal soul, the capacity for culture, the conscience, responsibility, the relation with God, which—though not redemptive—exists even in sin, language, the whole of cultural life.[2]

Brunner's book met with an immediate and harsh answer from Barth in a pamphlet *Nein: Antwort an Emil Brunner*. The unusual heat of Barth's response was due in part to the political situation in Germany, where natural theology had been exploited by pro-Nazi Christians. Against Brunner's reading of Calvin, Barth argued that Calvin constantly pointed to the Bible as the true source of the knowledge of God.

> The possibility of a real knowledge by natural man of the true God, derived from creation, is, according to Calvin, a possibility in principle, but not in fact, not a possibility to be realized by us. One might call it an objective possibility, created by God, but not a subjective possibility, open to man. Between what is possible in principle and what is possible in fact there inexorably lies the fall. Hence this possibility can only be discussed hypothetically: *si integer stetisset Adam* (Inst., I, ii, 1).[3]

Because the human race has fallen into sin, the content of its natural knowledge of God is nothing more than idolatry and superstition.[4] Therefore, the revelation of God in nature, whatever its original purpose may have been, serves only to render fallen human beings inexcusable and to justify the wrath of God against them.[5] As Barth understands Calvin, there is no knowledge of God the creator apart from the knowledge of God the redeemer.[6]

In his recent book, *John Calvin: A Sixteenth Century Portrait*, William J. Bouwsma, whose interest in Calvin's thought is more historical than theological, touches briefly on the problem of the natural knowledge of God in the context of Calvin's indebtedness to his cultural tradition. Unlike Karl Barth, Bouwsma is convinced that Calvin does in fact advocate a natural theology based on natural insight and innate religious instinct.[7] While Calvin is not altogether certain "how far or how deep the natural knowledge of God could go," he is convinced at the very least that nature unremittingly demonstrates God's existence.[8]

On the question of God's essence, Bouwsma believes that Calvin is more ambiguous. On the one hand, Calvin warns against speculative theology that attempts to know the essence of God from his works; on the other hand, he regards "every aspect of external nature" as "redolent with religious instruction."[9] Rivers and mountains, birds and flowers, even the human body itself, are important sources for the natural knowledge of God. Calvin is particularly interested in the heavenly bodies as theological tutors and regards astronomy as the alphabet of theology.[10] Yet in spite of the fact that Bouwsma has found impressive evidence for a kind of natural theology in Calvin's thought, he nevertheless concludes that the debate between Brunner, "for whom Calvin left a large place for the knowledge of God from nature," and Barth, "for whom he left little or none," "is futile because of Calvin's ambivalence; he can be cited on both sides of the issue."[11]

The appeal to Calvin's ambivalence with respect to the problem of natural theology, while understandable, may not be entirely justified.[12] Calvin outlines the main themes of his understanding of the natural knowledge of

God in his earliest theological writings. His views on natural law and the role of human conscience are, for example, already articulated in the 1536 edition of the *Institutes*. While Calvin modifies his views over time, he remains remarkably consistent in adhering to fundamental distinctions first drawn in the 1539 *Institutes* and the 1540 *Commentary on Romans*.[13]

In what follows, I want to examine one of Calvin's earliest discussions of natural theology—namely, his exegesis of Rom. 1:18–32—a passage in which the question of the natural knowledge of God is crucial to the development of Paul's argument. What I hope to demonstrate is that Calvin gives this passage a highly original, if problematic, reading that remains crucial to his later thought. In order to assess the originality of Calvin's interpretation of Paul, I intend to compare his exegesis with the exegesis of Augustine and four other well-known and widely cited interpreters, who inhabit to a greater or lesser degree Calvin's own intellectual and spiritual world.[14]

Paul had raised the question of the natural knowledge of God in the context of the problem of the moral responsibility of the Gentiles. If the ancient pagans had a knowledge of the true God, however rudimentary, they could be held responsible for their moral lapses and addiction to idols. By the same token, total religious ignorance would provide them with a legitimate excuse and relieve them of accountability to God.

Paul takes the line that the pagans did have a knowledge of God from nature and conscience. While this knowledge was primitive in comparison with the rich revelation of God entrusted to the Jews, the really decisive question for Paul was not how much the Gentiles knew, but what they did with what they knew. Although the Gentiles admittedly had little, they abused the little they had. God was therefore within his rights to hold them accountable for their sins and to punish them for their disobedience.

I

Augustine in his early commentary on Romans, the *Expositio quarundam Propositionum ex Epistola ad Romanos*, regards 1:18–32 as essentially unproblematic. The wiser Gentiles knew God the Creator through his creation. Their problem was not lack of knowledge, as Paul's sermon in Athens demonstrates (Acts 17:28), but pride, the root of all sins. They did not give thanks to God, who was the source of their wisdom, and so fell foolishly into idolatry. The reprimand of the Gentiles, however, is itself proof that they are not excluded from the realm of salvation but can attain grace through conversion. Augustine does not seem to have in mind a knowledge of God the Creator through creation possessed by all human beings, but only by some. The wiser Gentiles knew in fact what others could, but did not, know in principle.[15]

The late medieval exegetical tradition, of which Denis the Carthusian may be taken as representative, agreed with Augustine that Romans 1 contains no special problems.[16] There were, of course, a number of smaller exegetical points on which commentators differed, but the general thrust of Paul's argument seemed clear enough.

Denis admits that God has revealed truth to human beings in a variety of ways: through an infusion of wisdom, through angelic revelation, through the teaching of the saints, and through natural reason. Paul, however, is speaking about natural reason in Romans 1.[17] Through the influence of the light of natural reason, a rational soul can understand the creator by means of the created order, since effects bear some likeness to the cause in which they participate.[18] Specifically, one can know that God is just and wise, that God approves of what is just and disapproves of injustice, and that God deserves reverent worship.[19] One can even know the "invisible things" of God; namely, the perfections such as power, justice, and providence that are one in the simple, incorporeal being of God. Furthermore, Denis agrees with John Damascene that all human beings have an innate knowledge of the existence of God.[20] If the Gentiles have merited the wrath of God, it is not because they do not know the truth but because they do not obey it.

The themes sounded in Augustine and developed by Denis recur in the three Protestant commentators mentioned favorably by Calvin in the preface to his own commentary on Romans: Philip Melanchthon (Wittenberg, 1532), Heinrich Bullinger (Zurich, 1533), and Martin Bucer (Strasbourg, 1534).[21] But there are other themes as well. Important to Melanchthon's treatment of Rom. 1:18–32 is a Lutheran distinction between law and gospel.[22] As Melanchthon sees it, Paul posits a natural knowledge of God, but it is a knowledge of the law and not of the gospel.[23] What the Gentiles know through nature is that there is a God, that this God is just and requires justice, that he punishes the ungodly, and that he hears and saves whoever is obedient to the law. What cannot be known through natural reason alone is the gospel; namely, that God desires to remit sins, to be reconciled to the unworthy and unclean, and freely to account as just the unrighteous. To the extent that the natural knowledge of God posits the necessity for human worthiness, to that extent it is in conflict with the knowledge of God derived from the gospel.[24]

Melanchthon understands Paul to teach that the natural knowledge of God is implanted in the human mind by God and is not simply a conclusion derived from the observation of nature.[25] Indeed, reason would not marvel at the works of God in nature if it did not already have an innate, proleptic knowledge of God. The rise and fall of nations, the change of times and seasons, the punishment of the wicked and the terrors of conscience are all testimonies that there is a good and just God, to whom all human beings are responsible. By the exercise of reason the human mind can know that things do not exist through themselves but depend on a prior transcendent cause.

This natural knowledge ought not, however, to be confused with speculations concerning the essence of God. Natural knowledge of God is knowledge of God's will toward sinners, not of his hidden nature.[26] Paul is a practical, not a speculative, theologian.

Unfortunately, the natural knowledge of God has been partly obscured by original sin. Human nature is so weakened by the fall into sin that it neither constantly assents to the knowledge it has nor obeys the eternal law written in the mind.[27] Melanchthon is particularly offended by the position of the Epicureans, who deny the providential care of God for creation, and by the stubborn opacity of idolaters, who cling to a false persuasion of God in their hearts.[28]

If Melanchthon's discussion is dominated by a characteristically Lutheran distinction of law and gospel, Bullinger seems preoccupied with a typically Zwinglian concern with superstition and the cultic use of religious art.[29] Bullinger believes that idolators are particularly blameworthy because God has richly revealed himself to them in the natural order. Through the visible order they know that the invisible God is the omnipotent, true, wise, just, good, and supreme Being through whom all things subsist and by whom all things are governed.[30] This sentiment is found not only in Paul, but also in the Old Testament and in the writings of the pagan philosophers, especially in the writings of Seneca.[31] The Gentiles did not lack all knowledge of the truth and of true religion; rather, they abused the knowledge they had.[32] For Bullinger it is a short step from the pagan sin of idolatry to the cultic use of images by Christians.

The most extensive discussion of Romans 1 is found in Bucer's lengthy commentary on Romans.[33] Like Melanchthon, Bucer wants to emphasize both the external revelation of God in creation and the internal conception of God imprinted on the human mind. This innate *notio Dei* is so firmly implanted that it can never be expunged from the mind.[34] Bucer cites as proof of his contention the speech of the Stoic philosopher, Lucilius Balbus, in book two of Cicero's *De natura deorum*. For Bucer as for Melanchthon it is the innate knowledge of God that predisposes the mind to see the handiwork of God in nature.

Because God has revealed himself through nature and the human mind to the Gentiles, who do not worship him, it would seem that this revelation was given in vain. Bucer, however, wants to underscore Paul's point that God cannot be blamed for the failure of the Gentiles to make proper use of the witness of God in nature. Indeed, natural revelation takes away every human excuse.[35]

In his *Conciliatio locorum* Bucer distinguishes between two kinds of knowledge of God (*duplex notitia Dei*): (1) a general or natural knowledge of God given to all human beings who are sound of mind and body and (2) a full and solid knowledge of God, given by the Holy Spirit only to the elect, that generates love and reverence for God.[36] The former undercuts human excuses; the latter leads to eternal life. Therefore it can be rightly argued that the Gentiles both know God and do not know him.[37] They know God sufficiently to condemn themselves, but have no efficacious knowledge. While they know that God exists and glimpse something of his essence, they do not embrace and honor him as God.

The discussion has now moved far beyond the observation of young Augustine that wiser Gentiles knew God the Creator through creation but abused that knowledge through pride. Nevertheless, if we compare the exegesis of Denis the Carthusian with the exegesis of Melanchthon, Bullinger, and Bucer, we can, I think, point to a general consensus on the meaning of Romans 1 that incorporates Augustine's point in a more complex and nuanced vision. All agree that there is a general knowledge of God from creation that is accessible to human reason apart from grace. This knowledge rests in part on inferences drawn from observation of the created order (Denis, Melanchthon, Bullinger, Bucer) and in part on an innate knowledge implanted in the human mind by God (Denis, Melanchthon, Bucer).

All agree that human reason, on whatever grounds, knows that God exists. Melanchthon insists that what fallen human reason knows is God's will toward us and not God's essence, though the qualities Melanchthon insists are knowable—that God is just, that he punishes the ungodly, that he hears and saves whoever is obedient to the law—are simply accepted by other theologians as perfections belonging to the divine essence.

All agree that while the natural knowledge of God is not saving—and may even need to be corrected by the gospel (Melanchthon)—it is, nevertheless, real knowledge. The problem is not with the quality or even the quantity of knowledge gained by human reason through the natural order. The problem is human sin, which has so weakened human nature (Melanchthon) that it rejects or abuses the knowledge that it has (Denis, Melanchthon, Bullinger, Bucer). As a result, the natural knowledge of God serves only to render fallen human beings inexcusable. A subtheme in this discussion is a preference for Stoic philosophers (Bullinger, Bucer) and a distaste for Epicureans (Melanchthon, Bucer).

II

While Calvin repeats many of the themes developed by Denis, Melanchthon, Bullinger, and Bucer in his own exegesis of Paul, it is clear that Calvin intends to take the discussion in a somewhat different direction by focusing on the knowing subject and the noetic effects of sin. Calvin certainly agrees that human beings were "formed to be . . . spectator[s] of the created world" and endowed with eyes to see "the world as a mirror or representation of invisible things" and so to be led through the contemplation of creatures to the praise of their divine Author.[38] While Calvin, unlike Melanchthon and Bucer, does not speak of an innate knowledge of God, he does mention "a manifestation of God's character which is too forceful to allow men to escape from it, since undoubtedly every one of us feels it engraved on his own heart."[39] On the other hand, he immediately qualifies his sole reference to a knowledge "that God has put into the minds of all men," by adding, "He has so demonstrated his existence by His works as to make men see what they do not seek to know of their own accord, viz. that there is a God."[40]

Calvin repeats Paul's argument that pagans naturally know there is a God but "suppress or obscure" his "true knowledge."[41] While the natural order demonstrates the existence of God, it reveals, not God's essence, but knowledge accommodated to the limited capacity of human beings to comprehend God.[42] Calvin calls this a revelation of God's glory, which he defines as "whatever ought to induce and excite us to glorify God."[43] Calvin insists that all the works of God "clearly demonstrate their Creator."[44]

At this point Calvin breaks with the exegetical tradition since Augustine by distinguishing sharply between what is offered to natural reason and what is received. On the one hand, Calvin wants to insist that "the manifestation of God by which He makes His glory known among his creatures is sufficiently clear as far as its own light is concerned."[45] On the other hand, he wants to point to the fact of culpable human blindness. The difficulty is not with what is shown to fallen human reason through the natural order; the difficulty is with human misperception because of sin.[46]

The metaphor of blindness, however, is too strong. If blind, then ignorant; if ignorant, then not culpable. The earlier exegetical tradition did not have this problem because it admitted that natural reason knows both that God exists and that God is just, powerful, and providential. Such knowledge is not saving, but it is nevertheless authentic. Calvin realizes that blindness overstates Paul's case and retreats to the metaphor of severely damaged sight. "We are not so blind," he concedes, "that we can plead ignorance without being convicted of perversity."[47] Or, as he says elsewhere, "we see just enough to keep us from making excuse."[48]

The thrust of his argument, however, is that while human beings know that God exists, they misperceive his self-revelation in nature because of the noetic consequences of human sin. Since sin is a condition that is not natural to the human race, but a consequence of Adam's fall, the misperceptions of the revelation of God in nature are inexcusable. Fallen human beings therefore create fictitious new gods, imaginary pictures, insubstantial phantoms, which they worship in place of God.[49] Since all human beings, and not merely philosophers and intellectuals, seek "to form some conception of the majesty of God, and to make Him such a God as their reason could conceive Him to be," their "presumptuous attitude to God is not . . . learned in the philosophical schools, but is innate, and accompanies us, so to speak, from the womb."[50] Even Plato, "the most sound-minded" of the philosophers, disappoints Calvin, because he "sought to trace some form in God."[51] In the end, the content of the natural knowledge of God expressed as natural theology is idolatry.

One further note, mentioned by Calvin but not developed, is introduced by a reference to Heb. 11:3, which "ascribes to faith the light by which a man can gain a real knowledge [of God] from the work of creation."[52] Calvin suggests that creation, which is no longer an effective source of the knowledge of God for fallen human reason, can be reclaimed as a source by believers who view the world with the light of faith and not merely with the light of natural reason.

If we compare Calvin's exegesis with the exegesis of Denis, Melanchthon, Bullinger, and Bucer, we find some points of agreement among them. All agree that the created world demonstrates God's existence and that human beings without exception know by nature that there is a God. Calvin even agrees that the world is a mirror of God's glory, and that it reveals enough of God's will and nature to stimulate human beings to praise and glorify God.[53]

Calvin demurs, however, when the other interpreters of Paul argue that human beings have a reliable, if rudimentary, knowledge of the will or essence of God.[54] The problem is not with the objective revelation of God in nature but with the perception of God by fallen human reason. Human beings are very nearly blind because of sin. Since they know that there is a God and since they misperceive the self-revelation of God in creation, they worship idols in place of God. There is even a suggestion, not echoed by the other commentators, that faith will correct human blindness and enable human reason to reclaim creation as a reliable source for the knowledge of God.

III

These ideas, sketched in all too brief a form in the commentary on Romans, are expanded and developed in successive editions of the *Institutes*, beginning with the 1539 edition. For example, in the *Institutes* Calvin adopts the theme of an innate knowledge of God's existence (*sensus divinitatis*), advocated by Denis, Melanchthon, and Bucer, and missing or at best only hinted at in his interpretation of Romans 1.[55] Furthermore, his clumsy use of a blindness "not so blind" is replaced by a more satisfying appeal to the metaphor of sight dimmed by age.[56] Blindness is now an acute astigmatism that can be corrected by the light of faith and the spectacles of Scripture.

What is striking, however, is the singularity of Calvin's reading of Paul. In the judgment of Calvin's contemporaries, Paul does not stress an acute noetic impairment because of sin or distinguish sharply between what is revealed in nature and what is perceived by fallen human reason. The thrust of Paul's argument, indeed, runs in the opposite direction. The point that Paul makes is not how little the Gentiles knew, but, considering the circumstances, how much they did know and how little use they made of it. By stressing the damage human reason has incurred through sin, Calvin makes the argument for the moral responsibility of the pagans all the more difficult to sustain.

Other Protestant theologians, of whom Melanchthon may be taken as representative, tend to argue that God is revealed in nature, that this revelation, however limited and inadequate, is nevertheless perceived by fallen human beings, who, precisely because of their sinfulness, proceed to suppress, distort, deny, ignore, forget, and abuse what they know.[57] Calvin argues, rather, that God is revealed in nature, that this revelation is misperceived by fallen human beings, who, precisely because of their sinful and culpable misperception, proceed to suppress, distort, deny, and abuse the true knowledge of God offered to them through the natural order.

Calvin avoids the difficulties he has placed in his own path by arguing that human blindness is culpable; but it is an argument which, in the form Calvin presents it, is not embraced by Denis, Melanchthon, Bullinger, or Bucer. These four commentators are joined in their dissent by Desiderius Erasmus,[58] Faber Stapulensis,[59] Martin Luther,[60] Huldrych Zwingli,[61] Johannes Oecolampadius,[62] Erasmus Sarcerius,[63] Andreas Knöpken,[64] Johannes Bugenhagen,[65] Thomas de Vio (Cajetan),[66] Johannes Lonicer,[67] Jean de Gagney,[68] Jacopo Sadoleto,[69] Ambrosius Catherinus Politus,[70] Marino Grimani,[71] Johannes Arboreus,[72] Claude Guilliaud,[73] Conrad Pellikan,[74] Alexander Alesius,[75] Wolfgang Musculus,[76] Johannes Brenz,[77] Peter Martyr Vermigli,[78] Domingo de Soto,[79] and Andreas Hyperius.[80]

There are, of course, repeated expressions of concern by Calvin's contemporaries about the inadequacy of the natural knowledge of God. The Dominican theologian, Ambrosius Catherinus Politus, for example, is troubled by the fact that, even if the Gentiles knew something about God through the natural light of reason, they could not glorify God without the supernatural gift of grace. If God therefore commanded the Gentiles to do what they could not do without grace, how could they be held responsible for their failure? Catherinus resolves his dilemma by arguing that the Gentiles knew enough about God to ask for divine aid and that God would have gladly given his grace to any who sought it.[81]

Similarly, the Lutheran theologian, Johannes Brenz, agrees with Calvin that the natural knowledge of God was obscured by original sin. The fact that God gave Israel the law and the prophets in order to clarify and confirm the natural knowledge of God impressed on human reason is an incontrovertible argument for its inadequacy.[82] Nevertheless, the Gentiles, who had no knowledge of the Mosaic Law, the prophets, or the gospel, knew that God exists, that God is eternal, powerful, wise, good, and the governor of all things.[83] The obscurity that Brenz bemoans is a good deal clearer than the near blindness deplored by Calvin.[84]

The distinction between what is offered by God and what is received by fallen human beings is echoed in Calvin's eucharistic theology. The question had been posed many times whether unbelievers receive the body and blood of Christ when they take the elements of bread and wine. Calvin argues that the substance of Christ's body and blood is offered to the congregation in the eucharist, whenever it is celebrated, but can only be received by faith. Men and women who lack faith participate in the simple meal of bread and wine and not in the spiritual real presence of Christ. Christ is truly offered, whether faith is present or absent; Christ is truly received, only when faith is present.[85]

In short, Calvin draws a distinction between what is offered and received that becomes a guiding principle of his thought, even outside the context of natural theology. In spite of the human fall into sin, the created order continues to function as a theater of God's glory. The whole world is, to use Bouwsma's phrase, "redolent with religious instruction." While fallen human reason perceives that God exists, it misperceives what God is like. Only when reason is illumined by faith, can it once again see the world for what it is, a mirror of divine glory. On this fundamental point Calvin is, I think, sometimes ambiguous, but never ambivalent.

NOTES

1. Emil Brunner and Karl Barth, *Natural Theology*, trans. Peter Fraenkel (London: Geoffrey Bles, 1946), p. 37.

2. Ibid., p. 41.

3. Ibid., p. 106.

4. Ibid., p. 107.

5. Ibid., p. 108.

6. Ibid., pp. 108–9: "It is true that, according to Calvin, the knowledge of God in Christ includes a real knowledge of the true God in creation. Includes! This

means that it does not, as Brunner seems to think, bring forth a second, relatively independent kind of knowledge, so that the circle would become an ellipse after all—as if our reason, once it had been illuminated, had of itself (*per se*) gained the power of sight (Instit., II, ii, 25)!" The debate prompted by Barth and Brunner was continued and extended by several historians, especially by Edward A. Dowey, Jr., *The Knowledge of God in Calvin's Theology* (New York: Columbia University Press, 1952), and T. H. L. Parker, *Calvin's Doctrine of the Knowledge of God* (Grand Rapids, Mich.: Wm. B. Eerdmans, 1959).

7. William J. Bouwsma, *John Calvin: A Sixteenth Century Portrait* (New York: Oxford University Press, 1988), p. 103.

8. Ibid., p. 104.

9. Ibid., p. 104.

10. Ibid., p. 104.

11. Ibid., p. 262, n. 51.

12. The best treatment of the place of nature in Calvin's theology is found in Susan E. Schreiner, *Theater of His Glory: Nature and the Natural Order in the Thought of John Calvin*, Studies in Historical Theology 3 (Durham, N.C.: Labyrinth Press, 1991). See also the essay by Christopher B. Kaiser, "Calvin's Understanding of Aristotelian Natural Philosophy: Its Extent and Possible Origins," in Robert V. Schnucker, ed., *Calviniana: Ideas and Influence of Jean Calvin*, Sixteenth Century Essays and Studies 10 (Kirksville, Mo.: Sixteenth Century Journal Publishers, 1988), pp. 77–92. For a treatment of the distinction between natural and super-natural theology in Reformed theology from Calvin to Protestant orthodoxy, see Richard A. Muller, *Post-Reformation Reformed Dogmatics: Volume 1, Prolegomena to Theology* (Grand Rapids, Mich.: Baker Book House, 1987), pp. 167–93.

13. The critical edition of Romans by T. H. L. Parker contains the revised text of 1556, with variants noted for the 1551 and 1540 editions. While Calvin expands and revises his remarks on the natural knowledge of God in 1551 and 1556, the absolutely crucial distinction between the clarity of divine revelation and the blindness of fallen human reason is already clearly articulated in the 1540 exegesis of 1:20. Similarly I.v.1–2, 7, 9–11, 14–15, first appear in the 1539 *Institutes*.

14. T. H. L. Parker in his book, *Commentaries on the Epistle to the Romans 1532–1542*, compares Calvin's exegesis of 1:18–23 with the exegesis of Melanchthon, Cajetan, Bullinger, Sadoleto, Bucer, Haresche, Pellikan, Grimani, and Guilliaud. Parker has collected in one short volume a good deal of valuable information. He is, however, in my judgment overly cautious when he does not take up the idea of natural theology in these authors because working "with such short passages of commentary . . . would fail in almost every instance to do justice to the author [p. 7]." There is, of course, no doubt that Calvin's thought is richer than his few remarks on Romans 1 demonstrate, but what he and the other commentators say is enough, as Parker also observes, to "note agreements in general, agreements in intention and tendency [p. 7]."

15. "Expositio quarundam Propositionum ex Epistola ad Romanos, 3–7," in Paula Fredriksen Landes, ed., *Augustine on Romans*, Texts and Translations 23, Early Christian Literature Series 6 (Chico, Calif.: Scholar's Press, 1982), pp. 2–4.

16. Denis the Carthusian was one of the few medieval authors whose works were collected by the library of the Academy in Geneva. The standard work on the library of the Calvin's Academy is Alexandre Ganoczy, *La bibliothèque de l'Académie de Calvin*, Études de philologie et d'histoire 13 (Geneva: Librairie Droz, 1969). Although a beautiful edition of Denis was published in Cologne in 1533, Parker does not mention Denis in his own study of Romans commentaries, though he tracks other noncontemporary commentators such as Thomas Aquinas. Haymo of Auxerre, also unmentioned by Parker and appearing under the false name of Haymo of Halberstadt, is published in Cologne in 1539, *Haymonis Episcopi Halberstatten in d. Pauli Epistolas Omnes Interpretatio* (Cologne: Eucharius Cervicornus, 1539).

17. Denis the Carthusian, *In Omnes Beati Pauli Epistolas Commentaria* (Cologne: Peter Quentell, 1533), Vr.

18. Ibid., Vr: "Cum enim omnis creatura sit quidam radius sui creatoris, et omnis effectus sit quaedam participata similitudo suae causae (quam unumquodque producit sibi simile) certum est quod ex naturis creatis aliquomodo cognoscatur increata natura."

19. Ibid., IIIIv: "Per naturalem rationem de Deo scire potest, videlicet quod Deus sit iustus et sapiens, approbans bona, et reprobans mala, et quod ipsi soli sit cultus perfectissimus, utpote honor latriae, exhibendus."

20. Ibid., Vr: "Secundum Damascenum quoque omnibus naturaliter inserta est cognitio existendi Deum."

21. Parker omits from his discussion of commentaries in the period 1532–1542 the posthumously assembled exegesis of Zwingli, *In Evangelicam Historiam de Domino Nostro Iesu Christo, per Matthaeum, Marcum, Lucam et Ioannem conscriptam, Epistolasque aliquot Pauli, Annotationes D. Huldrychii Zvinglii per Leonem Judae exceptae et editae* (Zurich: Christophor Frouschouer, 1539), and the commentary by the Lutheran theologian Erasmus Sarcerius, *In Epistolam ad Romanos pia et erudita Scholia* (Frankfurt: Christian Egenolph, 1541). Moreover, Parker is not correct when he asserts that after 1542 and "before the Council of Trent" "no new commentaries came out . . . [p. viii]." See Antonio Brucioli, *Nuovo Commento in tutte le celesti et divine Epistole di San Paulo*, Vol. 7 (Venice: Francesco Brucioli, 1544); John Chrysostom, *In Omnes d. Pauli Epistolas Commentarii* (Antwerp: Jan Steelsius, 1544); and Veit Dietrich, *Annotationes Compendiariae in Novum Testamentum* (Frankfurt: Christian Egenolph, 1545).

22. Philip Melanchthon, *Commentarii in Epistolam Pauli ad Romanos* (Wittenberg: Joseph Clug, 1532). References are to Rolf Schäfer, ed., *Römerbrief-Kommentar 1532*, in *Melanchthons Werke in Auswahl* (Gütersloh: Gerd Mohn, 1965).

23. Ibid., p. 70: "Nam hanc notitiam de Deo naturaliter habent homines, quae quidem est notitia quaedam legis, non evangelii."

24. Ibid., p. 71: "Habet enim quandam legis notitiam, non evangelii, sicut in ipso conscientiae certamine experimur, ubi cum notitia naturali et notitia legis acerrime pugnat evangelium."

25. Ibid., pp. 71–72: "Quamquam enim, ut postea dicit, mens ratiocinatur aliquid de Deo ex consideratione mirabilium eius operum in universa natura rerum, tamen hunc syllogismum ratio non haberet, nisi etiam Deus quandam notitiam *kai prolepsin* indidisset mentibus nostris."

26. Ibid., p. 72: "Neque vero notitia Dei intelligi debet de speculationibus, in quibus quaeritur de essentia Dei, sed notitia Dei est notitia voluntatis Dei erga nos et notitia legis Dei, h.e. quod vere irascatur peccantibus, quod vere requirat iusta, quod iniustos puniat, quod exaudiat et servet iustos."

27. Ibid., p. 71: "Quamquam autem naturae hominis quaedam legis notitia de Deo insita est, tamen haec ipsa notitia peccato originis aliqua ex parte obscurata est et nunc obruitur in impiis per alias rationes, ut, cum vident impii bonis male esse, sceleratis bene esse, discedunt a naturali notitia propter has offensiones et iudicant Deum non curare, non respicere humana. Ita delabitur mens humana in Epicureas opiniones." Cf. p. 74: "Porro haec naturalis notitia aliqua ex parte obscurata est a peccato originis. Nunc enim tanta est imbecillitas naturae, ut non constanter assentiatur huic notitiae, sed patiatur eam nobis excuti. Nec affectus oboediunt isti legi aeternae in animis scriptae, non timent Deum, non confidunt Deo."

28. Ibid., p. 75: "Quod igitur hic dicit: 'Vani facti sunt per cogitationes suas', ad utrosque referatur, ad philosophos et idolatras, quod habuerint vanas, falsas et nihili opiniones de Deo et has falsas opiniones amplexi sint tamquam veritatem, sicut Epicurei mira securitate irrident omnes alios et se solos sapere gloriantur hoc nomine, quod ausint contemnere Deum."

29. Heinrich Bullinger, *In Sanctissimam Pauli ad Romanos Epistolam* (Zurich: Christophor Froschouer, 1533), see, especially, fol. 19v–28r.

30. Ibid., fol. 17v: "Et enim omnia in iis intelliguntur, nempe si opera Dei exacto iudicio pensitentur. Deus enim per se omnium rerum est subsistentia, omnipotens, summus, verus, aeternus, bonus, sapiens et iustus. Caeterum harum rerum certissmum argumentum est moles mundi, quae in Deo subsistit. Potentia et sapientia eius condita est, iustitia et veritate regitur, bonitate vero et pulcherrima est et utilissima: quae sane non posset nisi aeternus, omnipotens et vere summus esset."

31. Ibid., fol. 18r: "Certe ut ex multis unum proferam, unus Seneca plus syncerioris theologiae posteritati religuit, guam omnes fere omnium scholasticorum libri."

32. Ibid., fol. 18v.

33. Martin Bucer, *Metaphrases et Enarrationes Perpetuae Epistolarum d. Pauli Apostoli* (Strasbourg: Wendelin Rihel, 1536), pp. 82–100.

34. Ibid., p. 84: "Cum enim Deus se ipse hominibus revelet, ea quae de ipso fas est homines cognoscere, non possunt eos latere. Sic certe haec notio Dei, eum in omnia habere potestatem, et esse summum bonum, impressa et infixa est mentibus omnium, ut nemo, qui quod sentit verum, fateri velit, queat negare eam inditam divinitus. Quae enim non ab ipso naturae conditore in nobis notiones informantur, incertae, nec diuturnae, et eadem apud omnes esse solent. At Deum esse, omnibus innatum et quasi in animo insculptum est, et non solum una cum saeculis, aetatibusque hominum inveteravit, sed confirmatum auctumque semper est adeo, ut quamvis multis multo studio annitantur, nequeant tamen hanc Dei notionem ex animo expungere." See also the comments of Parker, *Commentaries on Romans*, pp. 108–10, on Bucer's adaptation of the Stoic concept of *notio* to Paul's argument.

35. Ibid., p. 86: "Omnis siquidem peccati defensio eo constat, quod quis non volens peccarit, viam quod quis ignorat non potest eligere, eoque videtur non volens

peccare, quod peccat ignorans. Hinc Paulus veniam se consequutum scribit, quod Christum blasphemasset per ignorantiam. Proinde ubi Deus tollit sui ignorantiam, tollit simul nobis omnem excusationem contemptus sui apud nos."

36. Ibid., pp. 87–88.

37. Ibid., pp. 87–88: "Ex hiis iam satis liquet, utrumque vere dici, impios nosse Deum, et non nosse. Norunt siquidem Deum, norunt quae recta sunt, quantum ad id sufficit, ut seipsi condemnare compellantur. Rursus non norunt, quia non norunt efficaciter, ita ut spiritus Domini, quo ista Dei notitia constat, praevaleat, et diversum carnis iudicium opprimat, sed praevalet hoc illi, omneque quod a spiritu Dei est veri iudicium profligat."

38. Translations into English are quoted from John Calvin, *Calvin's Commentaries: The Epistles of Paul the Apostle to the Romans and to the Thessalonians*, trans. Ross Mackenzie (Grand Rapids, Mich.: Wm. B. Eerdmans, 1973), pp. 29–39. The Latin text was edited by T. H. L. Parker, *Iohannis Calvini Commentarius in Epistolam Pauli ad Romanos*, Studies in the History of Christian Thought 22 (Leiden: E.J. Brill, 1981), p. 29, abbreviated as Calvin, *Comment.trius*.

39. Calvin, *Commentarius*, p. 29: "Hic tamen videtur voluisse indicare manifestationem qua proprius urgeantur quam ut refugere queant: ut certe eam cordi suo insculptam quisque nostrum sentit."

40. Ibid., p. 30: Hic aperte testatur, Deum omnium mentibus sui cognitionem insinuasse: hoc est, sic se demonstrasse per opera, ut illi necessario conspicerent quod sponte non quaerunt, esse scilicet aliquem Deum."

41. Ibid., p. 29: "**Veritas Dei**, veram Dei notitiam significat. Eam continere, est supprimere, seu obscurare."

42. Ibid., p. 29: "Quo verbo significat, Deum quantus est, minime posse mente nostra capi: sed aliquem esse modum intra quem se cohibere debeant homines: sicuti Deus ad modulum nostrum attemperat quicquid de se testatur. Delirant ergo quicunque scire appetunt quid sit Deus."

43. Ibid., p. 29: "Intelligit autem id totum quod pertinet ad gloriam Domini illustrandum: vel (quod idem est) quicquid nos movere excitareque debet ad Deum glorificandum."

44. Ibid., p. 29: "Deum per se invisibilis est: sed quia elucet eius maiestas in operibus et creaturis universis, debuerunt illinc homines agnoscere: nam artificem suum perspicue declarant."

45. Ibid., p. 30: "Sit ergo haec distinctio: Demonstrationem Dei qua gloriam suam in creaturis perspicuam facit, esse, quantum ad lucem suam, satis evidentem: quantum ad nostram caecitatem, non adeo sufficere."

46. In his treatment of Rom. 8:20–22, Calvin admits that nature has been damaged by the fall, but that God preserves it from collapse until its renewal at the end of time.

47. Ibid., p. 30: "Caeterum non ita caeci sumus, ut ignorantiam possimus praetexere quin perversitatis arguamur."

48. Ibid., p. 30: "Neque abs re: caecitate enim impedimur ne pertingamus ad scopum. Videmus eatenus nequid iam possimus tergiversari."

49. Ibid., p. 31: "Eiusmodi virtutes quum non recognoverint homines in Deo, sed somniarint tanquam inane phantasma: merito dicuntur illum sua gloria improbe

spoliasse." Ibid., pp. 31–32: "Postquam Deum talem finxerunt, qualem carnali suo sensu apprehendere poterant, longe abfuit quin verum Deum agnoscerent: sed factitium et novum Deum, vel potius eius loco spectrum sunt fabricati."

50. Ibid., p. 31: "Nemo enim fuit qui non voluerit Dei maiestatem sub captum suum includere: ac talem Deum facere qualem percipere posset suopte sensu. Non discitur inquam haec temeritas in scholis, sed nobis ingenita, ex utero (ut ita loquar) nobiscum prodit."

51. Ibid., p. 32: "Atqui talis audaciae scelere nemo eximi potest: non sacerdotes, nec legislatores: non philosophi, quorum maxime sobrius Plato, formam ipse quoque in Deo vestigat."

52. Ibid., p. 30: "Quare Apostolus ad Hebraeos, fidei tribuit istud lumen, ut in mundi creatione vere proficiat."

53. In this connection Muller, *Post-Reformation Reformed Dogmatics*, p. 185, rightly observes:

> The Barthian readers of Calvin go to great lengths to deny the existence of natural theology, while all that Calvin does is declare such theology useless to salvation. Calvin, in fact, consistently assumes the existence of false, pagan natural theology that has warped the knowledge of God available in nature into gross idolatry. Calvin must argue in this way because he assumes the existence of natural revelation which *in se* is a true knowledge of God. If natural theology were impossible, idolatrous man would not be left without excuse. The problem is that sin takes the natural knowledge of God and fashions, in fact, an idolatrous and sinful theology. The theology exists and man is to blame because it is sin and sin alone that stands in the way of a valid natural theology.

54. Calvin, *Commentarius*, p. 30: "Concipimus Divinitatem: deinde eam quaecunque est, colendam esse ratiocinamur. Sed hic deficit sensus noster, antequam assequatur aut quis, aut qualis sit Deus."

55. *Inst.* I.iii.1. Muller, *Post-Reformation Reformed Dogmatics*, p. 174, in discussing *cognitio insita*, prefers to speak of an intuitive knowledge basic to the mind to distinguish it both from innate knowledge in the Platonic sense and from discursive knowledge acquired by ratiocination.

56. *Inst.* I.vi.1.

57. Melanchthon, *Commentarii*, pp. 71, 74.

58. Desiderius Erasmus, *In Novum Testamentum Annotationes* (Basel: Jerome Froben and Nicholas Episcopius, 1535), pp. 346–47.

59. Jacobus Faber Stapulensis, *Epistole divi Pauli Apostoli: cum commentariis praeclarissimi viri Jacobi Fabri Stapulen.* (Paris: Jean de la Porte, 1517), fol. 54v–56r.

60. WA 56.11–13, 174–79.

61. Huldrych Zwingli, *In Evangelicam Historiam de Domino nostro Iesu Christo, per Matthaeum, Marcum, Lucam, et Ioannem conscriptam, Epistolasque aliquot Pauli, Annotationes D. Huldrychi Zuinglii per Leonem Iudae exceptae et aeditae* (Zurich: Christophor Froschouer, 1539), p. 409.

62. Johannes Oecolampadius, *In Epistolam b. Pauli Apost. ad Rhomanos Adnotationes* (Basel: Andreas Cratander, 1525), fol. 12r–15r.

63. Erasmus Sarcerius, *In Epistolam ad Romanos pia et erudita Scholia, pro Rhetorica Dispositione, ad perpetuum Coherentiae Filum, conscripta* (Frankfurt: Christian Egenolph, 1541), on Rom. 1:18–32.

64. Andreas Knöpken, *In Epistolam ad Romanos Interpretatio* (Nuremberg: Johann Petreius, 1524), on Rom. 1:18–32.

65. Johann Bugenhagen, *In Epistolam Pauli ad Romanos Interpretatio* (Hagenau: Johannes Secerius, 1527), on Rom. 1:18–21.

66. Thomas de Vio, Cardinal Cajetan, *In Omnes d. Pauli et Aliorum Apostolorum Epistolas Commentarii* (Lyon: Jacobus et Petrus Prost., 1639), pp. 5–7.

67. Johannes Lonicer, *Veteris cuiuspiam Theologi Graeci succincta in d. Pauli ad Romanos Epistolam Exegesis, ex Graecis Sacrae Scripturae Interpretibus desumpta* (Basel: Robert Winter, 1537), pp. 6–7.

68. Jean de Gagney, *Brevissima et facillima in omnes d. Pauli Epistolas Scholia* (Paris: Martin Durand, 1629), fol. 2r–2v.

69. Jacopo Sadoleto, *In Pauli Epistolam ad Romanos Commentariorum Libri Tres* (Venice: Joannes Antonius Nicolinus de Sabio, 1536), fol. 22v–23r.

70. Ambrosius Catherinus Politus, *Commentaria in omnes divi Pauli et alias septem canonicas Epistolas* (Venice: Vincent Valgrisius, 1551), pp. 16–18.

71. Marino Grimani, *In Epistolas Pauli, ad Romanos, et ad Galatas Commentarii* (Venice: Aldine, 1542), fol. 13r–14v.

72. Johannes Arboreus, *Doctissimi et lepidissimi Commentarii in omnes divi Pauli Epistolas* (Paris: Jean de Roigny, 1553), fol. 4v–5r.

73. Claude Guilliaud, *In omnes divi Pauli Apostoli Epistolas Collatio* (Paris: Jean de Roigny, 1548), fol. 6v–7v.

74. Conrad Pellikan, *In omnes apostolicae Epistolas, Pauli, Petri, Iacobi, Ioannis et Iudae Commentarii* (Zurich: Froschouer, 1539), pp. 15–17.

75. Alexander Alesius, *Omnes Disputationes de tota Epistola ad Romanos* (Leipzig: Georg Hantzsch, 1553), on Rom. 1:18–32.

76. Wolfgang Musculus, *In Epistolam Apostoli Pauli ad Romanos* (Basel: Johann Hervagius, 1555), pp. 30–31.

77. Johannes Brenz, *In Epistolam, quam Apostolus Paulus ad Romanos scripsit, Commentariorum Libri Tres* (Basel: Paul Queck, 1565), pp. 55–66.

78. Peter Martyr Vermigli, *In Epistolam S. Pauli Apostoli ad Romanos* (Basel: Peter Pernam, 1560), pp. 57–67. See also the discussion by Muller, *Post-Reformation Reformed Dogmatics*, pp. 170–172.

79. Domingo de Soto, *In Epistolam divi Pauli ad Romanos Commentarii* (Antwerp: Jan Steelsius, 1550), pp. 41–48.

80. Andreas Hyperius, *Commentarii in omnes d. Pauli Apostoli Epistolas* (Zurich: Christophor Froschouer, 1584), pp. 22–26.

81. Politus, *Commentaria*, p. 18: "Sicut enim Deus illuminavit eos, ut intelligerent quid esset eis faciendum ad salutem, ita non defuisset in praebendo opportunum (quo ea facere poterant) auxilium, si poposcissent."

82. Brenz, *Commentariorum*, pp. 62–63: "Indigemus igitur sacris literis, quae hanc obscuritatem et tenebras discutiant. Et in hunc usum promulgatus est Decalogus, et postea Prophetica scriptura explicatus: ut quae de Deo impressa erant humani rationi, illustrarentur et confirmarentur."

83. Ibid., p. 60: "Ex hoc mundo naturaliter cognosci potest, quod sit Deus, isque aeternus. Deinde ut essentia Dei per se non videtur, ita nec potentia, nec sapientia, nec bonitas, nec severitas eius videntur: proponuntur tamen humanae rationi, ex hoc mundo videnda. Cum enim ex administratione mundi intelligitur quod sit Deus: eodem intellectu comprehenditur etiam, quod is Deus sit potentissimus et sapientissimus."

84. The same point is made by Melanchthon earlier, *Commentarii*, pp. 71, 74.

85. *Inst.* IV.xvii.33–34.

3

Calvin and the Absolute Power of God

The medieval distinction between the absolute and the ordained power of God is a distinction in Christian theology between what God can do in view of his sheer and unlimited ability to act and what he has chosen to do in the light of his wise and sometimes inscrutable purposes. God cannot, of course, will his own nonexistence or suspend the principle of non-contradiction. Omnipotence does not extend to the production of non-sense. But apart from these limitations, the sovereignty of God is absolute. Whatever God chooses to do (excluding, of course, what is inherently self-contradictory), God can do.

That God can do a thing, however, does not mean that he will do it. One may, in this respect draw an analogy, however imperfect, between divine and human activity. Just as human beings choose to do only some of the things that they could in fact do, so, too, God restricts his choices to a limited number of the almost limitless possibilities which lie open to his will. To talk about what is possible for God to do is to talk about the absolute power of God (*potentia dei absoluta*). To focus on the choices and decisions that God has made, is making, or will make (the distinction is in the human mind and not in the utterly simple being of God) is to introduce the subject of the ordained power of God (*potentia dei ordinata*).

In the third book of the *Institutes* (III.xxiii.2) Calvin attacked the distinction between the absolute and the ordained power of God as a speculative doctrine that separates the omnipotence of God from his justice and transforms the compassionate Father of the biblical narratives into an arbitrary tyrant. Anyone who has ever tried to trace Calvin's relationship to his sources knows how difficult it is and how few clues Calvin himself provides. What clues there are in the text, however, suggest that Calvin is drawn to the position of Duns Scotus—and, to a lesser extent, William Ockham—on several controverted issues. Like Scotus, Calvin stresses the priority of predestination to glory over predestination to grace (III.xxii.9) and argues that whatever God wills, "by the very fact that He wills it, must be considered righteous" (III.xxiii.2). Like Scotus and Ockham, Calvin wishes to preserve the transcendent freedom of God and to stress the radical contingency of the world and of all created being. It therefore comes as a shock that Calvin refuses to accept the very distinction they used to safeguard God's transcendent freedom and to underscore the world's radical contingency.

Later Reformed theology did not agree with Calvin's harsh judgment. By the end of the century theologians like Amandus Polanus[1] in Basel and William Ames[2] in Franeker were routinely drawing a distinction between absolute and ordained power in their discussions of divine omnipotence. Even Francis Turrettini[3] in Geneva felt obligated to explain away Calvin's objection to the distinction as an objection to the abuse of this distinction by certain unnamed late medieval scholastics.

Although the distinction between the absolute and the ordained power of God is not a subject on which Calvin wrote extensively, he did return to it several times during the period from 1551 to 1563. The distinction is mentioned in his commentaries on Gen. 18:13, Gen. 25:29, Rom. 9:19, Isa. 23:9, Jer. 12:1, his sermons on Job, as well as in four of his polemical tracts and treatises. Since Calvin is not inclined to use the technical theological language of the medieval church, his repeated comments on this technical language indicate that the distinction touches on a subject of some importance to him. Calvin seems to object to the distinction as such and not to abuses in the application of the distinction. Yet he is eager to preserve in his own theology many of the points which the medieval distinction intended to protect.

Did Calvin understand this distinction correctly? Did he criticize it fairly? Is Turrettini right when he claims that Calvin's rejection of the distinction between the ordained and the absolute power of God is a rejection of its abuse? Or are there internal tensions in Calvin's theology that make him suspicious of this distinction quite apart from the history of its use? In order to answer these and similar questions we need to examine what Calvin says about the absolute power of God both in the context of the antecedent history of this concept and in the context of his own theological commitments.

I

The distinction between the absolute and the ordained power of God was first suggested by medieval theologians in the late eleventh century. By the twelfth century it was a distinction common to all the theological schools.[4] In the thirteenth century Thomas Aquinas discussed the distinction in his disputation *De Potentia Dei* q.1 a.5 as well in the *Summa Theologiae* I q.25 a.5 and in II *Summa contra Gentiles* c.23–30. Thomas used the distinction to make the point that God's actions are free and not subject to necessity. Although the created order expresses God's wisdom, justice, and goodness, it does not exhaust them. God could have created *de potentia absoluta* a quite different order of the world and yet one in which his wisdom, justice, and goodness would still have found adequate expression. Thomas made this point in order to reject all necessitarian doctrines of God, whether pagan, Islamic, or Christian in origin, and to emphasize the contingency of the created order.

This distinction, while important, remained marginal to theological debate until the time of Duns Scotus, when it was given broader application.[5] Theologians found increasingly fewer propositions that were, on the face of them, self-contradictory, and increasingly more theological problems that were illuminated by considering the church's teaching against the background of the hypothetical possibilities inherent in the absolute power of God. Theologians asked whether God could *de potentia absoluta* cause the intuitive cognition of a nonexistent,[6] grant pardon to a *viator* who lacked the habit of grace,[7] or institute a new morality.[8] Some even speculated whether God could have become incarnate in an irrational animal.[9] By invoking divine omnipotence, theologians thought they were better able, in the words of Paul Vignaux, to separate "the accidental from the essential in the object of an investigation."[10]

In addition to the role played by the distinction between the absolute and the ordained power of God in late medieval theology, the distinction was of major importance within the enterprise of natural philosophy in this period as well.[11] God's absolute power was appealed to repeatedly (most often without reference to his ordained power) in the critical examination of the tenets of Aristotelian natural philosophy and, especially, in extending the investigation of problems within that natural philosophy from the realm of what was physically possible from the perspective of an Aristotelian system to what was logically possible, an extension that was directly accommodated by the invocation of a divine power limited only by the logically contradictory. Aristotle had asked, for example, whether an actual infinite was physically possible;[12] his fourteenth-century commentators asked in addition whether such actual infinites were logically possible.[13] It is noteworthy that such appeals in natural philosophy to God's absolute power often did not mention this power as such, but tacitly introduced it into the course of an argument by a simple "God could (*Deus posset*)" or by using some hypothetical operation of God that was relevant to the point at issue. (For example, God seeing or perceiving the total infinity of points in a line[14] or God annihilating everything save a single physical body.[15])

The theological use of this distinction by Scotus and his disciples—and later by William Ockham and his school—has been the subject of considerable scholarly debate in the twentieth century. Occamism or nominalism (debate has centered for the most part on the use of the *potentia absoluta* by this school) has received a generally negative assessment among such important historians as Gilson,[16] Feckes,[17] Knowles,[18] Lortz,[19] Iserloh,[20] and Leff.[21] According to the critics of nominalism, its philosophy and theology are atomistic, skeptical, and fideistic. This understanding of Ockham in particular and of nominalist theology in general has been challenged by many scholars, chiefly E. A. Moody,[22] Paul Vignaux,[23] Gerhard Ritter,[24] Philotheus Boehner,[25] Erich Hochstetter,[26] Léon Baudry,[27] Heiko A. Oberman,[28] Leif Grane,[29] William J. Courtenay,[30] and Albert Lang.[31] While these historians have differed among themselves, they have contributed to a revisionist assessment of nominalism that is increasingly influential.

The revisionists admit that it is true that nominalists celebrate the absolute freedom and transcendence of God. God is *exlex*, free from all claims and demands external to his own will. Prior to his self-revelation, God is unpredictable and unknowable. One cannot apply human concepts of justice to the justice by which God guides his actions in history. God is a free and sovereign Lord who acts in a manner that cannot be anticipated and which appears at first glance scandalous and an affront to reason. The absolute power of God means not only that God is utterly free but that the created order is radically contingent.

But while God is radically free from external limitations, he is not free from limitations that he has imposed upon himself. According to nominalist theology, God enters into covenants that restrict his freedom and that he regards as permanently binding. God could, had he chosen to do so, justify a sinner who lacks an infused habit of grace or refuse to accept a *viator* who has one. The point is that he does not choose to do so *de potentia ordinata*. Having limited himself by his covenant to justify sinners who are infused by a habit of grace, he remains faithful to his decision. The fidelity of God to his covenants *de potentia ordinata* is a central theme of late medieval nominalism.

When the Scotists and Occamists celebrated the freedom and transcendence of a God, who, although under no natural obligation to his creation, nevertheless bound himself to fulfill the terms of certain freely assumed covenantal obligations, they were returning to a theme which had a long and venerable tradition in Western thought, beginning with St. Augustine and continuing through such early Franciscan theologians as Odo Rigaldi.[32] Ideas concerning covenant and promise that seem radical in the fifteenth century were already taught by Cardinal Laborans and his contemporaries in the twelfth century.[33] Indeed, the notion that human merit should be established primarily on the basis of the covenant and promise of God[34] rather than on ontological grounds is a dominant motif if one takes the whole Middle Ages and not merely the thirteenth century into account.

The absolute power of God, therefore, must always be kept in tension with his ordained power. The fidelity of God to his covenants is just as important to late medieval theologians as the fact of his utter transcendence and radical freedom. Second causes are not suspended, though God by his absolute power could dispense with them. The point which Scotus and Ockham make is that the present order is radically contingent, not that it is thoroughly unreliable.

The world is governed by divine justice. God is not erratic or arbitrary, even granting that the justice of his will cannot be discovered in advance by human reason. The fact that God is not constrained by external and previously established norms does not mean that he acts unwisely. God is guided by his own inner sense of justice, which, even if it cannot be predicted, commends itself to human reason as self-consistent and reasonable, once it is revealed. God is his own justice. He therefore acts in limited, defined ways. He is committed to uphold the natural order and the process of salvation in spite of their undeniably contingent character.

It is precisely at this point that a disagreement has arisen over the status of miracles. Does a miracle belong to the absolute or the ordained power of God? William J. Courtenay has argued that late medieval theologians use the term *the absolute power of God* to refer to the "total possibilities initially open to God, some of which were realized by creating the established order."[35] The unrealized possibilities remain only hypothetically possible. The ordained power of God, on the other hand, refers to "the complete plan of God for his creation," including both miracle and historical novelty.[36] That God does some things on what appears to be a random or haphazard basis, while he does other things with unvarying regularity, does not mean that the random and occasional acts are any less an expression of the ordained power of God. What God has done, is doing, or will do belongs to the realm of his ordained power, even if that act is the crossing of the Red Sea or the resurrection of Jesus Christ from the dead. A miracle is as much an expression of the ordained power of God as the sunrise or the movement of the tides.

Other historians, among them Francis Oakley[37] and Steven Ozment,[38] have cited authors who use the distinction between the absolute and the ordained will of God as a distinction between the way God normally acts and the way he acts on occasion. There is evidence, as Courtenay admits, that Pierre d'Ailly (IV *Sent.* q.1 a.2) and Gregory of Rimini (I *Sent.* d.42–44 q.1 a.2) understood the distinction between the absolute and the ordained power of God in the sense in which Oakley and Ozment have defined them. Even Gabriel Biel (IV *Sent.* d.1 q.1 a.3 dub.2 M; I *Sent.* d.17 q.1 a.3 H) suggested that the rite of circumcision, once established as a requirement for the believing community in the Old Testament by the ordained power of God, has been superseded by baptism and so has fallen back into the realm of the absolute power of God, where it remains a hypothetical but not a real requirement for the Christian church. John Eck, who lectured on the *Sentences* of Peter Lombard for the last time in 1542, appears to agree with this looser usage and to ascribe a miracle both to the absolute power of God and to what he called "special ordained power."[39] It may be that Courtenay's description of the absolute power of God as the realm of the merely hypothetical represents the majority opinion in the thirteenth and fourteenth centuries, but theologians in the fifteenth and sixteenth centuries seem to be more casual in their use of terms.

What remains constant in the history of the use of this distinction is the continuing attempt by medieval theologians to protect the freedom and transcendence of God and to stress, for whatever reasons, the contingency of the created order. Thomas and Ockham did not altogether agree about what threatens the doctrine of that freedom and they certainly differed with each other about what God had bound himself to do. This distinction remained serviceable to Christian theologians who disagreed about many other matters because they shared a common conviction that creation did not exhaust the possibilities open to God and that divine omnipotence stretches beyond the furthest bounds the human imagination can reach.

II

Calvin's rejection of the distinction between the absolute and the ordained power of God occurs in three contexts in his biblical commentaries.

Miracles

The first context is the question of the adequacy of the power of God to perform miracles. According to Genesis 18, when Sarah hears about the promise to Abraham of a son (or, more accurately, overhears the promise, since she is eavesdropping at the time), she "laughs within herself." It is not the laughter of joy, but of unbelief. Sarah is convinced that the natural obstacles—the advanced age of her husband and her own advanced age, compounded by her chronic infertility—are stronger than the Word of God. The angel, who has an unsettling ability to see around corners and to hear inaudible thoughts, rebukes Sarah for her silent laughter with the words, "Is anything too hard for the Lord?" Sarah's sin, as Calvin sees it, is that "she did wrong to God, by not acknowledging the greatness of his power."[40]

Sarah's laughter leads Calvin to make two points to his readers. The first is to warn them not to limit the power of God to the "scanty measure" of their own reason. They doubt God's promises because like Sarah they "sinfully detract from his power." But the second touches on the distinction between the absolute and the ordained power of God. God's power should only be considered in the context of God's Word, what God can do in the framework of his declared will.

> In this way the Papists plunge themselves into a profound labyrinth, when they dispute concerning the absolute power of God. Therefore, unless we are willing to be involved in absurd dotings, it is necessary that the word should precede us like a lamp; so that his power and will may be conjoined by an inseparable bond.[41]

Providence

The second context in which Calvin rejects the distinction between the absolute and the ordained power of God is the question of the goodness of providence, especially in the face of the continued prosperity of the wicked. Here the prophets Jeremiah and Isaiah stimulate Calvin to reflect on God's power. Jeremiah 12 deals with the "confusion" the faithful experience when they observe that the wicked not only prosper but plead their prosperity as a sign of God's favor. In such circumstances the faithful are tempted to conclude either that the world is governed by chance and therefore not by God or that the God who governs the world is, after all, unjust.[42]

The pagan notion that there are no gods and that the world is at the mercy of irrational fortune is not an idea that Jeremiah seriously entertains. He knows that there is a God and that this God governs the world by his providence. Jeremiah's task is therefore to show that this God is just and that "the disorder in the world"[43] does not reflect any disorder in God. The wicked have mistaken God's forbearance for God's favor. Indeed, the wicked are accumulating a "heavier vengeance" for themselves on the day of judgment by their continued abuse of God's patience.[44] What Jeremiah does not do is "set up the judgments of men against the absolute power of God, as the sophists under the Papacy do, who ascribe such absolute power to God as perverts all judgment and all order; this is nothing less than sacrilege."[45] What he does do is suggest to God (and to the wicked who are listening to this conversation) that it may be time on the basis of God's declared will in the Torah to bring this period of patience and forbearance to an end. God's justice may be slow but it has not arbitrarily been set aside.

Isaiah 23 deals with the judgment of God on the Princes of Tyre. Judgments on princes and nations are examples of God's providential ruling of the world. What Isaiah wants to avoid is the notion that the punishment of the Princes of Tyre was unmerited or that God is guided in his judgments by anything less than his own sense of justice and equity. It is, of course, true that the justice by which God guides his judgments is not always clear to us. But that is all the more reason never to separate God's "wisdom and justice from his power."[46] The Princes of Tyre were brought low, not because they occupied high station, but because they were proud.

> That invention which the Schoolmen have introduced, about the absolute power of God, is shocking blasphemy. It is all one as if they said that God is a tyrant who resolves to do what he pleases, not by justice, but through caprice. Their schools are full of such blasphemies, and are not unlike the heathens, who said that God sports with human affairs.[47]

Predestination

The third context in which Calvin considers the absolute power of God is provided by the doctrine of predestination. Calvin illustrates this problem with the story of Jacob and Esau as told in Genesis 25 and retold in Romans 9. In the commentary on Genesis, Calvin attacks the idea that Jacob's election was based on foreseen merit or Esau's rejection on foreseen demerit. Calvin repeats the Augustinian argument that since all are unworthy to be saved, election is wholly gratuitous. There is no cause outside the will of God for the election of Jacob and that will, which can never be called to account, is itself "the cause of causes."[48]

> And yet Paul does not, by thus reasoning, impute tyranny to God, as the sophists triflingly allege in speaking of his absolute power. But whereas he dwells in inaccessible light, and his judgments are deeper than the lowest abyss, Paul prudently enjoins acquiesence in God's sole purpose; lest, if men seek to be too inquisitive, this immense chaos should absorb all their senses.[49]

In his commentary on Romans 9, Calvin returns to the same set of issues. God is just, even though his justice may be hidden from us, and there is "no higher cause than the will of God."[50] The ungodly, however, wish to blame their predicament on God. They attempt to excuse themselves by accusing God of being a tyrant. As the ungodly see it, God made human beings as they are and, by condemning them, only condemns his own workmanship. In their view God is powerful, but it is a power without justice. "So also the sophists in their schools talk nonsense about what they call his absolute justice, as if God would forget his own righteousness and test his authority by throwing everything into confusion."[51]

When Calvin takes up the problem of the absolute power of God in the *Institutes* (III.xxiii.2), he does it in the context of predestination, specifically in response to the objection leveled against it in his commentary on Romans—namely, whether the doctrine of election makes God a tyrant. In responding to this question, Calvin takes a very Scotistic line: "God's will is so much the highest rule of righteousness that whatever he wills, by the very fact that he wills it, must be considered righteous." He combines this answer with the antispeculative position characteristic of the early Reformation: "it is very wicked merely to investigate the causes of God's will." In short, "when . . . one asks why God has so done, we must reply: because he has willed it." But when Calvin is asked to name this exalted will of God, this "cause of causes," this "law of all laws," he shrinks back from calling it God's absolute will.

> we do not advocate the fiction of "absolute might"; because this is profane, it ought rightly to be hateful to us. We fancy no lawless god who is a law unto himself.[52]

III

When we consider Calvin's rejection of the distinction between the absolute and the ordained power of God in the context of the history of that doctrine, three things, I think, become clear.

Antispeculative

Calvin rejects the distinction in part because he fears that it encourages the natural human tendency to speculate about the being and nature of God apart from revelation. God can only be known where he has made himself known. While Calvin is only too eager to recommend the boundless power of God as a comfort for believers, he does not want the godly to contemplate that power except through the spectacles of Scripture. To investigate the will of God apart from the revealed will of God in the Bible is to lose oneself in a labyrinth of vain speculations.

Power and justice

Calvin's principal objection to the distinction is that, in his judgment, it separates the power of God from his justice. We have seen already from our survey of the history of the distinction how unfair that judgment is and how close to Scotus Calvin veers in his own concept of the omnipotent will of God. Nevertheless, it is true that scholastic theologians were willing to consider *de potentia absoluta* in such hypothetical possibilities as the incarnation of Christ in an irrational animal or the justification of sinners without a created habit of grace. Such arguments served to underscore the wisdom and justice of God's decisions *de potentia ordinata*.

Calvin is unwilling to entertain even a hypothetical separation of God's power from his justice. Of course, Scotus and Ockham do not seriously intend to separate God's power from God's justice, except as an experiment in thought. But Calvin refuses to do even that. God's power and justice are so tightly bound together that they cannot be separated. What the scholastics regard as a useful experiment in thought, Calvin regards as shocking blasphemy.

Potentia inordinata

Because the distinction, even rightly understood, invites speculative reflection on God outside revelation and allows a hypothetical, if not an actual, separation of God's power from his justice, Calvin's rejection of this distinction must, I think, be understood as a rejection of the distinction as such and not as a protest against its abuse. At no time does Calvin suggest that there is a licit use for this distinction or that it can be salvaged for Christian theology. Calvin reads the distinction between the *potentia absoluta* and the *potentia ordinata*, not as a distinction between the absolute and the ordained power of God, but as a distinction between *potentia ordinata* and *inordinata*, between "ordered" and "disordered" power. What the scholastics call the absolute power of God is a disordered power because it disjoins God's power from his justice. In that sense all power of God, realized and unrealized, actual and potential, is *potentia ordinata*, power ordered by God's justice.

Calvin, who hates and fears disorder in a fallen world, refuses to accept the idea that the disorder and confusion in the world are in any sense a reflection of disorder in the will of God. Whatever God has done, is doing, or plans to do is an expression of his *potentia ordinata*, even if the justice that guides his will is secret and hidden from us. That ordered power is displayed in miracles, providence, and predestination. Indeed, even the impenetrable darkness outside revelation cannot rob the godly of their confidence that the hidden power of God is not the power of an arbitrary tyrant, but the infinite power of a just Father. As Calvin writes in his commentary on Isa. 23:9:

> we ought to contemplate the providence of God in such a manner as to ascribe to his almighty power the praise which it deserves for righteous government. Although the rectitude by which God regulates his judgments is not always apparent or made visible to us, still it is never lawful to separate his wisdom and his justice from his power. . . . in the school of Christ we are taught that the justice of God shines brightly in his works, of whatever kind they are, "that every mouth may be stopped" (Rom. 3:19), and that glory may be ascribed to him alone.[53]

In short, Calvin is not opposed to the points made by Scotus and Ockham about the freedom and transcendence of God and at times sounds more Scotistic that Scotus himself. But he finds it impossible to make those points by appealing to the theological distinction between the absolute and the ordained power of God. Absolute power is for him disordered power, omnipotence divorced from justice. The will of God may be hidden and mysterious; it may even contradict human concepts of justice, but it is not disordered. Calvin is therefore not only opposed to the abuse of this doctrine, as Turrettini speculated; he is opposed to the distinction as such.

NOTES

1. Amandus Polanus von Polansdorf, *Syntagma Theologiae Christianae* II c.29 (Geneva: Jacob Stoër, 1617).

2. William Ames, *Medulla Theologiae* I.vi.16–20. English translation by John Dystra Eusden, *The Marrow of Theology* (Durham, N.C.: Labyrinth Press, 1968, 1983).

3. Francis Turrettini, *Institutio Theologiae Elenchticae* loc.III q.21 a.3–5 (Edinburgh: John D. Lowe, 1847).

4. Cf., for example, Hugh of St. Victor, *De Sacramentis* II c.22, PL 176.214.

5. See, for example, Albert the Great, *De Caelo et Mundo* I tract.III c.6; Alexander of Hales, I *Sent.* q.21 m.3 a.1; Bonaventure, I *Sent.* d.44 a.1 q.1.

6. Philotheus Boehner, "The Notitia Intuitiva of Non-existents according to William Ockham," in *Collected Articles on Ockham* (St. Bonaventure, N.Y.: Franciscan Historical Institute, 1958), pp. 269–300.

7. Cf., for example, Gabriel Biel's discussion of the necessity of a habit of grace considered *de potentia absoluta* in I *Sent.* d.17 with the same habit considered *de potentia ordinata* in II *Sent.* d.27.

8. William Ockham, II *Sent.* q.19 a.1 ad 30; *Quodlibet* III q.13.

9. Duns Scotus, *Ox.* III d.2 q.1 a.1; William Ockham, III *Sent.* d.1 q.1 U; Gabriel Biel, III *Sent.* d.1 q.1 a.1 cor.2 E, III *Sent.* d.1 q.1 a.1 concl. resp.

10. Paul Vignaux, *Philosophy in the Middle Ages* (New York: Meridian Books, 1959), p. 173.

11. Cf. the role it plays as a fundamental postulate relative to natural philosophy in the pseudo-Ockham *Tractatus de principiis theologiae*, ed. L. Baudry (Paris, 1936), p. 45.

12. Aristotle, *Physics* III, ch. 4–8.

13. Blasius of Parma, *Quaestiones in Phys.*, III q.4; MS VA 2159, fol. 107v–111bv.

14. Henry of Harclay in MS Tortosa Cated. 88, fol. 88r.

15. Jean Buridan, *Quaestiones Phys.* (Paris, 1509), fol. 50v.

16. Etienne Gilson, *History of Christian Philosophy in the Middle Ages* (New York: Random House, 1955).

17. Carl Feckes, *Die Rechtfertigungslehre des Gabriel Biel und ihre Stellung innerhalb der nominalistischen Schule* (Münster i.W., 1925).

18. Dom David Knowles, *The Evolution of Medieval Thought*, 2d ed. (New York: Longmans, 1988).

19. Joseph Lortz, *Die Reformation in Deutschland*, 2 vols. (Freiburg i.Br., 1941; Eng. trans. New York: Herder, 1968).

20. Erwin Iserloh, *Gnade und Eucharistie in der philosophischen Theologie des Wilhelm von Ockham* (Wiesbaden, 1956).

21. Gordon Leff, *Bradwardine and the Pelagians* (Cambridge: Cambridge University Press, 1957); *Gregory of Rimini: Tradition and Innovation in Fourteenth Century Thought* (Manchester: Manchester University Press, 1961); *William of Ockham: The Metamorphosis of Scholastic Discourse* (Manchester: Manchester University Press, 1975).

22. E. A. Moody, *The Logic of William of Ockham* (London, 1935).

23. Paul Vignaux, *Justification et prédestination au XIVe siècle: Duns Scot, Pierre d'Auriole, Guillaume d'Occam, Grégoire de Rimini* (Paris, 1934); *Luther commentateur des Sentences* (Paris, 1935); *Nominalism au XIVe siècle* (Montreal, 1948).

24. Gerhard Ritter, *Studien zur Spätscholastik*, 3 vols. (Heidelberg, 1921–22, 1926–27).

25. Boehner, *Collected Articles on Ockham.*

26. Erich Hochstetter, *Studien zur Metaphysik und Erkenntnislehre Wilhelms von Ockham* (Berlin-Leipzig, 1927).

27. Léon Baudry, *Lexique philosophique de Guillaume d'Ockham* (Paris, 1949).

28. Heiko A. Oberman, *The Harvest of Medieval Theology: Gabriel Biel and Late Medieval Nominalism* (Cambridge: Harvard University Press, 1962); *Werden und Wertung der Reformation* (Tübingen: J.C.B. Mohr (Paul Siebeck), 1977); *The Dawn of the Reformation* (Edinburgh: T. & T. Clark, 1986).

29. Leif Grane, "Gabriel Biels Lehre von der Allmacht Gottes," *Zeitschrift für Theologie und Kirche* 53 (1956): 53–75; *Contra Gabrielem, Luthers Auseinandersetzung mit Gabriel Biel in der Disputatio contra Scholasticam Theologiam* (Gyldendal, 1962); *Modus Loquendi Theologicus: Luthers Kampf um die Erneuerung der Theologie 1515–1518* (Leiden: E.J. Brill, 1975).

30. William J. Courtenay, *Covenant and Causality in Medieval Thought: Studies in Philosophy, Theology, and Economic Practice* (London: Variorum Reprints, 1984).

31. Albert Lang, *Henry Totting von Oyta* (Münster: Aschendorff, 1937).

32. Odo Rigaldi, *Quaestiones de gratia*, Toulouse, Bibliothèque de la ville, Cod. 737, fol. 208a–220d; II *Sent.* d.26–29, ed. J. Bouvy, "Les questions sur la grâce dans le Commentaire des Sentences d'Odon Rigaud," *Recherches de théologie ancienne et médiévale* 27 (1960): 305–43 (d.26 and 27); "La necessité de la grâce dans le Commentaire des Sentences d'Odon Rigaud," *Recherches de théologie ancienne et médiévale* 28 (1961): 69–96 (d.28 and 29).

33. Cardinal Laborans, "De iustitia et iusto," ed. A. M. Landgraf, *FlorPatr* 32 (Bonn, 1932): 6–42.

34. Odo Rigaldi calls such merit *meritum ex pacto. Quaestiones de gratia* q.35 ad 1, fol. 220d.

35. William J. Courtenay, "Nominalism and Late Medieval Religion," in *The Pursuit of Holiness in Late Medieval and Renaissance Religion*, ed. Charles Trinkaus with Heiko A. Oberman (Leiden: E.J. Brill, 1974), p. 39.

36. Ibid., p. 39.

37. Francis Oakley, "Medieval Theories of Natural Law: William of Ockham and the Significance of the Voluntarist Tradition," *Natural Law Forum* 6 (1961): 65–83; "Pierre d'Ailly and the Absolute Power of God: Another Note on the Theology of Nominalism," *Harvard Theological Review* 56 (1963): 59–73; *The Political Thought of Pierre d'Ailly* (New Haven: Yale University Press, 1964); *The Western Church in the Later Middle Ages* (Ithaca-London: Cornell University Press, 1979).

38. Steven E. Ozment, *Mysticism and Dissent, Religious Ideology and Social Protest in the Sixteenth Century* (New Haven: Yale University Press, 1973).

39. John Eck, *In Primum Librum Sententiarum Annotatiunculae* d.42 a.5, ed. Walter L. Moore, Jr. (Leiden: E.J. Brill, 1976).

40. CO 23.255. For a brief introduction to the problem of the *potentia absoluta* in Calvin's thought, see François Wendel, *Calvin: Origins and Development of His Religious Thought* (Durham, N.C.: Labyrinth Press, 1963, 1987), pp. 126–29. Cf. Armand Aime LaVallee, "Calvin's Criticism of Scholastic Theology," (Ph.D. diss., Harvard University, 1967), 60–65, 291.

41. CO 23.255.

42. CO 38.130. Cf. CO 34.336.

43. CO 38.128.

44. CO 38.129.

45. CO 38.129.

46. CO 36.391.

47. CO 36.391.

48. CO 23.354.

49. CO 23.354.

50. T. H. L. Parker, ed., *Iohannis Calvini Commentarius in Epistolam Pauli ad Romanos* (Leiden: E. J. Brill, 1981), p. 211.

51. Ibid., p. 210.

52. *Inst.* III.xxiii.2.

53. CO 36.391.

4

Calvin and the First Commandment

The great controversies of the sixteenth century seem, at first glance, to have very little to do with the Ten Commandments or to deal with them as no more than a subtheme of the broader problem of the role and function of the law. Moreover, the law itself is not regarded by sixteenth-century theologians as synonymous with the Ten Commandments. Theological treatises on the law discuss, in addition to the Ten Commandments, such topics as natural law, human law, ceremonial law, and the long list of moral precepts found in the Bible, though not included in the Decalogue itself.

The Lutheran, Reformed, and Roman Catholic confessions of faith talk about the law of God without spending much, if any, time elucidating the Ten Commandments themselves. The impression created is that, while sixteenth-century Christians differed sharply about the relationship of faith and works or about the distinction between law and gospel, they did not quarrel over the meaning of "do not steal" or "honor your father and mother." Unfortunately, such an impression is incorrect. Some of the fiercest Reformation controversies centered on specific commandments and their meaning for the life of the Christian churches.

One can take, for example, the sixth (seventh) commandment and the prohibition of adultery. Zacharias Ursinus in his *Commentary on the Heidelberg Catechism* used this commandment to discuss sexual ethics in general and the institution of marriage in particular.[1] In the course of his exposition Ursinus outlined the degrees within which a lawful marriage may occur and the problems of consanguinity and affinity. Other commentators discussed clandestine betrothals, monastic vows, legitimate and illegitimate grounds for divorce, and the possibility of remarriage by innocent parties. The disagreement over the meaning and import of this commandment was so great that Protestant communities in sixteenth-century Europe could often be distinguished from Roman Catholic, not only by the doctrine of the eucharist they embraced, but by the cousins they were allowed to marry.[2]

One of the earliest, and certainly one of the most intense, controversies to erupt in the sixteenth century was the dispute over the first commandment. In the traditional numbering, retained by Lutherans and Roman Catholics but abandoned by the Reformed, the first commandment includes the prohibition of graven images of God. The controversy was precipitated in 1521 by Andreas Bodenstein von Carlstadt, Luther's senior colleague on the faculty of theology, who believed that the first commandment requires the radical simplification of worship and the elimination of all cultic art.[3] Luther responded to Carlstadt in 1522 in a series of sermons and again in 1525 in a longer treatise, *Against the Heavenly Prophets.*[4]

Huldrych Zwingli, who led the Reformed community in Zurich, came to conclusions similar to Carlstadt's, though on the basis of somewhat different reasoning, and articulated his position in his *Commentary on True and False Religion* (1525).[5] Zwingli was opposed by John Eck, a Roman Catholic theologian who had debated Luther and Carlstadt at Leipzig in 1519 and the Zwinglian party at Baden in 1526. Eck included a response to all three in the 1529 revision of his popular handbook, *Enchiridion of Commonplaces against Luther and Other Enemies of the Church.*[6] By the time John Calvin discussed the first commandment in the 1536 edition of his *Institutes of the Christian Religion* the lines between the confessional families had been drawn and the fundamental arguments advanced.

The positions defended by Lutheran, Reformed, and Roman Catholic theologians in the sixteenth century proved to have fateful consequences for the doctrinal and liturgical traditions of the churches they represented. What appeared at first to be a limited disagreement over the meaning of the first commandment prompted dissension over such related issues as the role of art in Christian worship, the nature of the Lord's Supper, the authority of the Old Testament for the Church, and the pace of ecclesiastical reform— issues that are still in dispute, even if the terms of disagreement have shifted with the passage of time.

I

In 1521 Andreas Bodenstein von Carlstadt, professor of theology in the University of Wittenberg as well as doctor in civil and canon law, proposed and helped to implement several measures for the reform of public worship in the churches of Wittenberg. Carlstadt was not alone in his desire to reform public worship and thought that he had the backing of his influential younger colleague, Philip Melanchthon, in addition to the support of the more radical elements in town. On Christmas Day, 1521, Carlstadt celebrated the eucharist in both kinds, wearing a simple nonliturgical gown and pronouncing the words of consecration in German.[7] While he was not directly involved in the acts of vandalism that took place in Wittenberg in 1521–1522, he did advocate the removal of images and defended a swift implementation of his reform program.

Carlstadt's argument for the removal of images hinged on his understanding of the first commandment.[8] In order to prevent idolatry and to promote the worship of the one true God, Moses had forbidden Israel to make graven images of God. This commandment, although addressed to Israel, is still binding for Christian churches, whose history has proven that they, too, are unable to make religious images without falling into idolatry and superstitious worship. Carlstadt called on the City Council of Wittenberg to act swiftly to remove images from the churches under its jurisdiction.

Luther, who had been in hiding for almost a year in the Wartburg castle following his refusal to recant at the Diet of Worms, returned to Wittenberg on March 6, 1522, to resume leadership of the Reform movement. Wearing the tonsure and cowl of an Augustinian friar, Luther preached a series of eight sermons in the City Church of Wittenberg from Invocavit Sunday, March 9, to Reminiscere Sunday, March 16. The third of these so-called Invocavit sermons, preached on Tuesday, March 11, attacked in explicit terms Carlstadt's understanding of the first commandment.[9]

Luther's argument has several elements in it. First of all, he disputed Carlstadt's exegesis. Although it is clear that the first commandment prohibits idolatry and the creation of images for use in idolatrous worship, it is not at all clear that the Old Testament prohibits the making of images. Moses, who gave the commandment against idols, also put carvings of cherubim on the ark of the covenant and erected a bronze serpent in the wilderness. Hezekiah broke the bronze serpent, not because Moses had no right to erect it, but because it had been abused as an object of veneration. The ban was not on images as such but on the improper use of images.

Furthermore, iconoclasts like Carlstadt were in danger of sacrificing Christian freedom and of transforming the liberating gospel of Christ into a dismal announcement of inescapable duties. Theologians who insist that churches must abolish images commit as grave an error as theologians who insist that they must be venerated. Images, like meat offered to idols, are nothing in themselves, or else Paul would have denounced the altars on Mars Hill or defaced the images of Castor and Pollux on the prow of his ship. What is at issue in the first commandment is whether God alone is honored and believed. The Word alone, and not the smashing of images, can free the human heart from idolatry and liberate it for the veneration of the true God.

Carlstadt did not respond to Luther in writing until November 1524, when he published in Basel a tract entitled *Whether One Should Proceed Slowly and Avoid Offending the Weak in Matters that Concern God's Will*.[10] The chief point that Carlstadt disputed is Luther's contention that Christian love requires the Church to have patience with weaker consciences and to proceed with great caution in enacting controversial reforms. Carlstadt attacked Luther's counsel of patience, first by a *reductio ad absurdum* and then by a telling illustration.

The first commandment is one of ten. Whatever applies to the other nine commandments, argued Carlstadt, ought to apply to the first as well. Does Luther counsel patience in enforcing the prohibition of stealing or of killing one's neighbor? Should adultery be permitted until weaker consciences are convinced that adultery is wrong? If patience is inappropriate in the enforcement of the sixth and seventh commandments, why is it appropriate in the enforcement of the far more important first commandment?[11]

Furthermore, Carlstadt was not convinced that Luther had correctly assessed the duty that love owes to the weak. If a child should pick up a sharp knife with which it could do itself or some other child a severe injury, should a parent stand idly by and allow the child to keep an object that is harmful or should the parent snatch the knife away, even though the child is distressed and cries inconsolably for the restoration of the dangerous object. The patient parent, who leaves the knife with the child, does not love the child. The duty love owes the weak is immediate intervention. If this is true with respect to the bodily injury inflicted by a knife, how much more is it true with respect to the spiritual injury inflicted by idols.[12] Carlstadt's guiding principle is summarized in these words: "each one should do what God commands, even though the whole world holds back and does not want to follow."[13]

Luther's longest response to Carlstadt was developed in his 1525 treatise, *Against the Heavenly Prophets*.[14] While Luther repeated and expanded many of the points made in his Invocavit sermons, he took the discussion in a new direction by introducing the subject of natural law and the question of the relationship of the Ten Commandments to it. The principles of natural law are the moral principles that are intelligible to human reason apart from special revelation. Natural law contains not only rules of human conduct in the narrow sense ("do not steal," "do not murder," "do not commit adultery"), but also such religious principles as the inalienable human conviction that there is a God to whom worship is owed.

The old distinction, that the Ten Commandments—in contrast to the judicial and ceremonial law—embody a moral law that has not been abro-

gated by the gospel, is simply false. Two commandments are clearly ceremonial in nature: the commandments concerning the observance of the
sabbath and the prohibition of the worship of images. Furthermore, the
validity of the Ten Commandments rests, not only the authority of Moses,
but on the conformity of the commandments to the principles of natural
law—that is, to the will of God as it can be known by human reason. The
law of Moses is nothing more than the *Sachsenspiegel* of the Jews. It is a law-
code for a particular people, embodying universal principles of natural law,
but adapted to the historical situation of ancient Israel.

When Moses told the Jews not to murder or steal, he was only articulating
principles of natural law also known to the pagans and embodied in their
law-codes. Even the commandment to keep the sabbath is an application
to the Jews of the natural principle that periodic times of rest are essential
for men and women. Just as the French are not bound by the particular
details of German law-codes (though they are bound by principles of natural law), so Christians are not bound by the detailed law-codes of Moses
whenever Moses goes beyond what natural law requires.

Natural law requires that God alone be honored and worshiped. The
prohibition of images, on the other hand, is a time-bound application of
this principle to the situation of the Jews. The principle that God alone is
to be honored and worshiped is still in effect (though it is fulfilled under
the gospel by faith alone). But the prohibition of images, like the prohibition of work on Saturday, is a commandment that has no validity for the
Christian church.

In his *Large Catechism*, which is included as one of the Lutheran confessional documents in the *Book of Concord*, Luther repeated for a lay audience
his sharp distinction between the prohibition of idolatry, which is absolute and universally applicable, and the ban on images, which is relative
and dependent on a specific historical context. Luther offered the example
of a wealthy man who worships money and property. Even though the rich
man constructs no images of God, he is an idolater who worships a false
God. Idolatry is always a matter of the heart; it is a matter of trusting completely in "creatures, saints, or devils" rather than in God who has created
and redeemed the world in Christ.[15]

II

Response to the controversy between Luther and Carlstadt came from two
quarters: from the Reformed theologian, Huldrych Zwingli, who alluded
to Luther's *Against the Heavenly Prophets* in his *Commentary on True and False
Religion*, and from the Roman Catholic theologian, John Eck, who responded
to all three—Luther, Carlstadt, and Zwingli—in his *Enchiridion*. Zwingli
agreed in the main with Carlstadt that the first commandment prohibits

the worship of images and the use of cultic art. Images are impermissible in Christian worship both because they are forbidden in the Old and New Testaments and because they are incapable of kindling love for God.[16]

Zwingli, however, shifted the focus of the debate by referring to Luther's attack on Carlstadt in the context of his discussion of the Lord's Supper.[17] To what extent is there a parallel between the veneration of cultic art and the adoration of the sacrament? Zwingli saw no difference between the veneration of images and icons in Christian worship and the veneration of the elements of bread and wine. A priest who places a consecrated host in a monstrance for adoration by the faithful is violating the first commandment as surely as if he were to erect a statue of Zeus or Aphrodite. He is substituting the creature for the creator, robbing God of the glory that belongs to God alone, and transferring it to a wafer. "God alone is to be worshiped," argued Zwingli, "and absolutely no creature," not even "Christ's pure humanity."[18]

In the *Second Helvetic Confession*, which summarizes the theology of Zurich at mid-century and which became the most widely used of all the Reformed confessions, Zwingli's successor, Heinrich Bullinger, repeated the argument of Carlstadt that images are forbidden by the Old Testament and the argument of Zwingli that the bodily presence of Christ is less profitable for the church than the perpetual presence of his Spirit. Against the Roman Catholic claim that images are books for the laity, Bullinger replied that the laity are taught mainly through the preaching of the gospel and the institution of the sacraments.[19]

John Eck, who had written his *Enchiridion* primarily against Luther and Melanchthon, found himself in rather grudging agreement with Luther's attack on Carlstadt's iconoclasm. As a Catholic theologian, Eck wanted to make a far more positive case than Luther for the usefulness of images, since they "instruct the simple, admonish the knowing," and "affect all."[20] But if Luther was not willing to embrace the whole teaching of the Catholic Church concerning images, he was at least wise enough to reject Carlstadt's arguments against them.

Eck listed five objections to images put forward by Carlstadt and other "heretics," who shared his point of view, and responded to each objection in turn.[21] Against the objection that images are forbidden in the Old Testament, Eck responded that idolatry and not images are forbidden; otherwise, Solomon would have sinned when he had twelve lions carved in his throne and Moses when he placed images of cherubim on the ark of the covenant. Against the objection that Hezekiah broke the bronze serpent made by Moses, Eck replied with Luther that it was the idolatrous abuse of the image by the Jews and not the image itself that was at fault.

Eck turned on its head the objection of Zwingli that the worship of God in spirit and in truth is worship without sensible images. For Eck spiritual worship and the proper use of images imply and complement each other. Images "admonish and remind" Christians to direct their worship to the invisible, incorporeal God. If that were not so, God would not have established the sacraments, which, like images, are sensible signs that point to transcendent realities.

To the objection that cultic art not only seduces the simple laity into idolatry but sometimes stimulates them to erotic fantasies, Eck denied the necessity, though not the possibility, of the misuse of religious art. Idolatry can be avoided by teaching the laity the meaning and purpose of images. Unclean thoughts can be avoided by forbidding painters to render what Eck calls "lascivious subjects."

Eck identified the fifth and final objection to images with the name of his former student, the Anabaptist theologian, Balthasar Hubmaier. According to Eck, Hubmaier appealed to the principle that the church may only do what is explicitly commanded in Scripture. If the Bible explicitly commands the church to have images of Christ and the saints, then it must create them. If the Bible does not, then the church may not. The absence of a command has the moral force of a prohibition.

Eck replied by demonstrating how unworkable such a principle is and how quickly it leads to consequences unacceptable even to Hubmaier. The Bible, for example, commands the keeping of the sabbath but lacks any command concerning the worship of God on Sunday. Did Hubmaier propose that Christians worship God on Saturday, for which there is a command, rather than on Sunday, for which there is none? If so, did Hubmaier recommend the reinstitution of Jewish sabbath regulations and dietary laws? If not, why not? In short, Hubmaier's argument seemed to Eck to collapse the church into the synagogue and to dissolve the boundaries between the two testaments.

The position of Eck was reaffirmed by the Council of Trent at its twenty-fifth session on December 4, 1563. Images are not idols because the "honor which is shown to them is referred to the prototypes which they represent."[22] Furthermore, images have an important role to play in the education of the laity, who are reminded of what they believe and inspired by the "stories of the mysteries of our redemption portrayed in paintings and other representations."[23] The Council even repeated Eck's concern to avoid abuses, including the painting and adorning of images "with a seductive charm."[24]

III

As a theologian of the second generation, John Calvin summarized, and often harmonized, the conflicting positions of the earlier reformers. In the controversy over the first commandment, however, Calvin sided unreservedly with Zwingli and Bullinger against Luther and Eck. Like Zwingli, Calvin dealt with the first commandment in the dual context of law and the eucharist.[25] While there is an echo of Luther's catechetical teaching in Calvin's summary of the first commandment (God "is to be feared and loved by us, beyond all else, that we recognize him alone as our God, and fix all our hope and trust in him"), the weight of Calvin's exposition falls on the prohibition of sensible images of God: "This commandment teaches God himself . . . is to be honored by such worship that we dare not attach anything physical to him, or subject him to our senses, as if he could be comprehended by our dull heads, or be represented in any form."[26]

Calvin's principal fire was directed against two arguments advanced by Eck and the Roman Catholic defenders of religious art: namely, that veneration is referred to the prototypes rather than to the images of Christ and the saints, and that images are pedagogically useful as the book of the unlearned. The first argument, that veneration is directed toward God rather than to pictorial representations of God, is rejected by Calvin as specious. Exactly the same argument could be advanced by devotees of any pagan religion. All idolaters regard their idols as visible signs of an invisible God. The ancient Romans were "not so senseless . . . as not to have understood God to be something else than wood or stones."[27] In the end, of course, the ancient Romans became dependent on the images they had created and could no longer imagine the presence of God apart from a physical presence in images.

The second argument, that images are the book of the unlearned, met with Calvin's scorn. The instruction of the laity ought to take place through the preaching of the Word. One sentence of clear catechetical instruction is worth five thousand crucifixes. Furthermore, many of the images the laity encounter in the churches are sexually provocative. "Indeed," contends Calvin, "brothels show harlots clad more virtuously and modestly than the churches show those objects which they wish to be seen as images of virgins."[28]

Like Zwingli, Calvin linked the problem of images to the problem of eucharistic piety. He repudiated the adoration of the eucharist for two reasons, one specific to the sacrament and one derived from the first commandment. The specific reason why Christ's body cannot be adored in the sacrament is that the risen humanity is seated at the right hand of God the Father in heaven. While Christ may be adored as ascended and exalted, the eucharistic bread and wine may not. Furthermore, to adore the sacrament is to adore the gift rather than the giver, to transfer to "creatures of bread and wine" the honor that belongs to God alone. What appears at first glance to be commendable Christian piety proves on closer scrutiny to be a regrettable lapse into idolatry.

Calvin developed these points further in his 1559 edition of the *Institutes*, especially in I.xi.1–15. Against the example of the cherubim on the ark of the covenant cited by Luther and Eck, Calvin responded that the cherubim with outspread wings, like the seraphim in prophetic visions, "signify that the splendor of divine glory is so great that the very angels also are restrained from direct gaze, and the tiny sparks of it that glow in the angels are withdrawn from our eyes."[29] The cherubim are not sensible signs of the invisible God but visible reminders of an ineradicable mystery. They do not so much disclose as conceal the incomprehensible essence of God.

Finally, Calvin felt obliged to answer the charge that his opposition to cultic art should be understood as an opposition to all sculpture and painting. He pled innocent to the charge of cultural Philistinism and protested that his opposition to religious sculpture and painting was only opposition to the portrayal of the invisible majesty of God. Artists have a perfect right to paint what "the eyes are capable of seeing."[30] Calvin, however, was still uneasy that artists, given half a chance, would take indecent liberties in their portrayal of the human body.

IV

The central point on which all participants in this controversy agreed was that the first commandment prohibits the worship of any God except the true God. Whether that could best be done without the use of images was the question on which no consensus could be formed. Luther and Eck argued against Carlstadt, Zwingli, and Calvin that the prohibition of idolatry did not entail the elimination of all visual art in Christian worship but only the prevention of its abuse. Their opponents regarded any visual representation of God as unavoidably idolatrous by its very nature. To portray God in painting or sculpture is to transfer to creatures the honor that belongs to God alone.

The debate turned on two issues: whether the Mosaic law forbade the making of all images and whether, if it did, the prohibition was binding on Christian churches. Eck attempted to refute Carlstadt and his allies by listing the images expressly sanctioned by the Old Testament, including images made by Moses himself. Luther moved the argument to a different level when he contended that the Ten Commandments derive their authority from natural law rather than from Moses. Even the principle involved in the first commandment—namely, there is one God to whom worship is owed—is a principle accessible to all human beings through the natural light of reason. The prohibition of images is only a statute of Jewish positive law, intended to enforce the prohibition of idolatry in the specific historical context in which Israel found itself and, as such, not binding on the church.

Reformed theologians, including Carlstadt, gave the Old Testament prohibition of images a privileged place as a universal injunction still valid for the liturgical life of the church. Eck had argued that images are licit because of their similarity to the sacraments as sensible signs pointing to a transcendent reality. While Calvin agreed with Eck that the eucharist is a sensible sign, he sharply distinguished the eucharist from other representations of God in the visual and plastic arts. Other sensible signs are idolatrous by nature and fall without exception under the prohibition of the Mosaic law. Sacraments are not idolatrous by nature, but only through abuse. In this connection the first commandment is a wall of defense against what Calvin regarded as an inadequate doctrine of the real presence of Christ in the eucharist.

The differences between the confessional families—Roman Catholic, Lutheran, and Reformed—are readily apparent. The images of Christ and the saints that are at home in a Roman Catholic parish are not yet welcome in a Presbyterian congregation. What is not so apparent, but what the sixteenth-century dispute helps us to see more clearly, is the nature of those differences. The original disagreement was not between Christians who embraced and Christians who rejected the first commandment, but between Christians who understood the first commandment differently. No one denied that the first commandment taught Christians to fear and love God beyond all else, to recognize him alone as their God, and to fix all their hope and trust in him. The quarrel was not over what to do, but how to do it.

NOTES

1. Zacharias Ursinus, *Catecheticas Explicationes* (NN: Ioannis Tornaesius, 1623). Cf. the English translation by G. W. Willard, *The Commentary of Dr. Zacharias Ursinus on the Heidelberg Catechism* (Columbus, Ohio: Scott and Bascom, 1851), pp. 589–95.

2. For an introduction to the issues involved, see Steven Ozment, *When Fathers Ruled: Family Life in Reformation Europe* (Cambridge: Harvard University Press, 1983).

3. For an introduction to Carlstadt and his controversy with Luther, see especially E. Gordon Rupp, *Patterns of Reformation* (Philadelphia: Fortress Press, 1969); James S. Preus, *Carlstadt's Ordinaciones and Luther's Liberty: A Study of the Wittenberg Movement 1521–22*, Harvard Theological Studies 27 (Cambridge: Harvard University Press, 1974); and Ronald J. Sider, *Andreas Bodenstein von Karlstadt*, Studies in Medieval and Reformation Thought 11 (Leiden: E.J. Brill, 1974).

4. WA 18.62–125, 134–214. Cf. Carlos M. N. Eire, *War against the Idols: The Reformation of Worship from Erasmus to Calvin* (Cambridge: Cambridge University Press, 1986), pp. 54–73.

5. Emil Egli, Georg Finsler, and Walther Köhler, *Huldreich Zwinglis Sämtliche Werke*, Vol. 3 (Leipzig, 1914), abbreviated as ZW 3. English translation edited by S. M. Jackson and C. N. Heller, *Zwingli: Commentary on True and False Religion* (Durham, N.C.: Labyrinth Press, 1981).

6. Johannes Eck, *Enchiridion locorum communium adversus Lutherum et alios hostes ecclesiae (1525–1543)*, ed. Pierre Fraenkel, Corpus Catholicorum 34 (Münster: Aschendorff, 1979). Cf. John Eck, *Enchiridion of Commonplaces against Luther and Other Enemies of the Church*, trans. by Ford Lewis Battles (Grand Rapids, Mich.: Baker Book House, 1979). According to Battles, the *Enchiridion* went through ninety-one editions by 1600 (p. 4*).

7. Sider has provided a translation of Carlstadt's sermon at this eucharistic service in Ronald J. Sider, *Karlstadt's Battle with Luther* (Philadelphia: Fortress Press, 1978), pp. 7–15.

8. Carlstadt's position is outlined in *Andreas Karlstadt, Von Abtuhung der Bilder*, ed. Hans Lietzmann, Kleine Texte 74 (Bonn: A. Marcus und E. Weber, 1911), pp. 1–22.

9. BoA 7.370–72.

10. The German text was edited by Erich Hertzsch, *Karlstadts Schriften aus den Jahren, 1523–25*, Teil 1 (Halle: Max Niemeyer, 1956), pp. 74–97.

11. Ibid., pp. 76–77.

12. Ibid., pp. 88–89.

13. Ibid., p. 76.

14. WA 18.62–125, 134–214.

15. Theodore G. Tappert, ed. and trans., *The Book of Concord: The Confessions of the Evangelical Lutheran Church* (Philadelphia: Muhlenberg Press, 1959), pp. 365–71.

16. ZW 3.901–02.

17. ZW 3.817.

18. ZW 3.817.

19. Arthur C. Cochrane, ed., *Reformed Confessions of the 16th Century* (Philadelphia: Westminster Press, 1966), pp. 229–30.

20. Eck, *Enchiridion locorum*, p. 194.

21. Ibid., pp. 195–98.

22. *Denz.* 986.

23. *Denz.* 987.

24. *Denz.* 988.

25. OS 1.42–45, 143–45.

26. OS 1.43.

27. OS 1.43.

28. OS 1.44.

29. *Inst.* I.xi.3.

30. *Inst.* I.xi.12.

5

Calvin and Abraham

It is possible to be so familiar with a subject that we no longer see its peculiar features. Roger Fry, the English art critic, spoke of a specialization of vision that prevents us from observing familiar objects around us until artists awaken us to the distinctive reality of what we have overlooked by lending us their eyes.[1] Historical discoveries are often very much like an aesthetic awakening. Only a relatively small percentage are prompted by the discovery of wholly new and previously unknown evidence. The great majority are stimulated by fresh insight into evidence so familiar that its significance has been underestimated or disregarded.

The fascination of the sixteenth century with the Bible forms a case in point. Historians have paid very little attention to the history of the interpretation of the Bible in the sixteenth century. The career of John Calvin provides an excellent example of such neglect. Although Calvin considered himself to be primarily an interpreter of the Bible and although his sermons and commentaries outnumber in length and quantity his systematic and polemical writings, far more is known about Calvin as a systematic or polemical theologian than as an interpreter of the Bible. What makes this situation particularly ironic is that Calvin regarded his primary theological work, the *Institutes of the Christian Religion*, as a handbook or introduction for beginners to study Scripture. Calvin hoped that the *Institutes* would uncover the architectonic structure of Scripture, so that inexperienced readers of the text might find their way in it. Alexandre Ganoczy has described this relationship as a hermeneutical circle: from the text to the *Institutes* and back to the text again.[2]

I

The letter to the Romans was particularly important to Calvin and his contemporaries. In it Paul discusses such themes as human sin, the place of the law, justification by faith, Christian ethics, the moral claims of the state, and the continuing significance of Israel in the history of salvation. Indeed, the first biblical commentary that Calvin ever wrote was a commentary on Romans (1540), a work which he twice revised and expanded (1551, 1556).[3] Furthermore, Romans plays a significant role in Calvin's other theological writings, particularly in the successive editions of the *Institutes*. In the first edition of the *Institutes* in 1536, Calvin cites Romans 162 times; by 1559 and the last Latin edition of the *Institutes*, the list has grown to 573 citations. It is surprising, therefore, that so little has been written on Calvin as an interpreter of Paul. In recent years several scholars have turned their attention to aspects of the problem. In an unpublished thesis, John R. Walchenbach examined Calvin's use of Chrysostom in his interpretation of I Corinthians.[4] Benoit Girardin discussed the rhetorical style of Calvin's lectures on Romans.[5] T. H. L. Parker commented on texts, translations, and editions.[6] The most extensive work has been done by Alexandre Ganoczy, who has devoted his attention to Calvin's hermeneutics in three publications.[7]

Although the literature on Calvin and Paul is modest, the exegetical tradition on Romans is extensive and rich. In addition to Calvin the book was commented on in the sixteenth century by more than seventy Lutheran, Reformed, Catholic, and Radical theologians, including such figures as Erasmus,[8] Colet,[9] Sadoleto,[10] Lefèvre d'Étaples,[11] Luther,[12] Cajetan,[13] Melanchthon,[14] Bugenhagen,[15] Knöpken,[16] Oecolampadius,[17] Bullinger,[18] Pellikan,[19] Catherinus Politus,[20] de Soto,[21] Brenz,[22] Musculus,[23] Olevian,[24] Hemmingsen,[25] Sarcerius,[26] Toledo,[27] Cruciger,[28] and Bucer.[29] There are partial or complete commentaries by Patristic authors from Origen[30] to Ambrosiaster[31] and by medieval commentators from Peter Abelard[32] and Haymo of Auxerre[33] to Hugh of St. Cher[34] and Nicholas of Lyra.[35] Whereas Calvin did not know or cite the whole of this literature, he did know a substantial portion of it as his own comments on the text make clear.

What I propose to do in what follows is to place Calvin's commentary on Romans, or at least a small portion of it, in the context of the sixteenth-century debate on the meaning and significance of this book. By doing so, I intend to show that Calvin's comments on Paul can only be properly understood and evaluated within that context. Since Romans is far too large a book to consider in one essay, I shall concentrate on Romans 4, a chapter that appeals to the example of Abraham as an illustration of the doctrine of justification by faith.

The principle that underlies Paul's interpretation of the Abraham story is that temporal priority indicates theological priority as well. Abraham is justified by his faith in Genesis 15, prior to his circumcision in Genesis 17 or the giving of the Mosaic law in Exodus 20. Justification by faith is therefore more fundamental to the process of the redemption of sinners than the rite of circumcision or obedience to the law. Furthermore, Abraham is not only the father of the Jews, who accept the rite of circumcision, but of Gentiles who are justified by faith without it. Indeed, Genesis 15 shows that Abraham is the father of all believers, Jew or Gentile, circumcised or uncircumcised. Paul confirms his reading of the Abraham story by appealing to Psalm 32 by David, which locates true blessedness in the nonimputation of sins.

What becomes immediately clear when we read Calvin's commentary on Romans 4 in the context of other sixteenth-century commentators on the same text is that, to an astonishing degree, the questions which perplex him and the solutions which he proposes are not original with him but are found in the antecedent exegetical tradition. Calvin is part of a long theological discussion over the meaning of Paul, a discussion which he did not initiate but to which he feels himself obliged to respond. To understand what Calvin is doing in his own commentary on Romans, we need to bear in mind what demands the literary genre of commentary places on all commentators in the sixteenth century.

A commentary, to put it in its simplest form, is an explanation of a literary work or body of writings regarded as particularly authoritative by some group. The writings need not be biblical. Commentaries were written in the sixteenth century on philosophers, theologians, lawyers, poets, and playwrights as well as on the books of the Bible. There were even commentaries on commentaries, like Cajetan's commentaries on Thomas's commentaries on Aristotle. What distinguishes a commentary from other forms of literature is not only that it requires an authoritative text to interpret, but also that it is aware of, uses, and corrects previous commentaries. Commentators are limited, therefore, both by the primary work on which they are commenting and by the weight of accumulated exegetical opinion. Earlier commentaries may be rejected, but they may not be ignored.

Just as there are dogmatic traditions, which are transmitted from generation to generation in the Christian church, so, too, there are exegetical traditions. When Calvin mentions the case of Phinehas the priest in connection with the story of Abraham's justification by faith (4:6) or compares Abraham's state of mind in Genesis 17 with the Virgin Mary's astonishment at the annunciation (4:20), he is repeating exegetical traditions of which he is not the author and which he shares with interpreters who represent in all other respects fiercely competing confessional loyalties. Paul himself mentions neither Phinehas nor the Virgin Mary. References to them belong to the extrabiblical exegetical lore that accompanies the canonical text. Interpreters who differ about the doctrine of justification by faith can agree about the relevance of the case of Phinehas to the problem of Abraham's justification.

II

When Calvin began to write his commentary on Romans 4, he was confronted with an exegetical literature that had already identified several clusters of problems in the text. The first cluster of problems was primarily technical. Erasmus reminded his contemporaries that a debate had raged since the time of Origen whether the phrase "according to the flesh" in 4:1 refers to the phrase "Abraham our father" or to the verb "has found."[36] If the phrase refers to "Abraham our father according to the flesh," then Paul is addressing a Jewish or Jewish Christian audience. If the phrase refers to "found according to the flesh," then Paul is already referring to the inadequacy of circumcision and law keeping as a means of justification. Not surprisingly, interpreters from the same theological party divide over this question.[37]

Also troubling to the grammarians is the meaning of the words "sign" and "seal" (*signum* and *signaculum*) in 4:11, especially as those words are applied to the rite of circumcision.[38] Is there a theological and not merely a lexical difference between sign and seal? If so, what is that difference and how does it affect the interpretation of this passage?

A second and far larger cluster of issues centered on the adequacy of St. Paul's interpretation of Genesis. For example, has Paul made too much of Genesis 15:6, "Abraham believed God and it was reckoned to him for righteousness," since he seems to imply that Abraham lacked faith before Genesis 15? Abraham's justification must antedate Genesis 15, since Hebrews 11 asserts that Abraham acted in faith when he left his homeland, an event reported in Genesis 12.[39] Some interpreters are also troubled that there is no mention of Christ, the promised seed, in Genesis 15.[40] How can there be justification by faith without reference, however vague and ambiguous, to the coming Redeemer?[41]

More serious still, Gen. 15:6 is the only verse that ascribes Abraham's justification to faith. While Bucer mentions this fact in order to commend Paul as a careful reader of Scripture, other interpreters are less certain that the matter can be settled so easily.[42] According to Num. 25:6–9, Phinehas, the grandson of Aaron the priest, stopped a plague in the Israelite camp by killing an idolatrous Jew and his Midianite mistress. Psalm 106:31 celebrates the zealous action of Phinehas and announces in language that echoes Gen. 15:6 that his act was counted to him for righteousness. In other words, while Abraham was justified by faith, Phinehas was justified by works. Or to state the matter even more sharply, Phinehas was justified by a double homicide. On what theological principle is Gen. 15:6 and the faith of Abraham given precedence over Ps. 106:31 and the zeal of Phinehas?[43]

The problem is exacerbated by the contention of James 2:21 that Abraham was justified by his works, specifically by his act of offering Isaac as a sacrifice to God.[44] Can the disagreement be settled by admitting that faith itself is a work, indeed, the chief work which Abraham does?[45] Does Paul really mean to contend, when he claims that Abraham was justified by faith, that Abraham was justified by faith alone? Or is some synthesis of faith and works the biblical solution? After all, Gen. 22:16–18 praises the works of Abraham and ties the promise of the covenant to his obedience.

Paul's exegesis raises other troubling questions as well. For example, were the promises given to Abraham really about spiritual matters or about earthly?[46] When Paul asserts that Abraham is the father of all believers, he seems to be twisting the promise of an earthly posterity in the land of Israel (principally Jewish) into the promise of spiritual descendants scattered throughout the world (both Jewish and Gentile, though principally Gentile). Furthermore, if Paul is correct and Abraham was justified by faith while still an uncircumcised Gentile, his justification by faith did not free him from the obligation to be circumcised. Should believing Gentiles who are justified by faith in imitation of Abraham also follow him in accepting the rite of circumcision? Beza asks the related question whether Jews, following Abraham's example (first faith, then circumcision), should abandon the practice of the circumcision of infants.[47]

Paul claims that Abraham did not waver through unbelief, but Genesis 17 paints an altogether different picture. According to Gen. 17:17, Abraham like Sarah began to laugh when he heard the promise of a son.[48] Suspicions aroused by texts like this raise the further question whether the works of Abraham were genuinely good. Were the works of this extraordinary friend of God nothing more than splendid vices? Not many commentators think so, though the question is nevertheless voiced.[49]

Similarly, Paul argues that Abraham regarded his body "as good as dead" so far as his procreative powers were concerned. But according to Genesis 25, Abraham married a second wife named Keturah after the death of Sarah, by whom he had six more sons in addition to Isaac and Ishmael.[50] That does not sound like the activity of a man who has lost his sexual potency.

Paul's citation of Ps. 32:1–2, a psalm traditionally ascribed to David, also stimulates some debate about the meaning of true blessedness.[51] Paul locates beatitude in pardon and the nonimputation of sin, whereas Psalm 1 locates it in good works and keeping the law. Is the clash between Psalm 1 and Psalm 32 significant and, if so, how does Paul justify his exclusive choice of Psalm

32? The papal court theologian, Ambrosius Catherinus Politus, argues that Psalm 32, insofar as it refers to the sacrament of penance, refers to the remission of guilt but not the penalty of sin.[52] The penalty for postbaptismal sin is not deleted but only reduced to temporal works of satisfaction.

A third cluster of issues focuses on the sacraments and their efficacy. The contention of Paul that Abraham was not justified by circumcision and the works of the law could be, and indeed had been, interpreted to mean that Abraham was not justified by obeying the ceremonial law.[53] Scholastic theologians were inclined to downplay the importance of what they regarded as the Jewish sacraments of circumcision and passover because of a distinction they drew between the old and the new law.[54] Sacraments of the new law, like baptism and the eucharist, were always powerful because they rested on the grace of God and not on human response for their efficacy. Sacraments of the old law, however, were only effective if recipients of those rites received them in an appropriately pious frame of mind. Since efficacy depended on a proper human disposition, it is not surprising that Paul stressed Abraham's faith and minimized the importance of the ceremonial rite. Thomists like Catherinus Politus rejected this reading of the text and insisted that Paul was teaching the impossibility of meriting grace but not the impossibility of meriting final salvation.[55] Protestants rejected both Catholic formulations of the problem, but were hard pressed to offer an alternative reading of the text.

Finally, Calvin had to confront questions about the rhetorical structure of Paul's argument. Melanchthon, in particular, was keen to uncover the rhetorical devices that Paul used to further his theological argument.[56] His analysis was widely copied and repeated, by his theological enemies as well as his friends. But even interpreters who were less interested in rhetoric than Melanchthon were quick to point out that generalizations based on one example, like Paul's generalization based on the example of Abraham alone, were inherently weak and untrustworthy. An argument is not proven by a single instance.[57]

III

Calvin discusses both of the technical problems raised by his contemporaries. Although he can see, like Bullinger, the point of attaching the phrase "according to the flesh" to the verb "has found" in 4:1, he agrees with Bucer that the natural sense of the passage seems better served by linking "according to the flesh" to the phrase "Abraham our father." Paul was conceding to the Jews that Abraham was their biological ancestor in order to impress upon them the importance of following his example of justification by faith.[58]

Calvin also agrees with Erasmus, who repeats the Patristic discussion, that there is an important difference in 4:11 between sign (*signum*) and seal (*signaculum*) or, as Calvin prefers to translate the Greek, (*sigillum*). Circumcision is a sign in two principal senses. It points beyond itself to the blessed seed, Jesus Christ, through whom God will effect the reconciliation of the world, and it symbolizes the removal by God of everything from human nature that impedes a life of integrity and holiness.[59]

More important to Calvin than the notion that circumcision is a sign is its character as a seal. Abraham was already justified by faith. Circumcision served as a seal to ratify the righteousness he had received while still uncircumcised. Though circumcision does not confer righteousness, it does imprint the promises of God on the human heart and confirms the certainty of grace. In that respect circumcision is like all the other sacraments.[60]

In contrast to Melanchthon, Calvin engages in very little rhetorical analysis of Paul. While Melanchthon and Bucer mention Paul's use of synechdoche (a figure of speech denoting the whole in the part), Calvin only mentions Paul's use of enthymema (an incomplete syllogism) in 4:2. In this respect, Calvin differs from Lutheran interpreters of Romans, who repeat and amplify Melanchthon's rhetorical analysis in their own commentaries.[61]

Calvin spends a good deal of time defending Paul's reading of the Old Testament, particularly Genesis 15, and reconciling his views with evidence that seems to undercut them. While it is true that Genesis 15 does not allude to Jesus Christ as the blessed seed (as, for example, Genesis 12 does), the fatherly favor of God includes as a matter of course eternal salvation by Christ.[62] Furthermore, the example of Phinehas, whose deed was accounted to him for righteousness, does not invalidate the general principle embodied in the example of Abraham that righteousness is a gift given to faith.

Calvin reminds his readers that one act, even an act of intense zeal for God, cannot justify. Only the perfect obedience described in Lev. 18:5 can form the basis for justification by works. Phinehas must first have been justified by his faith in order to have elicited from God this favorable judgment on his works.[63] God clothes sinners with the righteousness of Christ before he accepts their works. God accepts Phinehas because of his faith, and therefore accepts his works because he has accepted the person. The works of Phinehas are accounted to him for righteousness only in this secondary and subordinate sense. As Calvin understands the mind of Paul, "all works would be condemned of unrighteousness, if justification were not by faith alone."[64]

It is in this context that Calvin wants to understand the tension between Psalms 1 and 32. The blessing that is pronounced on the righteous who obey the commandments of God and who meditate on them day and night is "useless" until the righteous have first been "purified and cleansed by the remission of sins."[65] Psalm 32 takes precedence over Psalm 1 because the forgiveness of sins takes precedence over the life of Christian discipleship. Holy living is the effect of faith, not its cause. To insist on the priority of the righteousness of works over the righteousness of faith is to destroy the cause with its own effect. As that principle was true in the case of Abraham and David, so, too, it is true in the case of Phinehas.

The contention of James that Abraham was justified by his works, especially by the binding and offering of Isaac, does not undercut Paul's argument. Calvin has already attempted to reconcile the disagreement of Paul and James in his commentary on 3:28. Paul is discussing how men and women attain righteousness in the presence of God; James is discussing "how they prove to others that they are justified."[66] Paul is concerned with the justification of the ungodly; James with the justification of the already just. Calvin refers readers who wish a further discussion of this matter to his *Institutes*.

The question whether Paul has twisted earthly promises to Abraham into heavenly promises is given an impressive answer by Melanchthon, which both Bucer and Calvin repeat. Melanchthon insists that the principal object of faith is the promised mercy of God.[67] This object always exists in faith, even if faith is turned toward external objects. Abraham believes the promise of an earthly posterity only because of a deeper trust in the mercy and goodness of the God who has promised it. It is the apprehension of the divine mercy in the earthly promise that justifies Abraham.

> The passage quoted is taken from Gen. 15.6, in which the word *believe* should not be restricted to any particular expression, but refers to the whole covenant of salvation and the grace of adoption which Abraham is said to have apprehended by faith. . . . If we take this position, it is clear that those who think Paul wrested the Mosaic statement from its context, do not understand the principles of theology.[68]

Similarly, Calvin cites a traditional explanation of the laughter of Abraham in Genesis 17.[69] Abraham laughs not because he doubts the promise of a son, but because he is astonished by it.

> Like the Virgin Mary, when she inquired of the angel how his message would come to pass, and other similar instances in Scripture, Abraham asked how this could happen, but it was the question of a person struck with wonderment. When, therefore, a message is brought to the saints concerning the works of God, the greatness of which exceeds their contemplation, they break out into expressions of wonder, but from wonder they soon pass on to a contemplation of the power of God.[70]

However, Calvin does not follow the line of Melanchthon's argument in extolling the great works of Abraham. As Melanchthon understands the issue, Paul praises all the works and virtues of Abraham, including the ceremonial works. If Abraham was not justified before God with all his great works, it is easy to see how ordinary men and women are not justified on the basis of their own lesser deeds.[71] Calvin, on the other hand, is not interested in the human estimate of Abraham's works. Before God Abraham had nothing to offer "except the acknowledgment of his own misery."[72] The only righteousness that matters to Paul is the righteousness God gives to faith. In this context human virtue is not merely flawed; it is irrelevant.

Calvin also believes that Paul is correct when he calls Abraham's body "as good as dead" prior to the birth of Isaac, in spite of the fact that Abraham became the father of six additional sons after the death of Sarah. Calvin is not willing to agree with Augustine that the infertility of Sarah was the only obstacle to the birth of Isaac.[73] He is also unwilling to accept the suggestion of some commentators that Abraham's second wife, Keturah, stimulated him sexually in a way that Sarah no longer could.[74] Rather, Calvin believes, along with Origen and Oecolampadius, that when God restored Abraham's virility, he did it in such a way that those powers did not decline after the death of Sarah.[75]

The circumcision of Abraham as a sign and seal of the righteousness of faith raised for Calvin, and for his contemporaries, the question of the sacraments and their efficacy. Calvin begins by rejecting several interpretations of Abraham's circumcision from the antecedent Patristic and medieval tradition. He resists, first of all, the use of Psalm 32 as a description of the sacrament of penance. In the sacrament of penance the guilt of post-baptismal sins is deleted, but the penalty of those sins is reduced to temporal punishment rather than remitted. Calvin calls this teaching a half-remission and rejects it as an absurdity.[76]

In the same way he rejects the sharp distinction in medieval Catholic thought between sacraments of the old law and sacraments of the new. The notion that sacraments of the new law, like baptism and the eucharist, are effective *ex opere operato* (on the basis of the performance of the rite), whereas sacraments of the old law, like circumcision and the passover, are weaker because they are effective *ex opere operantis* (on the basis of the disposition of the recipient) is ruled out by Calvin as an unacceptable distinction.[77] No sacrament is effective on the basis of the performance of the rite without the active faith of the recipient. To be sure, baptism has replaced circumcision in the new covenant, so that children of Abraham by faith no longer need to be circumcised.[78] But just as Abraham was justified by his faith and not by his circumcision, so, too, Christians are justified by their faith and not by their baptism. So far as the basic principle of justification by faith is concerned, the old covenant and the new stand on the same level.

Paul's viewpoint does not mean to imply that faith is a meritorious virtue that wins justification by its own intrinsic worth, even though faith is relentless in its pursuit of moral virtue. Nor does he propose to teach that sacraments are empty signs that depend on the faith of the recipients for their meaning. Sacraments seal the righteousness of faith and so make believers more certain of the grace they have received.[79] Unlike Peter Martyr Vermigli, who spends thirty-three pages of his Romans commentary developing his doctrine of the sacraments, Calvin, who is committed to what he calls "lucid brevity," reserves his detailed discussion of the sacraments for Book IV of the *Institutes*.[80]

IV

It is clear from the evidence I have presented that Calvin's interpretation of Romans 4 is very much conditioned by the antecedent exegetical tradition, which sets most of the questions and many of the answers he adopts. Historians who read Calvin's commentaries in isolation may be surprised by the extent of his dependence on tradition, since Calvin himself provides few clues in the text to indicate what he is doing. In the preface to his commentary on Romans, he mentions the works of Melanchthon, Bullinger, and Bucer. In Romans 4 itself he cites Augustine, Erasmus, and Bucer. All of his other attributions are exceedingly vague. The impression conveyed is that Calvin has written an independent work with occasional help and stimulation from other commentaries. Only by reading Calvin in context do we discover the corporate nature of his exegesis.

The exegetical tradition he uses is not limited to questions and answers but also includes what I have called "exegetical lore." The comparison of Abraham's laughter to the astonishment of the Virgin Mary, the contrast between Phinehas's justification by works and Abraham's justification by faith, and the challenge to Paul's interpretation posed by Abraham's second wife and six additional sons, are not ideas and problems first suggested by Calvin, but form a body of interpretive material passed on from generation to generation in the church. This exegetical lore does not have the status of a dogmatic tradition, but exercises a similar control over the work of interpretation. Calvin comments within a framework provided by the exegetical traditions of his predecessors. Some of these traditions he challenges and rejects; others he modifies. What he does not do, however, is ignore those traditions. His own exegesis is not only a conversation with the text of Paul, but also with the traditions of Pauline exegesis.

It is evident from Calvin's own exegetical practice that the Reformation principle of *sola Scriptura* (Scripture alone) cannot and does not mean that Romans is interpreted in isolation from the generations of interpreters who have labored on the text before him. Even the principle that Scripture is its own interpreter needs to be qualified in light of Calvin's de facto practice. The story of the zeal of Phinehas is certainly a biblical story; the application of this story to the story of Abraham is a Christian tradition. The process is extrabiblical in its mode, if not in its content.

I do not mean to imply that Calvin's commentary is utterly devoid of original ideas or that Calvin himself is nothing more than a quotation from his ancestors. Calvin's writings are full of penetrating comments on the biblical text that reflect his own special angle of vision. What I want to suggest is that Calvin's contribution to Pauline scholarship must be understood first as a response to the exegetical traditions he inherited. He demonstrates his genius as an interpreter in his creative treatment of those traditions. Therefore to read Calvin in isolation is to misread him. Only by placing his exegesis in context can we understand it properly.

NOTES

1. Roger Fry, "An Essay in Esthetics," in *A Modern Book of Esthetics: An Anthology*, ed. Melvin Rader (New York: Henry Holt and Company, 1952), p. 51.

2. Alexandre Ganoczy, "Calvin als paulinischer Theologe," in *Calvinus Theologus*, ed. Wilhelm Neuser (Neukirchen: Neukirchener Verlag, 1976), pp. 39–69.

3. T. H. L. Parker, ed., *Iohannis Calvini Commentarius in Epistolam Pauli ad Romanos*, Studies in the History of Christian Thought 22 (Leiden: E.J. Brill, 1981), abbreviated as Calvin, *Commentarius*.

4. John R. Walchenbach, "John Calvin as Biblical Commentator: An Investigation in Calvin's Use of John Chrysostom as an Exegetical Tutor" (Ph.D. diss., University of Pittsburgh, 1974).

5. Benoit Girardin, *Rhetorique et théologique: Calvin, le Commentaire de l'Epître aux Romains* (Paris: Beauchesne, 1979).

6. T. H. L. Parker, *Calvin's New Testament Commentaries* (Grand Rapids, Mich.: Wm. B. Eerdmans, 1971); *Commentaries on the Epistle to the Romans, 1532–1542* (Edinburgh: T. & T. Clark, 1986).

7. Alexander Ganoczy and Klaus Müller, *Calvins Handschriftliche Annotationen zu Chrysostomus: Ein Beitrag zur Hermeneutik Calvins* (Wiesbaden: Steiner Verlag, 1981); Alexandre Ganoczy and Stefan Scheld, *Herrschaft-Tugend-Vorsehung: Hermeneutische Deutung und Veröffentlichung Handschriftlicher Annotationen Calvins zu Sieben Senecatragödien und der Pharsalia Lucans* (Wiesbaden: Steiner Verlag, 1982); Alexandre Ganoczy and Stefan Scheld, *Die Hermeneutik Calvins: Geistesgeschichtlice Voraussetzungen und Grundzüge* (Wiesbaden: Steiner Verlag, 1983).

8. Desiderius Erasmus, *Paraphrases in Omnes Epistolas Pauli* (Basel: Froben, 1523); *In Novum Testamentum Annotationes* (Basel: Froben, 1535).

9. John Colet, *Opera*, ed. J. H. Lupton (London, 1867–76).

10. Jacopo Sadoleto, *In Pauli Epistolam ad Romanos Commentariorum, Libri Tres* (Venice: Joannes Antonius et Nicolinus de Sabio, 1536).

11. Jacques Lefèvre d'Étaples, *Epistole divi Pauli Apostoli: Cum commentariis praeclarissimi viri Jacobi Fabri Stapulensis* (Paris: Jean de la Porte, 1517).

12. Martin Luther, *Der Brief an die Römer*, WA 56 (Weimar: Hermann Böhlaus Nachfolger, 1938).

13. Thomas de Vio (Cajetan), *Epistolae Pauli et aliorum Apostolorum ad Graecam veritatem castigatae, et iuxta sensum literalem enarratae* (Paris: Carola Guillard et Jean de Roigny, 1540).

14. Philip Melanchthon, *Commentarii in Epistolam Pauli ad Romanos* (Wittenberg, 1532); citations are from the critical edition, *Römerbrief-Kommentar 1532*, ed. Rolf Schäfer, in *Melanchthons Werke in Auswahl* 5 (Gütersloh: Gerd Mohn, 1965).

15. Johann Bugenhagen, *In Epistolam Pauli ad Romanos Interpretatio, ipso in schola interpretante, a Doctore Ambrosio Maiobano, ut licuit, excepta* (Hagenau: Johannes Secerius, 1527).

16. Andreas Knöpken, *In Epistolam ad Romanos Interpretatio* (Nuremberg: Johann Petreius, 1524).

17. Johannes Oecolampadius, *In Epistolam b. Pauli Apostoli ad Romanos Adnotationes* (Basel: Andreas Cratander, 1525).

18. Heinrich Bullinger, *In sanctissimam Pauli ad Romanos Epistolam Commentarius* (Zurich: Christophor Froschouer, 1533).

19. Conrad Pellikan, *In omnes apostolicae Epistolas, Pauli, Petri, Iacobi, Ioannis et Iudae Commentarii* (Zurich: Christophor Froschouer, 1539).

20. Ambrosius Catherinus Politus, *Commentaria in omnes divi Pauli et alias septem canonicas Epistolas* (Venice: Vincent Valgrisius, 1551).

21. Domingo de Soto, *In Epistolam divi Pauli ad Romanos Commentarii* (Antwerp: Jan Steelsius, 1550).

22. Johannes Brenz, *In Epistolam, quam Apostolus Paulus ad Romanos scripsit, Commentariorum Libri Tres* (Basel: Paul Queck, 1565).

23. Wolfgang Musculus, *In Epistolam Apostoli Pauli ad Romanos: Commentarii* (Basel: Johann Hervagios, 1555).

24. Caspar Olevian, *In Epistolam Pauli ad Romanos notae* (Geneva, 1579).

25. Niels Hemmingsen, *Commentarius in Epistolam Pauli ad Romanos* (Leipzig, 1562).

26. Erasmus Sarcerius, *In Epistolam ad Romanos pia et erudita scholia* (Frankfurt: Christian Egenolphus, 1541).

27. Francisco de Toledo, *Commentarii et Annotationes in Epistolam beati Pauli Apostoli ad Romanos* (Lyons: Jean Pillehotte, 1603).

28. Caspar Cruciger, *In Epistolam Pauli ad Romans scriptam Commentarius* (Wittenberg: Johannes Crato, 1567).

29. Martin Bucer, *Metaphrases et Enarrationes perpetuae Epistolarum d. Pauli Apostoli. Tomus Primus* (Strasbourg: Wendelin Rihel, 1536).

30. PG 14.

31. *Ambrosiastri qui dicitur Commentarius in Epistulas Paulinas; Pars Prima, In Epistulam ad Romanos*, ed. H. J. Vogels, CSEL 81 (Vienna, 1966).

32. *Petri Abaelardi Opera Theologica*, Vol. 2, ed. E. M. Buytaert, CCh, Continuatio Mediaevalis 12 (Turnholt: Brepols, 1969).

33. PL 117.

34. Hugh of St. Cher, *Tomus Septimus in Epistolas D. Pauli, Actus Apostolorum, Epist. septem Canonicas, Apocalypsim B. Joannis* (Venice: Nicolaus Pezzana, 1732).

35. Nicholas of Lyra, *Glossae in universa Biblia. Postilla* (Nuremberg: Anton Koburger, 1481).

36. Erasmus, *Annotationes*, p. 359.

37. Oecolampadius, *Adnotationes*, fol. 38r; Bullinger, *Commentarius*, fol. 61r; Bucer, *Metaphrases*, pp. 213–14; Pellikan, *Commentarii*, p. 46; Musculus, *Commentarii*, p. 88; Peter Martyr Vermigli, *In Epistolam S. Pauli Apostoli ad Romanos* (Basel: Peter Pernam, 1559), p. 219.

38. Erasmus, *Annotationes*, p. 360. Cf. Musculus, *Commentarii*, pp. 93–94; Oecolampadius, *Adnotationes*, fol. 40v–42r.

39. Oecolampadius, *Adnotationes*, fol. 38v; D. Andreas Hyperius, *Commentarii in Omnes d. Pauli Apostoli Epistolas* (Zurich: Christophor Froschouer, 1584), p. 75; Aegidius Hunnius, *Epistolae divi Pauli Apostoli ad Romanos Expositio Plana et Perspicua* (Frankfurt: Spies, 1590), pp. 162–63; Alfonso Salmeron, *Commentarii in Omnes Epistolas B. Pauli et Canonicas. Tomus Decimus Tertius* (Cologne: Antonius Hierat et Johannes Gymnicus, 1604), pp. 387–88.

40. Brenz, *Commentariorum*, pp. 324–35.

41. Oecolampadius addresses the problem of justifying faith without a sure knowledge of Christ, *Adnotationes*, fol. 40r; Hyperius argues that Abraham would never have believed the promise in Genesis 15, had he not already believed the promise concerning Christ, the blessed seed, in Genesis 12, *Commentarii*, p. 75.

42. Bucer, *Metaphrases*, p. 218.

43. Many sixteenth-century commentators mention specifically the case of Phinehas: Bucer, *Metaphrases*, p. 215; Brenz, *Commentariorum*, pp. 234–36; Hemmingsen, *Commentarius*, pp. 133–34; Hyperius, *Commentarii*, p. 76; Christoph Cornerus, *In Epistolam d. Pauli ad Romanos Scriptam Commentarius* (Heidelberg: Johann Spies, 1583), fol. 59v; Alexander Alesius, *Omnes Disputationes de tota Epistola ad Romanos* (Leipzig: Georg Hantzsch, 1553), Disputatio 10; Nicholas Selnecker, *In Omnes Epistolas d. Pauli Apostoli Commentarius Plenissimus* (Leipzig: Jacob Apelius, 1595), p. 130; Vermigli, *Ad Romanos*, p. 223; Salmeron, *Commentarii*, p. 387; Augustin Marlorat, *In Pauli Epistolas, Catholica Expositio Ecclesiastica* (Geneva: Pierre Sanctandreanus, 1593), p. 21.

44. Bucer, *Metaphrases*, p. 212; Melanchthon, *Römerbrief*, p. 131; Musculus, *Commentarii*, pp. 92–93; Oecolampadius, *Adnotationes*, fol. 39v; Tilemann Hesshusen, *Explicatio Epistolae Pauli ad Romanos* (Jena: Gunther Huttichius, 1572), fol. 113r.

45. Bucer, *Metaphrases*, p. 216.

46. Melanchthon, *Römerbrief-Kommentar*, pp. 127–28; Bucer, *Metaphrases*, pp. 214–15.

47. Theodore Beza, *Annotationes Majores in Novum Dn. Nostri Iesu Christi Testamentum, Pars Altera* (Geneva: Robert Stephanus, 1594), p. 49.

48. Cajetan, *Epistolae*, fol. 26r–26v; De Soto, *Commentarii*, p. 131; Claude Guilliaud, *In Omnes Divi Pauli Apostoli Epistolas Collatio* (Paris: Jean de Roigny, 1548), fol. 25v.

49. Cf., for example, the relatively positive assessment of Oecolampadius, *Adnotationes*, 38v, with the relatively negative assessment of Beza, *Annotationes*, p. 46.

50. Oecolampadius, *Adnotationes*, 45r; Musculus, *Commentarii*, p. 103; de Soto, *Commentarii*, p. 131.

51. Bucer, *Metaphrases*, p. 213.

52. Catherinus Politus, *Commentaria*, p. 46.

53. Bucer, *Metaphrases*, p. 214.

54. An excellent discussion of the theological issues involved in a scholastic reading of Romans 4 is offered by the fifteenth-century commentator, Denis the Carthusian, *In Omnes Beati Pauli Epistolas Commentaria* (Cologne: Peter Quentel, 1545), fol. 10v–11r.

55. Catherinus Politus, *Commentaria*, p. 46.

56. See especially *Beilage* I and II of Melanchthon, *Römerbrief-Kommentar*, pp. 373–92.

57. Hemmingsen, *Commentarius*, p. 125; Calvin mentions the same point in his treatment of 4:23.

58. Calvin, *Commentarius*, p. 80.

59. Ibid., pp. 86–87.

60. Ibid.

61. Erasmus Sarcerius finds twenty-two enthymemata in Romans 4. See his *Scholia* on 4:1.

62. Calvin, *Commentarius*, pp. 80–82.

63. Ibid., pp. 84–85.

64. Ibid., p. 85.

65. Ibid.

66. Ibid., p. 77.

67. Melanchthon, *Römerbrief-Kommentar*, pp. 127–28.

68. Calvin, *Commentarius*, p. 81.

69. Guilliaud, *Collatio*, fol. 25v.

70. Calvin, *Commentarius*, pp. 96–97.

71. Melanchthon, *Römerbrief-Kommentar*, pp. 123–24.

72. Calvin, *Commentarius*, pp. 80–81.

73. Ibid., pp. 95–96.

74. Musculus outlines the various schools of interpretation on this question, *Commentarii*, p. 103.

75. Calvin, *Commentarius*, pp. 95–96. In his commentary on Gen. 25:1 (1554), Calvin suggests that Abraham married Keturah before Sarah died, though he still believes in a miraculous restoration of Abraham's sexual vitality.

76. Calvin, *Commentarius*, p. 84.

77. Ibid., pp. 88–89.

78. Ibid., p. 88.

79. Ibid., pp. 86–87.

80. Calvin first refers readers to his commentaries in the 1539 edition of the *Institutes*, prior to the publication of the first edition of the Romans commentary in 1540.

6

Calvin and Tamar

In 1550, John Calvin, whose commentary on Genesis would not be published until 1554, lectured on the story of Judah and Tamar in Genesis 38.[1] Judah was the fourth son of Jacob by his first wife Leah. Tamar was not Judah's wife or even his concubine. She was his daughter-in-law and the widow of his two sons, Er and Onan. But it is not the relationship of Tamar to Judah's sons but to Judah himself that gives the story its primary significance. Judah becomes the unwitting father by Tamar of twin boys, Perez and Zerah, in what Christian tradition regards as one of the more famous cases of incest in the Bible.

The main elements of the story can be quickly summarized. Tamar was a Canaanite woman, who was given in marriage to Er, Judah's eldest son. According to the biblical text, Er was so wicked (the precise nature of his wickedness remains unspecified in the text) that God brought his miserable life to an end. Judah then commanded his second son, Onan, to marry Tamar with the understanding that the first born child of this union would be regarded as the child of Er rather than of Onan. Onan was willing to sleep with Tamar, but he was unwilling to impregnate her. At the very last moment, he interrupted his sexual relations with her so that she could not bear a child. For this offense against the unwritten law, God took Onan's life as he had taken the life of Onan's brother Er.

Not surprisingly, Judah was disturbed by the loss of two sons and, fearing that Tamar was somehow to blame, postponed a marriage with his youngest son, Shelah. Judah sent Tamar back to her father's house to live

as a widow. He promised that he would eventually send for her to become
Shelah's wife. However, time passed, Shelah matured, and Judah made no
move to fulfill his promise to Tamar.

After waiting in vain for Judah to act, Tamar decided to take matters
into her own hand. She heard that her father-in-law was going to Timnath
to shear his flocks of sheep. She removed the clothing that marked her as a
widow, put on a veil, perfumed herself, and sat where the road to Timnath
forks in two directions. When Judah, himself newly widowed, sees Tamar
at the side of the road, he assumes that she is a prostitute (perhaps a temple-
prostitute) and attempts to engage her services. She agrees to accept a kid
as payment for her sexual favors. However, since Judah has not yet reached
his flocks, she asks for his staff, as well as his seal and its cord, as a pledge
for the payment owed. Judah agrees and the bargain is concluded.

When Judah reaches his flocks, he sends a friend back to the crossroads
with the promised payment. But Tamar has disappeared. When he asks
people in the vicinity whether they have seen a temple-prostitute, they deny
having seen anyone like that ply her trade at the fork in the road. So Judah's
friend returns with the kid to Judah, who decides to drop the matter and
let the unknown prostitute keep the pledge he gave her.

Three months later, Judah is notified that Tamar is pregnant. Judah is
outraged and condemns her to be executed by fire. Before the sentence can
be carried out, Tamar produces Judah's staff, cord, and seal and claims that
the father of her child is the owner of these articles. Judah instantly realizes what has transpired and cancels the sentence against her. "She is more
in the right than I am," confesses Judah, "because I did not give her to my
son Shelah."

The story ends with the account of the difficult birth of twin boys, Perez
and Zerah. Tamar has successfully tricked Judah into redeeming his dead son
Er. It is not clear whether Tamar was ever given to Shelah as a wife. The narrative only asserts that Judah never had intercourse with Tamar again.

I

Among the commentaries Calvin consulted in his exposition of Genesis was
the multivolume commentary by Martin Luther.[2] Luther had lectured on
the story of Judah and Tamar in late 1543 or early 1544. His lectures on
Genesis 38 were reconstructed from student notes and published posthumously. Although Calvin was not altogether in sympathy with Luther's
exegetical method and even quarreled with him over points of interpretation, he nevertheless took Luther's exposition into account in his own lectures on Genesis.

Luther's lectures on this story were delivered at a time when very few new commentaries on Genesis had been written. By 1545, the year Luther completed his nine-year cycle of lectures on Genesis, Thomas Cardinal Cajetan had completed a commentary on Genesis (1531)[3] as had Huldrych Zwingli at Zurich (1527),[4] Conrad Pellikan at Basel (1536),[5] and Wenzeslaus Linck at Wittenberg (1543).[6] Johannes Oecolampadius had commented on Genesis 1–16 (1536)[7] and there were partial commentaries by Philip Melanchthon (1523),[8] Augustinus Steuchus Eugubinus (1535),[9] Wolfgang Capito (1539),[10] and Paul Fagius (1542),[11] none of whom interpreted Genesis 38. The great burst of commentary writing on Genesis took place after 1545 when new commentaries were composed by such figures as Peter Becker (Artopoeus), Martin Borrhaus, Antonio Brucioli, Andreas Hyperius, Luigi Lipomani, Wolfgang Musculus, Jerome Oleaster, Peder Palladius, Ambrosius Catherinus Politus, Nicholas Selnecker, Peter Martyr Vermigli, Jerome Zanchi, and, of course, Calvin himself.

Luther relied more on older commentaries than on the writings of his contemporaries for exegetical insight and stimulus. His favorite medieval commentator was the fourteenth-century Franciscan interpreter, Nicholas of Lyra, whom he repeatedly cited throughout his lectures.[12] Lyra wrote *Postilla* on both the literal and moral senses of the Bible. More than most of his predecessors, Lyra attempted to utilize the rabbinic traditions of exegesis in his exposition of the Old Testament. Even though he was primarily concerned with the literal sense of the text, he did not consider it in isolation from Christian theology. By appealing to a double-literal sense, a literal-historical sense concerned with the story line and a literal-prophetic sense concerned with the story's theological significance, he broadened the meaning of letter to include matters that had earlier been relegated to the spiritual sense of the text.

Lyra was only one of several medieval exegetes who wrote on Genesis 38. The thirteenth-century French Dominican, Hugh of St. Cher,[13] and the fifteenth-century monastic reformer, Denis the Carthusian,[14] also wrote standard commentaries on Genesis. All three commented extensively on the literal sense of the text, which they recognized as primary. For them, as for the medieval tradition generally, the literal sense was the only sense of the text from which theological arguments could be drawn.

Printed editions of their commentaries were easily accessible in the early sixteenth century. Lyra's *Postilla super Genesim* went through several printings at Nuremberg and Basel in the 1480s and 1490s, while Hugh's *Repertorium* on Genesis was printed in Nuremberg in 1502 and Basel in 1503. Denis's *Enarrationes* were released in a new edition in Cologne in 1534. In order to provide a context for the interpretation of Genesis 38 by Luther and Calvin,

I want to recreate a composite late medieval Christian reading of the Tamar story, using these three standard commentators.

II

The first question that preoccupied medieval commentators is what Er, Tamar's first husband, did to merit death. The text, of course, is silent. All three commentators speculate that Er must have done what his brother Onan did, though for different reasons.[15] Er must have had sexual relations with Tamar, but in such a way as to prevent pregnancy. Nicholas of Lyra suggests that Er practiced a primitive form of birth control because he was so libidinously attached to Tamar that he did not want to spoil her beauty by impregnating her.

In medieval Christian ethics it was never enough to restrict sexual activity within the boundaries of marriage. Married couples were also obligated to observe certain rules of sexual conduct. By refusing to impregnate his wife, Er treated Tamar like a prostitute and defrauded her of the children that were rightfully hers and which gave her status in ancient Jewish society.

The case of Onan, Er's brother and Tamar's second husband, is simple enough. Onan was willing to sleep with Er's widow, but unwilling to impregnate her. Unlike Er, Onan was not concerned with preserving Tamar's beauty. He simply did not want the firstborn child of his marriage to Tamar attributed to his dead brother.[16]

When Onan died, Judah, fearing these multiple deaths were the fault of Tamar, sent her back to her father's house. Tamar, who knew (as Denis asserts) that Christ would descend from the line of Judah, waited for him to keep his promise.[17] When she realized that Judah had denied his third son to her as a bridegroom, she decided to have sexual intercourse with her father-in-law. She was driven, not by her libido, but by a desire for the posterity that had been promised her. Hugh of St. Cher, who seems a little embarrassed by the ease with which Tamar seduced the recently widowed Judah, observes that while Judah was wrong to cohabit with Tamar, he at least had the decency to attempt to redeem his pledge and pay her the price agreed upon.[18]

When Judah learns that Tamar had behaved like a common prostitute and was pregnant through her wanton conduct, he orders her to be burned. The order to subject her to death by fire prompts a lively debate among the medieval commentators. What sexual transgression did Tamar commit to merit such a harsh punishment? Since both Judah and Tamar were widowed, they appear to have committed fornication, i.e., illicit heterosexual activity between unmarried consenting adults. While not to be encouraged and certainly a mortal sin, fornication was by no means the most serious fault in the medieval catalog of sexual sins. Far more serious was simple adultery, i.e., illicit heterosexual activity between two consenting adults, one of whom was married. If Shelah was betrothed to Tamar, then, perhaps, she should be regarded as already married at the time of her encounter with Judah. Hugh and Lyra agree and opt for adultery, whereas Denis merely reports both possibilities without choosing between them.[19] Paul of Burgos, who comments on Lyra's exegesis, rejects out of hand the notion that Tamar was married.[20]

Complicating the situation still further is the fact that Judah and Tamar violated the forbidden degrees. They are related as father and daughter by affinity rather than consanguinity, since Judah is Tamar's father-in-law rather than her biological father. But that is a distinction without a difference, since no sharp division was made in the later Middle Ages between consanguinity and affinity and since all sexual activity within the forbidden degrees was regarded as incestuous. According to medieval sexual ethics, Judah and Tamar committed adultery and incest, he unwittingly, she knowingly.[21] For his part Judah was only dimly aware of a casual act of fornication with an anonymous prostitute, who made off with his seal, staff, and cord.

Even if it is granted that Tamar committed adultery and incest, it is puzzling why Judah ordered her to be burnt. According to the later law of Moses, foreshadowed in the Levirate marriage of Onan with Tamar, she should have been executed by stoning for her crimes. The commentators surmise that she was subject to severer penalties because she was the daughter of a Canaanite priest. Lyra and Denis are concerned, however, to scotch the notion that Tamar was the daughter of Melchizedek, the mysterious priestly figure who receives tithes from Abraham, as some earlier commentators had argued.[22] When Tamar was born, Melchizedek was long dead.

The story builds to the confrontation between Judah and Tamar. When she is brought out, she sends Judah's seal, staff, and cord to him with the words, "The father of my child is the man to whom these things belong." Judah immediately recognizes the pledge he gave to an unknown prostitute on the road to Timnath and confesses that Tamar is more righteous than he is. The Latin word he uses is *iustior*.

Judah's confession that Tamar is "more righteous" than he troubles the medieval commentators. While they recognized that Judah had failed to live up to his obligation to guarantee his line through Er and had committed a casual act of fornication with a prostitute, they also acknowledged that Tamar had knowingly deceived her father-in-law and committed adultery and incest.[23] Although they admitted that Tamar's deceit kept the family line intact, they found no morally untainted characters in this story. All four principal actors—Er, Onan, Judah, and Tamar—committed mortal sin. Perhaps, Hugh suggests, it would be better to concede that Tamar was not more just than Judah but only less unjust.[24]

III

Luther was concerned with many of the questions that troubled medieval commentators. Like them he worried about the moral responsibility of the principal figures in the story—Er, Onan, Judah, and Tamar—though he broadened the cast of characters to include a chorus of Tamar's relatives, who were dismissed as mere bystanders in medieval exegesis. Like them he professed astonishment at the severity of Judah's sentence and explored the relationship of Tamar to a priestly line. Like them he was puzzled by the unqualified confession of Judah that Tamar was more righteous than he.

Yet, for all the similarities, there are important differences as well. The first dissimilarity is Luther's preoccupation with matters of chronology. Luther had worked out a chart derived from the ages of the patriarchs at their death. On the basis of this chronology, Luther advanced the astonishing claim that Judah was only twelve years old when he married Bathshua and twenty-seven when he defiled his daughter-in-law.[25] More important, Luther's reconstructed chronology enabled him to support the hypothesis of Lyra (sharpened by Paul of Burgos) that Melchizedek had been dead for fifty years when Tamar deceived Judah.[26] It was therefore highly improbable that Melchizedek could have been her father. Luther was himself of the opinion that Tamar belonged to a priestly line only by marriage to the family of Jacob.[27]

A second difference between Luther's exegesis and the exegesis of his predecessors lies in what appears to us as Luther's psychologizing of the biblical text. Luther was not alone among medieval theologians in his expansion of the spare narrative offered in the Bible or in his attempt to offer credible human motivations for the actions of biblical characters. Medieval theologians and preachers were quite willing to provide the additional links that tie the narrative of the biblical stories more tightly together. The fact that Hugh, Lyra, and Denis did not do it in their commentaries on Genesis 38 does not mean that they had any principled objections against it when it was done by someone else.

Luther could discuss the motivations of the biblical characters with considerable self-confidence because he drew no overly sharp lines between then and now, yesterday and today, the world of the Bible and the world of sixteenth-century Germany. The men and women in Genesis looked forward to a Redeemer who was yet to come, whereas sixteenth-century Christians looked back to a Redeemer who lived, taught, died, and was raised from the dead. Having conceded that important difference, Luther was hard pressed to find any other. What makes a human being human has not changed very much over the centuries. Judah, Er, Onan, and Tamar share a common humanity with Luther and his contemporaries. Therefore, the inner life of Luther and his contemporaries provides a key to unlock the innermost secrets of Judah, Er, Onan, and Tamar.

Four examples of Luther's approach will suffice. The first example concerns Onan.[28] Luther suggested an additional reason for Onan's disobedience to his father's command (though the command was not merely Judah's but God's). Onan was motivated not only by jealousy of his elder brother, but by a hatred for the commandment itself. It is a burdensome thing to be forced to take a woman as a wife whom one does not desire. Onan therefore mistreated his unwanted and undesired wife by exciting her sexually only to deny her the children she wished. By doing so, he violated an order of nature and received the punishment he deserved.

Example two concerns Judah.[29] Luther was puzzled by Judah's failure to recognize Tamar. Although she was veiled, Judah could see her eyes and hear her voice. Luther's explanation rests on the proposition that "imagination takes away perception and reflection."[30] The sexual appetite of the recently widowed Judah had so focused his mind and imagination that he took Tamar at face value and accepted her for what she pretended to be. To Judah the eyes and voice of Tamar were the eyes and voice of an anonymous prostitute.

The third example concerns the anonymous bystanders who deny they have seen a prostitute at the fork in the road to Timnath and who later denounce Tamar for having played the harlot. Luther is convinced they are not anonymous at all but are actually Tamar's relatives.[31] They were in on Tamar's deception from the first and may even have put her up to it. They covered her escape by denying all knowledge of a prostitute. Only when they were absolutely certain that Tamar was pregnant with Judah's child did they triumphantly denounce her to Judah. They could hardly wait to see the expression on Judah's face when he was handed his seal, cord, and staff and discovered with horror that he was the father of his own grandchildren.

The final example concerns Tamar herself.[32] Luther believes Tamar was driven to deceive Judah by her longing for children and not by her sexual passion. Tamar knew full well that Shelah was obligated by divine command to become her husband. She also knew that she had done nothing to merit the contemptuous treatment she had received from Judah. Judah had rejected her without cause.

Tamar was driven to take desperate measures by Judah's unjustified behavior. Perhaps she knew that Judah had had sexual relations with prostitutes before and so would be highly susceptible to seduction.[33] Perhaps

she regarded Judah as a good man and only tried to deceive him because
she could think of no other way to gain her rights. In any event, Luther
regarded Tamar as an extraordinary woman (*mirabilis mulier*), who forced
Judah against his will to obey God's command, even if not in the way God
commanded.[34] She was prepared to try something even more desperate if
this ruse failed.

Luther nurtured no romantic illusions about biblical families. He rejected
any approach to Genesis which treated its stories of often dysfunctional
families like an ancient Jewish collection of the *Lives of the Saints*.[35] Unlike
Ignatius Loyola, whose conversion to a more authentic Christianity was
profoundly shaped by his reading of the biographies of saints, Luther confessed that he found more comfort in the failings of the saints than in their
virtues.[36] Such a confession ought not to be confused with a kind of *Schaden-
freude* that takes delight in the misdoings or misfortunes of others. Luther
wanted only to underscore the importance of a grace that overcomes human
weakness and unreliability. If God could save the very great sinners who
inhabit the pages of Genesis, then he can certainly save half-hearted and
unimaginative sinners like you and me.

Unlike Hugh, Lyra, or Denis, Luther focused on the christological framework within which the story of Judah and Tamar should be read. Luther
observed that Tamar was a Gentile and that the ancestry of Jesus of Nazareth
includes both Jews and Gentiles. If the story of Tamar and Judah teaches
its readers nothing else, it teaches them that a Canaanite woman was the
mother of the whole tribe of Judah and therefore the remote mother of
Christ.[37] This genealogical fact established for Luther the important
theological point that the inclusion of Jews and Gentiles in the redeemed
people of God was intended by God from the very beginning.[38]

The story of Judah and Tamar also demonstrated to Luther that fallen
human sexuality provides the context within which the incarnation should
be understood. Jesus Christ was not born from a line of ancestors who were
beyond reproach in their sexual morality. "God allows [Christ] to be conceived in most disgraceful incest," says Luther, "in order that he may assume
the truest flesh."[39] Just as all human beings are given life through fallen
human sexuality, so Jesus Christ was born from a flesh truly "polluted by
Judah and Tamar."[40]

Of course, the flesh that Jesus assumed in the womb of the Virgin Mary
was sanctified by the Holy Spirit.[41] But it was sanctified because it was
sinful. Otherwise Christ would not be flesh of our flesh and bone of our
bone. "Judah, the very eminent patriarch, a father of Christ, committed this
unspeakable act of incest," concludes Luther, "in order that Christ may be
born from a flesh outstandingly sinful and contaminated by a most disgraceful sin."[42] The context for Bethlehem is the road to Timnath.

Finally, Luther dealt with the confrontation between Tamar and Judah and Judah's puzzling confession that Tamar was more righteous than he. Luther was well aware that Judah's remark must be understood within the context of the covenant line. God had commanded Judah to give Tamar to Shelah and Judah had refused. By deceiving Judah, Tamar had redeemed her dead husband Er and had preserved the line of Judah that leads to Christ.

On the other hand, Luther was concerned with the violation of Christian sexual morality embodied in this story. On the face of it, it seemed to Luther and his predecessors that Judah was guilty of nothing more serious than an absent-minded act of fornication, whereas Tamar, who knew exactly what she was doing, involved Judah in incest.[43] But Luther was convinced that such a reading of the text is superficial. By disobeying God's command and so preventing the birth of children to his dead son by Shelah, Judah was guilty of sacrilege and homicide.[44] Furthermore, his sin was greater than Tamar's because, unlike her, he was a teacher and ruler of the church. And so on both levels, the covenant-lineal and the ethical-moral, Tamar was more righteous than Judah.

IV

Luther concluded his exposition of Genesis 38 with the words: "I have preferred a simple explanation to the invention of allegories."[45] On one level, of course, that statement is self-evidently true. Unlike Hugh of St. Cher, Luther does not suggest that Judah is a type of Christ, Tamar a type of the church, Shelah a representative of the chorus of the apostles, or Er an enduring example of a bad prelate.[46] Luther takes the ancient narrative at face value and tries to explain the gaps in the biblical story by drawing on his own experience of human nature.

On the other hand, one could object that Luther and his medieval predecessors created problems for themselves by reading Genesis 38 within the framework provided by Christian sexual morality. In its original setting the story does not appear to be about incest (though Tamar was condemned by Judah for sexual misconduct) but about the redemption of a dead brother's line. What Tamar wanted was not a forbidden sexual experience (as Denis and Luther admitted) but the children that were owed her by her kinsmen within the family of Judah.

For Luther and his generation, however, the question of a Levirate marriage was not moot. It had been pushed into the center of theological discussion by the appeal of Henry VIII to European universities for support of his petition to annul his marriage to Catherine of Aragon.[47] Henry supported his claim for an annulment by citing the prohibition in Leviticus of marriage between a brother and his sister-in-law. In answering Henry's argument sixteenth-century theologians found themselves caught between two conflicting sets of texts from Leviticus and Deuteronomy. On the one hand, Lev. 18:16 and 20:21 forbade a brother to marry his sister-in-law. On the other hand, Deuteronomy 25 advocated exactly such a policy. Neither set of texts authorized a father-in-law to redeem the line of a dead son, though that was not the question posed by Henry.

William Tyndale attempted to reconcile the conflicting texts by arguing that Leviticus forbade a marriage between a brother and his brother's wife only when the first brother was still living. The Catholic theologian, Felix de Prato, elaborated Tyndale's thesis by insisting that a Levirate marriage was allowed, if the first brother were dead and had left no offspring. If there were living children, then the prohibition in Leviticus took precedence over the permission in Deuteronomy. Zwingli argued on the basis of Lev. 18:16 that marriage with a sister-in-law was condemned by natural and divine law under all circumstances, whereas Thomas Cardinal Cajetan argued that on the basis of Mosaic law Henry VIII was obligated to marry Catherine of Aragon. Melanchthon suggested that, under certain circumstances, bigamy was preferable to a divorce, while Luther concluded that neither text had any lingering power to bind Christian consciences. In short, when Christian theologians limited themselves to the Old Testament, they found that the ambiguity of the evidence forced them to look elsewhere for a resolution.

The Tamar story resolved itself for Luther into the question of the relation of the two testaments. If there is one people of God throughout time, then the question of Tamar's significance cannot be answered on the basis of Genesis alone. Tamar, the Gentile, is the mother of Christ, who conceived him by waylaying an unsuspecting Judah on the road to Timnath. While Luther disapproved of her sexual morality, he nevertheless admired her force of character and initiative. Desperate times call for desperate measures.

Although Luther accepted the traditional view that Tamar achieved her objective by knowingly committing incest, he placed her act in a larger theological context. Tamar the Canaanite was for Luther a witness to the universality of God's saving purpose, a sign that there is neither Jew nor Gentile, male nor female, in the redemptive plan of God.

She was also a sign of the reality of the incarnation. Luther insisted that the incarnation did not take place in a world of unfallen human sexuality. Christ was conceived in what Judah regarded as an insignificant encounter with a nameless prostitute and in what Tamar realized was a desperate deception of a man who held the power of life and death over her. There is a direct line for Luther from the tiny hut on the road to Timnath in which Perez and Zerah were conceived to the stable in Bethlehem in which Christ was born. Redemption embraces human sexuality as it is and not as it should be. The flesh Christ assumed and purified was fallen human flesh. Christ came from the incest of Judah and Tamar to redeem the world from sin, including its sexual sins.[48] That is the gospel message Luther found embedded in the Tamar story.

V

Calvin's exposition of Genesis 38 is far briefer than Luther's and shifts the reader's attention from the theological to the moral meaning of the text.[49] Calvin found the story of Judah and Tamar to be full of moral lessons. He observes, for example, that a long life is a gift of God though a short life is not necessarily a punishment; that one ought not to blame others for adversity but assume responsibility for oneself and abandon one's own sins; that a good reputation before other men and women is desirable, but ought not to be purchased at the cost of a good conscience before God; that widows should dress modestly; that fornication is a vice deplored even by those who practice it; that lust is easily aroused unless God restrains it; that people who are not governed by the Spirit are more concerned about the opinion of the world than about the judgment of God; that one ought never to condemn anyone unheard; and that "whoever attempts to destroy the distinction which nature draws between what is base and what is honorable, engages, like the giants, in open war with God."[50]

While Calvin emphasized the moral meaning of the Tamar story, he agreed with Luther that it had important implications for Christian theology as well. The theological context for Calvin's discussion is not the nativity story on which Luther had drawn but the Pauline account in Philippians 2 of Christ's self-emptying and humiliation.[51] Judah and Tamar serve as unwitting witnesses to the *kenosis*. Calvin regarded their incest as proof that Christ assumed human flesh "with the design of making himself of no reputation."[52] Christ was born into the family of Judah in order to show that he "derives no glory from his ancestors" and "no glory in the flesh."[53] Christ's glory is in the cross alone.

The fundamental premise on which Calvin built his interpretation of Genesis 38 is the premise accepted by Hugh and Lyra and rejected only by Paul of Burgos: namely, that Tamar was a member of Judah's family as long as there was a living brother capable of redeeming his dead brother's line.[54] Unless Judah released her from his family, she was obligated to bear children for her dead husband. She could not marry into another family or engage in sexual intercourse without committing adultery. Calvin realized that this duty was not spelled out in a legal code, but gave expression to a "mere instinct of nature."[55]

Calvin rejected the tradition that Er committed the same sin as Onan or that he abused his wife in private. Er's life was cut short because he was a notorious public sinner.[56] As a punishment for his wickedness, he fell victim to a sudden death, which Calvin and his contemporaries regarded as a "scourge of God," since it did not allow sinners to set their affairs in order and prepare their souls to meet God.[57]

When Onan refused to do his duty by Tamar and was also punished by God, Judah, who blamed Tamar unjustly, perpetrated a fraud.[58] He retained Tamar in his family, refused to release her from the obligation to bear children for Er, and yet withheld his son, Shelah, the only relative through whom this duty could have been redeemed. When it became clear to Tamar what had happened, she longed for revenge against Judah and plotted to seduce him.[59] There was nothing impulsive or spontaneous about her decision to seduce Judah. She was willing to commit adultery and incest to gain her ends. Calvin conceded that her ultimate goal was just, but he deplored without reservation or mitigation the means she employed to achieve it.

Although Calvin found little to admire in Tamar (certainly less than Luther found), he regarded Judah as equally blameworthy. Not only had Judah perpetrated a fraud on Tamar, but he had also demonstrated no qualms of conscience over a proposed liaison with a prostitute.[60] Even while Judah was at a distance from the fork in the road to Timnath, long before he had seen the beauty of the woman with whom he proposed to have sexual relations, he lusted for her. Only after he had slept with Tamar did he have any sense of shame at all. He concluded that it would be better to drop the search for the anonymous prostitute than to stir up unnecessary scandal. To Luther's question why Judah did not recognize Tamar, Calvin responded merely that God darkened his mind because he had quenched the light of the Spirit. Judah was a foolish old man, driven by passions he ought long since to have mastered.

Alone of all the commentators, Calvin was not surprised by the severity of Judah's judgment.[61] Calvin rejected the medieval contention that execution by fire was a punishment reserved for the daughters of priests. Death by fire was an appropriate punishment for the crime of adultery in Judah's world. Such a punishment was sanctioned by common consent in order to strengthen the sanctity of marriage. When Judah pronounced sentence over Tamar before hearing her, he was only stating a penalty that was not in dispute, although its foundation was not in law but in a certain "divine instinct."[62]

Calvin was less astonished by the fact that Tamar was threatened with fire than that Judah was not. Although Tamar might have sent Judah's pledge to him privately in order to escape execution through quiet diplomacy, she chose to denounce him as an adulterer equally deserving of punishment. As soon as news of their adultery and incest became public, it "was the duty of all to rise up against them."[63] But without Judah's leadership, the question of punishment was dropped. The phrase, "she is more righteous than I," meant only that "he had been, unjustly and without cause, angry against a woman, by whom he himself might rather have been accused."[64] Calvin conceded, however, that Judah was genuinely penitent when he confessed his sin. As a sign of his penitence Judah never had sexual intercourse with Tamar again.

VI

Throughout their interpretation of the Tamar story, Luther and Calvin engaged issues raised by the antecedent exegetical tradition. Why Er was punished, whether Tamar had committed adultery or fornication, why Judah ordered her to be burnt, were questions that had been discussed before by Jewish and Christian interpreters of the Bible. When Luther explored Tamar's relationship to Melchizedek and Calvin asserted without qualification that she had committed adultery with Judah, they were responding to questions raised by a long exegetical tradition, even when, as in the case of Melchizedek, they did not embrace the traditional answer.

Calvin differed from Luther in his interest in the moral sense of the Tamar story. His exegesis of Genesis 38 is dense with moral observations and rich in practical wisdom. At times Calvin sounds like La Rochefoucauld, as when, for example, in describing Judah's behavior toward Tamar, he utters the maxim "they who are rigid in censuring others, are much more pliant in forgiving themselves."[65] Tamar and Judah are instructive examples for the godly of moral misconduct. Calvin reads their story from the perspective of the third use of the law.

Luther, on the other hand, conceded that he was helped more by the faults of the saints than by their virtues. The dismal history of Judah's family provided him with a fresh incentive to hope in God's mercy. He found comfort in the thought that God, who was merciful to great sinners like Tamar and Judah, would certainly be merciful to him. For Luther, Tamar was a schoolmistress who drove him to Christ.

Nevertheless, in spite of their differences, Calvin followed Luther in setting the story of Tamar and Judah in a theological framework. Unlike Hugh, Lyra, and Denis, both linked Genesis 38 with the mystery of the incarnation. For Calvin, Tamar was a sign of the reality of the self-emptying and humiliation of Christ; for Luther, she was a sign that Christ had united with sinful flesh. While Luther focused on the reality of the humanity Christ assumed, Calvin concentrated on the prerogatives of divinity he set aside. Neither was content to regard the story of Judah and Tamar as nothing more than the sad chronicle of a dysfunctional family.

Calvin insisted, as Luther had before him, that there is no wickedness (including the wickedness of Er, Onan, Judah, and Tamar) that Christ cannot redeem. Christ died for all the sins of the world, its passions and sexual sins as well as its vanities and folly. The family of Judah is a reminder to Calvin that no one should trust in anything human for salvation. Genesis 38 therefore provides for Calvin the occasion for a great *sursum corda* in which he encourages his readers to turn their gaze from Judah and Tamar to Christ and, content with Christ alone, put their trust in nothing else.[66]

NOTES

1. For the dating of Calvin's commentary, see T. H. L. Parker, *Calvin's Old Testament Commentaries* (Edinburgh: T. & T. Clark, 1986), p. 29.

2. Calvin cites Luther by name in his exposition of Gen. 7:3, 11:10, 11:21, and 13:14.

3. Thomas de Vio (Cajetan), *In Omnes Authenticos Veteris Testamenti Historiales Libros et Iob, Commentarii* (Rome, 1531).

4. Huldrych Zwingli, *Farrago Annotationum in Genesin* (Zurich: Christophor Froschouer, 1527).

5. Conrad Pellikan, *Commentaria Bibliorum, Tomus Primus in quo continentur V. libri Mosis* (Zurich: Christophor Froschouer, 1536).

6. Wenzeslaus Linck, *Annotationum in die fünf Bücher Mose. Eyn schöne Vorred Doctoris Martini Lutheri* (Strasbourg: Balthasar Beck, 1543).

7. Johannes Oecolampadius, *D. Io. Oecolampadius in Genesim Enarratio* (Basel: Johann Bebel, 1536).

8. Philip Melanchthon, *In obscuriora aliquot capita Geneseos Annotationes* (Hagenau: Johann Secerius, 1523).

9. Augustinus Steuchus Eugubinus, *Cosmopoeia, vel de mundano opificio, expositio trium capitum Genesis, in quibus de creatione tractat Mosis* (Lyon, 1535). Eugubinus, Bishop of Kisami, Canon Regular of St. Savior, was Vatican librarian.

10. Wolfgang Capito, *Hexaemeron Dei Opus Explicatum* (Strasbourg: Wendelin Rihel, 1539).

11. Paul Fagius, *Exegesis sive Expositio Dictionum Hebraicorum literalis et simplex, in quatuor capita Geneseos, pro studiosis linguae Hebraicae* (Isen, 1542).

12. Nicholas of Lyra, *Postilla super Genesim, Exodum, Leviticum, Numeri, Deuteronomum, Iosue, Iudicum, Regum et Paralippomenon, cum additionibus Pauli Episcopi Burgensis replicisque Mathie Dorinck cumque textu plano incluso* (Nuremberg: Anton Koburger, 1498). For the history of the printings of Lyra in this period, see Karlfried Froehlich, "The Printed Gloss," in the *Biblia Latina cum Glossa Ordinaria* (Brepols-Turnhout, 1992), pp. xii–xxvi. This book is the facsimile reprint of the editio princeps by Adolph Rusch of Strasbourg (1480/81).

13. Hugh of St. Cher, *Repertorium apostillarum utriusque testamenti* (Basel: Johann Amerbach, Johann Petri, and Johann Froben for Anton Koburger, 1503–1504).

14. Denis the Carthusian, *Enarrationes piae et eruditae, in quinque Mosaicae legis libros* (Cologne: Peter Quentel, 1534).

15. Denis, *Enarrationes*, fol. 115v; Hugh, *Repertorium*, fol. 55v; Lyra, *Postilla*, cap. 38.

16. Denis, *Enarrationes*, fol. 115v; Hugh, *Repertorium*, fol. 55v; Lyra, *Postilla*, cap. 38.

17. Denis, *Enarrationes*, fol. 115v.

18. Hugh, *Repertorium*, fol. 56.

19. Denis, *Enarrationes*, fol. 116; Hugh, *Repertorium*, fol. 56v; Lyra, *Postilla*, cap. 38.

20. Lyra, *Postilla*, cap. 38.

21. Denis, *Enarrationes*, fol. 116.

22. Denis, *Enarrationes*, fol. 116; Lyra, *Postilla*, cap. 38.

23. Denis, *Enarrationes*, fol. 116; Hugh, *Repertorium*, fol. 56v; Lyra, *Postilla*, cap. 38.

24. Hugh, *Repertorium*, fol. 56v.

25. Martin Luther, *Luthers Werke*, WA 44 (Weimar: Hermann Böhlaus Nachfolger, 1915), p. 309. (Remaining references abbreviated according to the pattern WA 44.309.)

26. WA 44.332.

27. WA 44.332.

28. WA 44.315–17.

29. WA 44.323.

30. WA 44.323: "Respondeo: Imaginatio alienat sensus et cogitationem."

31. WA 44.329–32.

32. WA 44.321–22.

33. WA 44.323–24.

34. WA 44.325: "Fuit mirabilis mulier, ac videtur amplius tentatura fuisse, si spe sua frustrata esset."

35. WA 44.309.

36. WA 44.322.

37. WA 44.312.

38. WA 44.314–15.

39. WA 44.324: "Deus sinit eum concipi in incoestu foedissimo, ut assumeret verissimam carnem."

40. WA 44.324: "Et tamen revera erat caro polluta ex Iuda et Tamar."

41. WA 44.324.

42. WA 44.311: "Summus Patriarcha Iuda, pater Christi hunc infandum incoestum commisit, ut nasceretur Christus de carne excellenter peccante et turpissimo peccato contaminata."

43. WA 44.314: "Ex hac Thamar ortus est Messias, licet per stuprum et incoestum."

44. WA 44.332.

45. WA 44.337: "Hactenus vero historia Iudae et Thamar, quam simpliciter potius explicare, quam allegorias fingere libuit."

46. Hugh, *Repertorium*, fol. 55v.

47. For a fascinating discussion of the issues involved, see Guy Bedouelle, "The Consultations of the Universities and Scholars Concerning the 'Great Matter' of King Henry VIII," in *The Bible in the Sixteenth Century*, ed. David C. Steinmetz (Durham, N.C.: Duke University Press, 1990), pp. 21–36.

48. WA 44.311: "Caro Christi oritur ex incestuoso concubitu, similiter et caro Virginis, matris eius, et totius posteritate Iudae, ideo, ut significaretur ineffabile illud consilium misericordiae Dei, quod assumpsit carnem sive naturam humanum ex carne contaminata et horribiliter polluta."

49. Calvin's interpretation occupies less than ten columns. CO 23.491–501.

50. CO 23.500: "Hoc turpis et honesti discrimen quod natura dictat, quicunque tentant convellere, Deo palam gigantum more bellum inferunt."

51. CO 23.493.

52. CO 23.493: "Deinde scimus in eo maxime fulgere divitias Dei, quod Christus carnem nostram induens, in nihilum redigi voluit."

53. CO 23.493: "Interea meminerimus Christum nihil gloriae mutuarias suis maioribus, imo nihil habere gloriae in carne repositum, cuius praecipuus et maxime illustris in cruce triumphus fuit."

54. CO 23.496.

55. Calvin uses the phrase "solo naturae instinctu." See CO 23.495.

56. CO 23.494.

57. CO 23.494: ". . . quoque mortis celeritas inter Dei flagella deputanda est."

58. CO 23.496.

59. CO 23.496–97.

60. CO 23.497–98.

61. CO 23.498–99.

62. CO 23.499: "Hoc divino instinctu factum esse constat."

63. CO 23.500.

64. CO 23.500: ". . . sed comparative loquitur, ac si diceret se iniuste et sine causa iratum fuisse mulieri, a qua potius accusandus fuerat."

65. CO 23.500: ". . . hinc colligimus, qui duriter aliis succensent ad dandam sibi veniam esse plus quam flexibiles."

66. CO 23.493: "Denique probis infame oportuit esse ipsius genus, ut eo uno contenti nihil extra eum quaeramus: . . ."

7

Calvin and Isaiah

In 1885 Frederic W. Farrar, chaplain to Queen Victoria and later Dean of
Canterbury, delivered the Bampton Lectures at Oxford on the subject of
the history of interpretation. The book is a triumph of what the late Sir
Herbert Butterfield of Cambridge called "Whig" historiography. Farrar
admired about the past precisely those elements in it most like the present
and regarded the present, indeed, as the inevitable culmination of all that
was best in the past. The history of exegesis became for Farrar the history
of "more or less untenable" conceptions of the Bible, "a history of false sup-
positions slowly and progressively corrected."[1] Not surprisingly, Farrar
admired Antioch over Alexandria, Luther over Thomas Aquinas, Calvin over
Luther, and the moderns over all. Farrar catalogued with obvious delight
every strained allegory, every factual inaccuracy, every philological howler
committed by precritical exegetes in the name of biblical interpretation.
While he admitted that ancient commentaries are full of practical instruction aimed at moral and spiritual edification and that much of this instruction is "of the highest intrinsic value," he nevertheless warned that frequently such material "has but a slender connexion with the text on which
it is founded."[2]

The question that needs to be asked a century after Dean Farrar's lectures is not whether Farrar's bleak evaluation of the history of exegesis needs
to be corrected but how and to what extent. As a case study for this inquiry
I want to take one of the more spectacular oracles of First Isaiah, the vision
of the prophet in the Temple (Isa. 6:1–13), and examine the treatment of

this passage in the history of Christian exegesis. Although it is doubtful that the book of Isaiah was ever as popular a subject for commentators as the book of Genesis or the Gospel of John, there is still a significant body of commentaries on it. Among the Greek Fathers, Origen, Eusebius of Caesarea, Theodore Heracleensis, Cyril of Alexandria, Theodoret of Cyr, John Chrysostom, Hesychius, Didymus the Blind, and Procopius of Gaza either preached homilies or wrote commentaries on Isaiah. Jerome alone among the Latin Fathers wrote a commentary on the whole book, a commentary which, as Jerome freely admits, is heavily indebted to the Greek exegetical tradition stemming from Origen. If we discount, however, the partial commentaries of Augustine, Godefrid, Alan of Lille, and Joachim of Fiore, we will still have complete commentaries from such medieval expositors as Walafrid Strabo, Haymo of Auxerre, Rupert of Deutz, Hervaeus of Bourg-Dieu, Thomas Aquinas (including his reflections on Isaiah 6 in the preface to his commentary on John), Albert the Great, Hugh of St. Cher, Nicholas of Lyra, and Denis the Carthusian. By 1567 Oecolampadius (1525), Zwingli (1529), Luther (1532), Münster (ca. 1540), Brenz (1550), Castellio (1551), Musculus (1557), Calvin (1559), and Bullinger (1567) had all published at least one edition of a commentary on Isaiah. If we add the sixteenth-century Roman Catholic commentators Vatable and Forer to the Protestant commentators already mentioned, we find that we have a substantial, if somewhat diffuse and unwieldy, body of Christian literature on Isaiah.

In order to give a sharper focus to this reevaluation I will concentrate on Calvin's exegesis as the vantage point from which to survey the history of the precritical interpretation of Isaiah. I want to focus particularly on five interrelated questions: (1) how often did Calvin comment on Isaiah 6 and in what contexts? (2) what exegetical issues interested Calvin and how did he resolve them? (3) was Calvin's exegesis altogether new or did it fit into a longer history of commenting on the text? (4) what characterizes the precritical tradition of exegesis on Isaiah, especially as that tradition is exemplified in the exegesis of Calvin? (5) and, finally, is the precritical tradition still valuable to us, whose exegetical starting-point is the historical-critical method?

I

If we consult the first edition of the *Institutes* (1536), we find that Calvin makes only one allusion to Isa. 6:5 (OS 1.234) in order to emphasize that prophets preach folly if they proclaim their own word rather than bear the Word of the Lord. In the final Latin edition of the *Institutes* (1559), Calvin repeats this allusion (IV.viii.3) and adds eleven new ones: seven in book one, one in book two, two in book three, and one additional in book four. Calvin seems much impressed with John's interpretation of Isaiah's vision as a vision of the glory of the Son and uses Isaiah 6 against Servetus and the anti-Trinitarians (I.xii.11, I.xiii.23). This vision describes the dread and wonder that one experiences in the presence of God (I.i.3) and contains a warning that one cannot see the incomprehensible essence of God (I.xi.3). Calvin finds in this pericope proof not only for the deity of the Son but also (especially in view of Acts 28:25–26) for the deity of the Holy Spirit (I.xiii.15).

There are a cluster of allusions dealing with the doctrine of election and its consequences. While Calvin believes that Isaiah teaches that those who extinguish the light of nature befuddle themselves (I.iv.2), he denies that the hardening of the reprobate can be explained by appeals to divine fore-knowledge or permission (II.iv.3) and even admits that preaching can lead the nonelect to greater hardness of heart (III.xxiv.13). He will not concede, however, that the doctrine of election makes exhortations to godly living pointless (III.xxiii.13). For the rest, Calvin seems primarily concerned with the implications of Isaiah 6 for ecclesiological questions, such as the author-ity of the prophets over false Roman notions of teaching authority (IV.viii.3) and the unity of the covenant of God under two different testaments (IV.xvi.6). In short, Calvin finds in Isaiah 6 resources for dealing with such theological topics as the incomprehensibility of God, the doctrine of the Trinity, the nature of the proper worship of God, the mystery of election and reprobation, and the authority of the Church in the Old and New Testaments.

When we turn from the *Institutes* to Calvin's sermons, we find that Calvin preached two series of sermons on Isaiah. The first series, begun in 1546, was not taken down by a secretary and so was lost, though Colladon claims that these sermons became the basis of the 1551 commentary on Isaiah. The second series of sermons ran from July 16, 1556, to sometime just before September 4, 1559, when Calvin began to preach on Genesis. While Calvin's sermons were esteemed in Elizabethan England (indeed, Arthur Golding's translation of Calvin's 159 sermons on Job went through five editions in ten years), they have fared less well in more recent history. Although Denis Raguenier had transcribed 2,042 of Calvin's sermons (all of which were delivered extempore), the Genevan Library in 1805 disposed of forty-four of the original forty-eight sermon manuscript volumes, pricing them accord-ing to their weight. Later, of course, the officials of the library realized their mistake and attempted to recover the volumes which had been sold, but 35 volumes eluded recovery. Some had been purchased by the Bodleian, some by Bern, some by the Bibliothèque Nationale. Of the 2,304 sermons that we know were transcribed by Raguenier or others (including the 780 sermons published while Calvin was still alive), we have the text of 1,460. Over 800 sermons have simply disappeared. Unfortunately, the sermons of Calvin on Isaiah 6 were among the sermons that were lost.

The best and most authoritative text of Calvin's interpretation of Isaiah 6 is the Latin commentary of 1559. Behind it lies Calvin's experience with the text in his French sermons of 1546, his Latin and French commentaries of 1551 and 1552, and his French sermons of 1556–1559. While Calvin claimed in his dedicatory letter (1559) to Queen Elizabeth I of England that he had "bestowed so much care and industry" on the final edition of his commentary "that it ought justly to be reckoned a new work," there is reason to believe that Calvin exaggerated and that the changes are less sweeping than he suggests, more matters of style than of substance.[3] Nevertheless, as the final form of Calvin's exegesis of Isaiah 6, the 1559 commentary represents the distillate of his repeated exegetical work on the text.

II

All of the theological issues that Calvin discussed in the *Institutes* when he alluded to Isaiah 6—the incomprehensibility of God, the doctrine of the Trinity, the nature of worship, the mystery of election, and the authority of the Church—are repeated in one form or another in the 1559 commentary, though without lengthy systematic development. In addition to these theological issues, Calvin raises some exegetical problems, such as the order and composition of Isaiah, the nature of Isaiah's vision, and the character of the prophetic message which he bears. Since we cannot discuss in a brief chapter all of the theological and exegetical issues which Calvin raises, we shall limit ourselves to these last three exegetical issues, indicating their relationship to larger doctrinal questions as Calvin feels it is appropriate to do so.

The Order and Composition of Isaiah

Because Isaiah 6 is dated by the prophet himself as a vision that occurred "in the year that King Uzziah died," Calvin feels himself obliged to comment briefly on the historical circumstances surrounding this oracle. There are two historical-critical problems that Calvin finds in the antecedent exegetical tradition and that he attempts to resolve. We know that these are traditional problems because Calvin introduces them with the words "some think."

Calvin shows himself extraordinarily reluctant to name the commentators with which he disagrees. It is, of course, a fairly common medieval convention to refer to theologians with whom one disagrees as "some" commentators and to be much more explicit in listing by name the authorities with whom one agrees. But Calvin seems to carry such anonymity further than medieval custom requires. That this is a conscious policy T. H. L. Parker has shown by quoting a letter of Calvin to Francis Burkhard, secretary of the Elector of Saxony: "If others have gone wrong on something, I reprove it without mentioning names and without violence, and indeed I bury errors in silence unless necessity forces."[4]

This policy, admirable in itself, makes it exceedingly difficult to locate Calvin's sources and to retrace the series of preliminary steps which led him to an exegetical decision. Fortunately, however, one of the two historical-critical problems discussed by Calvin in Isaiah 6 is relatively easy to run down. Calvin mentions in the opinion of "some" that the death of Uzziah means leprosy, which was a kind of civil death.[5] This is the opinion of the Jewish commentator Rashi, based on a Talmudic saying and repeated by the later Jewish commentator Ibn Ezra.[6] While Calvin may have read this exegetical judgment in Jewish sources, it seems far more likely that he came across it in the commentary of the Franciscan expositor, Nicholas of Lyra, who cites Rashi by name.[7]

Calvin, however, accepts death in its literal sense and is convinced that Isaiah prophesied in the interval between the onset of the leprosy of Uzziah and his subsequent death.[8] The blindness of the people about which Isaiah so feelingly speaks in chapter 6 is a blindness that he has already experienced and the vision is intended to encourage him in the further discharge of an office that he has already accepted and undertaken.

When Calvin accepts a literal reading of "death," he agrees with the vast majority of Patristic, medieval, and Reformation commentators. He does not suggest, however, some of the possible exegetical implications of a literal meaning of the text developed in the preceding tradition. Jerome argued that God could not be seen in a temple defiled by Uzziah's illicit offering of incense any more than we can see God so long as we are ruled by the leprosy of sin.[9] The death of Uzziah was the precondition for the vision of God. Other Fathers, such as Eusebius,[10] Chrysostom,[11] and Cyril,[12] suggest that there was no prophetic oracle during the reign of Uzziah after he was struck down with leprosy and argue that the death of Uzziah marked the resumption of prophecy. Theodore of Moepsuestia in his commentary on Amos rejected the notion that there was an interruption in prophecy during the reign of Uzziah, though he was unable to prove that any of the prophecies were delivered after Uzziah's sacrilege in the temple.[13] Theodoret of Cyr agreed that there was a cessation of prophecy between the sacrilege in the temple and the death of Uzziah but blamed Isaiah for this cessation rather than the king.[14] Had Isaiah denounced the act of the king in the temple, prophecy would not have come to an end. Chrysostom and, to some extent,

Cyril disagree with this interpretation. Chrysostom finds no reason to impugn the character of Isaiah or blame the temporary loss of prophecy on him.

Of this Patristic debate or the suggestion that prophecy was interrupted during the reign of Uzziah, Calvin mentions not a word. In Calvin's view Isaiah prophesied throughout the reign of Uzziah and that, while the death of Uzziah was marked by the "various commotions . . . produced by the change of kings," it did not mark the resumption of prophecy or the lifting of a penalty imposed by God on Judah for the sacrilege of its king or the cowardice of its prophet.[15]

The second historical-critical problem is somewhat more difficult to trace down to its roots. Calvin reports the opinion of "some" commentators that chapter 6 is misplaced and belongs really at the beginning of the book of Isaiah, prefatory even to chapter 1. Calvin cites three reasons which have been given in support of this judgment on the composition and order of Isaiah: (1) first of all, Isaiah in chapter 6 declines an office which he already appears to exercise in chapters 1–5; (2) furthermore, he talks like a novice and seems to be unacquainted with the demands of his office; and (3) finally, Isaiah claims that this is the first vision of God which he has received and that he was the recipient of no prior ecstatic experience. Calvin dismisses all of these arguments as "feeble and unsatisfactory." He regards Isaiah in the temple as so "overpowered by the presence of God," "like one who had lost his senses," that he forgot that he had been a prophet and the recipient of previous oracles. The principal reason, however, why this overwhelming vision of the presence of God was delayed until Isaiah had begun his work as a prophet was in order to confirm him in the discharge of his office. He could have been disheartened by the "hard-hearted obstinacy of the people" and unsettled by the "changes of times and kings." It was only after Isaiah had begun to prophesy that God appeared to him. The new vision was necessary in order to encourage him to persevere. Therefore the order of chapters at the beginning of the book of Isaiah is the correct one.[16]

It is very difficult to know who the "some" are who argue that Isaiah 6 has been misplaced. Oecolampadius in 1525 also mentions that this is the opinion of "some" commentators, though he gives so much less detail than Calvin does that he cannot be Calvin's primary source.[17] Zwingli,[18] Luther,[19] and Brenz[20] do not mention the problem at all. The suggestion that Isaiah 6 is misplaced is not found in Origen,[21] Eusebius, Theodore, Cyril, Theodoret, Chrysostom, Procopius of Gaza,[22] Jerome, Walafrid Strabo,[23] Haymo of Auxerre,[24] Rupert of Deutz,[25] Ibn Ezra, Hervaeus of Bourg-Dieu,[26] Thomas Aquinas,[27] Albert the Great,[28] Hugh of St. Cher,[29] Nicholas of Lyra, or Denis the Carthusian.[30] Clearly, whoever the "some" commentators are to whom Calvin alludes, they represent an exegetical minority. The majority of expositors, like Calvin, seem to be satisfied with the canonical ordering of chapters 1–6.

The Nature of Isaiah's Vision

Far more interesting to most Patristic and medieval commentators than the order and dating of Isaiah's vision are the theological and epistemological implications of Isaiah's claim, *vidi dominum* ("I saw the Lord"). How is it possible, the commentators wonder, to see a God whose essence is invisible and cannot be seen? Yet Isaiah attributes to this invisible God "a throne, a robe and a bodily appearance." What did Isaiah see and how did he see it?

Both Nicholas of Lyra and Denis the Carthusian mention the suggestion of Pseudo-Dionysius that what Isaiah saw was an "angel." Nicholas, who is always sympathetic to Jewish readings of Old Testament texts, softens what other commentators regard as the trinitarian setting of this vision by pointing out that the threefold repetition of the *sanctus* ("Holy, holy, holy is the Lord of hosts") was an ancient Hebraic way of giving greater expression to the notion of divine sanctity. None of the Christian interpreters, however, picks up the comment of Ibn Ezra that the heavenly conversation which Isaiah overhears ("Whom shall I send and who will go for us?") is in fact a conversation between God and the seraphim.

The Christian commentators feel themselves bound by John 12:41 to regard the theophany as in some sense a revelation of Christ and by Acts 28:25–26 to regard the voice which speaks to Isaiah as the voice of the Holy Spirit. Coupling these verses with the threefold *sanctus*, the Pauline and Johannine notions that the Son is the image of the Father, and the trinitarian traditions of Christian theology, most Christian commentators, including Calvin, conclude that the vision is a vision of Christ, but a vision that involves in one way or another the whole Trinity. Only Zwingli among the early Protestants keeps his options open by calling it a vision of an image, type, form, or even sacrament of God. Calvin argues that while Isaiah saw the glory of Christ, what he saw cannot be limited to the person of Christ, since the word *Adonai* ("Lord") is applied to God "in an absolute and unrestricted manner."[31] Furthermore, while Calvin accepts the traditional view that the repetition of the *sanctus* points to the doctrine of the Trinity, he regards such proof by itself as weak. The heretics have a point when they object that three denotes the perfection of holiness and may say more about the "unwearied perseverance" of the angels in singing the praise of the holiness of God than it does about the trinitarian doctrine as such. Still Calvin is willing to agree with the "ancients" that the passage is trinitarian, however reluctant he may be to use the passage polemically.

The early Christian Fathers do not spend time discussing the epistemological implications of Isaiah's vision. Theodoret warns that the fact that God has appeared under many forms to the patriarchs and prophets does not mean that God is polyform. His essence is simple, without parts, invisible and inaccessible. For the rest Theodoret prefers to talk about the nature of God apophatically and to insist that the Son who knows the nature of the Father has never revealed it.

By the later Middle Ages, however, scholastic commentators show an interest in the psychology and epistemology of prophetic vision. Nicholas of Lyra refers his readers back to his comments on the nature of prophecy at the beginning of his commentary on the Psalms, while Albert the Great and Denis the Carthusian discuss the nature of Isaiah's vision is some detail. Though not all scholastic commentators agree exactly in their outline of the structure of the problem, there seems to be a fairly wide consensus that Isaiah's vision was not corporeal, but imaginative and intellectual. No one standing beside Isaiah would have seen what he saw, as everyone at Belshazzar's feast saw the handwriting on the wall. The images that Isaiah saw were implanted in his imagination by God. The prophet was also given an understanding of the intellectual signification of those images; otherwise, it would have been a hallucination rather than a prophetic vision. What Isaiah saw, he saw with his mind. Nevertheless, he was not given intuitive knowledge of the nature of God, but only knowledge by abstraction.

Calvin seems to prefer to return to the simpler discussion of this verse which marked Patristic exegesis. Rather than engage in extended epistemological discussions, he simply invokes one of his most characteristic theological principles—the principle of accommodation. "When God exhibited himself to the view of the Fathers, he never appeared such as he actually is, but such as the capacity of men could receive."[32] The vision of the throne, the robe, and the bodily appearance was adapted to the capacity of Isaiah "to perceive the inconceivable majesty of God." What is true of Isaiah's vision is true of all human knowledge of God from whatever source. No human being knows God as he is but only as he has adapted himself to the limitations and capacities of human nature. All knowledge of God is accommodated knowledge.

The Character of the Prophetic Message

In his vision Isaiah was given a troubling message: "Go and say to this people: 'Hear and hear, but do not understand; see and see, but do not perceive.'" It appears on the face of it that Isaiah has been commissioned as a messenger of bad news, a herald of an inevitable judgment to come that cannot be avoided. Everything Isaiah says, so the vision seems to imply, will harden the people of Judah in their obstinate defiance of God. Is God the author of the opposition to his own message? Has he foreordained the resistance that Isaiah meets? Is there a possibility of free response to Isaiah's message or has divine predestination foreclosed the possibility of repentance? It is not an easy question to answer and it is clearly a question which troubles the Christian interpreters of Isa. 6:9–10.

Theodoret of Cyr speaks for the overwhelming majority of Patristic commentators when he stresses human freedom and responsibility rather than divine foreordination. The infirmities of the congregation to whom Isaiah preaches are not the work of nature; they are the result of deliberate choice. Nature did not blind the eyes of Isaiah's listeners; the listeners themselves have closed them. What is at stake is not the weakness of physical organs but the stubborn refusal to believe. God has predicted Judah's response; he has not preordained it. Judah will persist in its perversity until destruction is brought down around its ears. Like most of the Patristic and medieval commentators, Theodoret feels himself bound by John 12:39–40 to regard the destruction which is foretold as the final destruction by Vespasian and Titus. For the rest, the spirit of torpor that overcomes the Jews was "given" by God only in the sense that God has permitted them to be overwhelmed by the accumulated consequences of their own free decisions.

Jerome feels that the point of the passage is that God has left Israel in its unbelief in order to have mercy on the Gentiles and that the text celebrates the mercy of God rather than his cruelty—especially since repentance is still a possibility for at least a remnant of the Jews. Neither the freedom of the human will (Theodoret) nor the mercy of God (Jerome) is seriously in question.

Denis the Carthusian feels that what we have in this oracle is a prophetic denunciation of future evils, not a command or exhortation to commit evil. Although people may hear the words of the prophet, they will not understand internally what he is saying. Denis is keen to distinguish what happens consecutively from what happens causally. It is true that hardness of heart follows consecutively on the denunciation which the prophet preaches. It is not true that the proclamation of the prophetic message is itself the cause of that hardness of heart. Judah is blind because it deserves to be and the attitude of God toward this blinding is permissive rather than active. Walafrid Strabo, Haymo of Auxerre, Rupert of Deutz, Hervaeus of Bourg-Dieu, and Thomas Aquinas all echo to a greater or lesser extent the exegesis of Jerome.

When we come to the Protestant reformers, the stress remains on the responsibility of the congregation to whom Isaiah preaches for their own blindness. Luther, who believes in predestination, nevertheless believes that Isaiah is not invoking predestination at all when he bemoans the voluntary obtuseness of Judah. Johannes Brenz, the Lutheran reformer of Schwäbisch Hall, who gives one of the two or three very allegorical interpretations of Isaiah 6, is convinced that the blindness of the Jews which concerns Isaiah is blindness concerning the gospel of Christ. Zwingli interprets this verse in the context of sixteenth-century eucharistic controversies and explains the blindness of the Jews as a blindness with respect to Christ's word that he would give them his flesh to eat.

Even Calvin stresses, both in his commentary on Isaiah 6 and in his commentary on John 12:39–40, the responsibility of unbelievers for their predicament. In the commentary on John (1553), Calvin makes an important point not made by other commentators.[33] God wills that Isaiah speak his Word. It is accidental to that Word and not essential to it that it blinds the men and women who hear it. In itself the Word is life-giving. When it meets adamant unbelief, however, it leaves the unbelieving hearers in a far worse state than it found them. In other words, the Word of God is never ineffectual. It either produces death or life. It never leaves things as they are.

In his commentary on Isaiah, Calvin makes the same point. God foretells a state of affairs for which unbelievers themselves are responsible. "Such blinding and hardening influence," says Calvin, "does not arise out of the nature of the Word, but is accidental, and must be ascribed to the depravity of man."[34] On the other hand, Calvin is willing to admit, when pressed for an answer, that "if you enquire into the first cause, we must come to the predestination of God."[35] Still, having said this, Calvin shows no eagerness in his commentary to discuss predestination. What he prefers to stress instead is the function of this oracle as an encouragement to Isaiah.

Only in the *Institutes* does predestination come to the fore. There Calvin attacks the Patristic notion that the hardening of unbelievers takes place through foreknowledge or permission (II.iv.3). Indeed, Calvin refers his readers to I.xviii, the chapter in which he attacks the notion of permission as Epicurean, epitomized by his image of "God in a watchtower," a lazy deity who is an idle spectator of a history which he neither can nor will influence. Calvin wishes to talk about the ways in which God carries out his judgments through Satan as a minister of his wrath. God is not merely passive in the process of the hardening of sinners, in spite of the fact that sinners are responsible for their own condition. Something more is involved, even though that "something more" ought not to become the object of curious speculation.

III

Christian interpreters of Isaiah 6 show very little interest in the allegorical interpretation of their text. Hugh of St. Cher suggests an allegorical inter-

pretation of the seraphim and Luther offers an alternative allegorical interpretation, almost as a theological exercise. Only the Lutheran Brenz is thoroughly committed to an allegorical interpretation of Isaiah 6 as its sole
meaning. Most interpreters are concerned with the literal-grammatical
interpretation of Isaiah. The fact that they are willing to consider that the
vision of Isaiah was a vision of the glory of Christ does not mean that they
are any the less interested in the literal sense, but only that the literal sense
of the Old Testament must be subordinate to the literal sense of the New.
For Christian interpreters the Old Testament is not attached to the Talmud
(though they make use of Jewish insights) but to the New Testament. There
are only two possibilities for them: Old Testament plus Talmud or Old
Testament plus New. There is no such thing as the Old Testament in itself
abstracted from the religious communities in which it lives.

On the whole, Christian interpreters seem conservative about the canonical shape of the text as it has been received from the synagogue by the church.
Most Christian interpreters think that Isaiah did in fact prophesy before
Isaiah 6 and that chapters 1–5 contain early oracles. At the same time most
interpreters agree that there was an interruption in the prophetic activity
of Isaiah associated with the sacrilege of Uzziah in the temple, a reading
which Calvin rejects. Very few authors are impressed with the suggestion
of Rashi that the death of Uzziah was the civil death created by his leprosy.
Some interpreters think that the vision in Isaiah 6 and the oracles in 1–5
all occur in the same year, the year in which King Uzziah died, an interpretation to which Calvin himself does not subscribe. In short, while commentators do raise historical-critical questions only very few interpreters
(Calvin calls them vaguely "some" commentators) seem inclined to rear-
range the canonical order of the oracles. Calvin even draws a spiritual les-
son from an order that places Isaiah 6 after 1–5.

Even though Christian interpreters are reluctant to tamper with the
canonical shape of Isaiah, they do not regard the canonical shape itself as
theologically determinative. They are not interested in the theology of a
redactor of whom they have never heard. The theological context for considering an oracle of Isaiah is not merely the theology of First Isaiah as a
whole or even the theology of First Isaiah as reinterpreted in the New
Testament, but the theology of the Christian church in the whole sweep
of its historical development. God did not become a Trinity at the Council of Nicaea, though Nicaea clarified what had always been true. The God
who created the world, who called Israel out of bondage, who revealed
himself in the temple to Isaiah, was and is one God eternally subsisting
in three Persons. Therefore it is not anachronistic to detect hints of the
trinitarian nature of God in the vision of Isaiah, though Isaiah himself
may have seen more than he explicitly understood; it is simply sound

exegesis. The hermeneutical key to the Old Testament is the *regula fidei* of the Christian church.

There seems to be a tendency in the history of exegesis, arrested by the Protestants who wish in this instance to return to an earlier form of exegesis as preferable, to use materials and methods in the exegesis of a text drawn from the general cultural history of Western civilization. Medieval interpreters are fascinated by the epistemology and status of prophetic vision. They do not attempt to explain prophetic ecstasy by appealing solely to other biblical traditions or to the traditions of Christian theology. They unashamedly make use of philosophical traditions which had their origins in Greek antiquity, but which have been commented on for centuries by generations of pagan, Islamic, Jewish, and Christian interpreters.

Secular learning has its rightful place in the exegesis of Scripture and a question cannot be shunted aside as irrelevant or unanswerable simply because the Bible does not give an answer to it. Universal natural truths concerning prophetic ecstasy are as true of Isaiah in the temple as they are of any other religious ecstatic: pagan, Islamic, Jewish, or Christian. The explanations which are offered are, of course, not historical but philosophical. Exegetes are not interested in particular but relative "truths," limited in their cultural application. They are interested in universal and unchanging truth, transcending every particular instance of its application.

The Christian exegetical tradition appears to be conservative both in its method of procedure and in its exegetical results. All the later commentators seem to know and quote the earlier commentators whose writings have been widely preserved. While commentators disagree (although disagreement seems to oblige dissidents to offer a reasoned explanation for their opinion), and while at times those disagreements take on a polemical tone, nevertheless the disagreements demonstrate that commenting is not an art that begins *de novo* with each generation. It belongs to the art of commenting to read all the commentators who have gone before. This exegetical tradition serves as a check on the singular opinions of various enthusiastic commentators and acts as a control on the practice of exegesis as such.

Indeed, it appears on occasion that the exegetical tradition may even be more conservative than the traditions of dogmatic theology. Calvin joins the almost universal chorus of previous commentators on Isa. 6:9–10 when he is reluctant to talk about predestination in the context of his commentary on Isaiah 6. When he does talk about predestination in the *Institutes* in the context of dogmatic theology, Calvin is not at all hesitant to quote Isa. 6:9–10 in support of this discussion. The shift of contexts seems to give him greater freedom. In the context of the genre of commentary he seems restrained by the overwhelming weight of the exegetical tradition, not to deny that predestination is suggested by the words of Isaiah (Calvin does not have an uncritical respect for the opinions of the Greek Fathers), but to stress rather (even if on his own terms and in his own way) the importance of human responsibility.

IV

Which brings us back to Frederick Farrar. It is difficult to recognize the exegesis of Isaiah 6 we have just examined in the general description of the history of exegesis which Farrar offered. To be sure, it is true that the older consensus on the historical-critical setting of Isaiah 6 would find few supporters among modern commentators, but the older discussion of these questions does not seem arbitrary or strained, even by modern standards. The judgment of Christian commentators that Isaiah saw the glory of Christ was an exegetical conclusion forced on the commentators by the New Testament itself, though there was a tendency on the part of some commentators—including Calvin—to soften the hard edges of that exegesis. The discussions of free will (Theodoret of Cyr), divine mercy (Jerome), and predestination (Calvin) stimulated by Isa. 6:9–10 may have gone far beyond the intentions of the author of the text, but one could not say that the theological discussion had no intrinsic connection to it. While the precritical exegesis of Isaiah 6 is not an exegesis we can simply adopt, it is still not accurate to regard it as arbitrary and strained, of value only for its homiletical asides.

It is no answer to Farrar to point out that there is a good deal in ancient commentaries which is surprisingly modern, even from a historical-critical or philological viewpoint, or to argue that the modern reader can find insight into the "literal" sense of the text in precritical commentaries. That is to admit his principle that precritical exegesis is good in the proportion that it anticipates or agrees with modern exegesis. Nor is it an answer to reply with a *tu quoque* and to list the exegetical atrocities which have been committed from time to time in the name of the historical-critical method, though such a list is disquietingly easy to compile.

The principal value of precritical exegesis is that it is not modern exegesis; it is alien, strange, sometimes even, from our perspective, comic and fantastical. Precisely because it is strange, it provides a constant stimulus to interpreters, offering exegetical suggestions they would never think of or find in any modern book, forcing them again and again to a rereading and reevaluation of the text. But if they immerse themselves not only in the text but also in these alien approaches to the text, they may learn in time to see with eyes not their own sights they could scarcely have imagined and may learn to hear with ears not their own voices too soft for their own ears to detect.

NOTES

1. Frederic W. Farrar, *History of Interpretation* (Grand Rapids, Mich.: Baker Book House, 1979), p. xiv.

2. Ibid, p. vii.

3. The critical edition (CO 36) does not include the dedicatory letters of Calvin to Edward VI and Elizabeth I. They are, however, readily available in the English translation in the Edinburgh edition reprinted by Baker, *Calvin's Commentaries* 7, pp. xvi–xxv.

4. T. H. L. Parker, *Calvin's New Testament Commentaries* (Grand Rapids: Wm. B. Eerdmans, 1971), p. 86.

5. CO 36.125.

6. For Ibn Ezra on Isaiah 6, see M. Friedländer, ed. and trans., *The Commentary of Ibn Ezra on Isaiah*, Vol. 1 (London, 1873; rpt. New York: Philipp Feldheim, n.d.), pp. 33–38.

7. For Nicholas of Lyra, I used the edition *Glossae in Universa Biblia. Postilla* (Nuremberg: Anton Koburger, 1481). I also consulted the 1498 Koburger edition.

8. CO 36.124–26.

9. Jerome, *Commentariorum in Esaiam Libri I–XI*, S. Hieronymi Presbyteri Opera Pars 1.2, CCh 73 (Turnholt: Brepols, 1963), pp. 83–95.

10. Eusebius of Caesarea, PG 24.121–32.

11. John Chrysostom, PG 56.67–77.

12. Cyril of Alexandria, PG 70.169–92.

13. Theodore of Moepsuestia, PG 66.241–304.

14. Theodoret of Cyr, *Commentaire sur Isaïe*, Vol. 1, Sources Chrétiennes 276 (Paris: Du Cerf, 1980), pp. 254–79.

15. CO 36.125–26.

16. CO 36.124–26.

17. Johannes Oecolampadius, *In Iesaiam Prophetam Commentariorum Libri VI* (Basel: Andreas Cratander, 1525).

18. Huldrych Zwingli, SS 5.609–14.

19. WA 31^2.47–54.

20. Johannes Brenz, *Tomus Quartus Operum Ioannis Brentii* (Tübingen: Gruppenbachius, 1580), pp. 191–96.

21. Origen, PG 13.219–24.

22. Procopius of Gaza, PG 87.1929–52.

23. Walafrid Strabo, PL 113.1242–45.

24. Haymo of Auxerre, PL 116.753–58.

25. Rupert of Deutz, PL 167.1277–79.

26. Hervaeus of Bourg-Dieu, PL 181.84–95.

27. Thomas Aquinas, *In Isaiam Prophetam Expositio*, Opera Omnia 14 (rpt. of Parma ed. New York: Musurgia Publishers, 1949), pp. 454–58.

28. Albert the Great, *Postilla super Isaiam*, Opera Omnia 19 (Münster Westf.: Aschendorff, 1952), pp. 85–100.

29. Hugh of St. Cher, *In Libros Prophetarum*, Opus Admirabile 4 (Venice: Nicolaus Pezzana, 1732), pp. 16–18.

30. Denis the Carthusian, *Enarrationes Piae ac Eruditae in Quatuor Prophetas Majores*, Opera Omnia 8 (Monstrolii: Typis Cartusiae S.M. de Pratis, 1899), pp. 370–80.

31. CO 36.126.

32. CO 36.126.

33. CO 47.297–98.

34. CO 36.137.

35. CO 36.138.

8

Calvin and the Divided Self of Romans 7

The inexperienced, who do not take into consideration the subject with which the apostle is dealing or the plan which he is following, suppose it is human nature which he is here describing. . . . But Paul, as I have already stated, is not here describing the bare nature of man, but is depicting in his own person the character and extent of the weakness of believers. For some time Augustine was involved in the same error, but after closer examination of the passage he not only retracted the false teaching which he had given, but in his first book to Boniface he proves by many powerful arguments that it can only be understood of the regenerate.[1]

In his commentary on Rom. 7:14–25 Calvin alludes to an important shift in Augustine's interpretation of Paul. The issue in this exegetical shift is whether Paul is speaking of fallen human nature when he writes in 7:15, "I do not do what I want, but I do the very thing I hate," or whether he is describing a conflict initiated by grace and experienced only by believers. Calvin prefers the position of older Augustine, who argued that grace places the believing self in conflict with itself, to the position of young Augustine, who understood Romans 7 as a reference to human nature untouched by grace.[2] According to Calvin, good exegesis follows the older Augustine; bad exegesis, that is, the exegesis of the "sophists" and scholastics, does not.

For the most part, Calvin's allies—Oecolampadius, Melanchthon, Zwingli, and Bullinger—agree with him that Romans 7 describes a conflict experienced only by believers. Even Calvin's implacable Lutheran critic, Tilemann

Hesshusen, accepts Romans 7 as a description of the inner conflict of the regenerate and alludes explicitly to the exegetical shift that placed Augustine in opposition to "Origen, Pelagius, monks, and countless others."[3] Paul's anguished cry, "O wretched man that I am," describes human life under grace (as old Augustine rightly taught) rather than under law (as young Augustine wrongly believed).

The issue is important for Calvin because it goes to the heart of what he regards as a correct assessment of human nature. If human beings outside of grace are equally fallen, it follows that they are equally insensitive to God. The intense spiritual conflict of Romans 7 is impossible for human nature untouched by grace.[4] While sinners have a vague sense that there is a God and even catch momentary glimpses of his glory, they are not, and cannot be, torn between the good they would but cannot do and the evil they cannot but would avoid. What Paul is describing is the weakness of believers, who experience an inner torment that only the faithful know.

Since Calvin prefers the exegesis of the older Augustine, he is suspicious of the exegesis of any theologian who does not. From Calvin's perspective, a preference for the exegesis of the younger Augustine is the sign of a defective anthropology.[5] Sinners are not divided against themselves, but believers are. To read Romans 7 as a description of human nature as such is to misread the human situation. It is the presence of grace, and grace alone, that challenges the hegemony of sin. Theologians who obscure that fact can be accused of minimizing the pervasive impact of the fall on human nature.

On the other hand, Calvin's position is not without its exegetical difficulties. Paul's description of life in the Spirit is difficult to reconcile with Calvin's characterization of the Christian life as an existence marked by inner conflict and repeated failure. If the person described in Romans 7:14 as "carnal, sold under sin" is a believer, then Calvin must explain how the same person can elsewhere be described as "set free from sin" (6:18) and "not in the flesh" (8:9). The exegetical data seems far easier to account for if, as the young Augustine argued, 7:14 refers to life under the law and the contradictory texts to life under grace.

I

Some interpreters in the sixteenth century do in fact prefer the exegesis of the young Augustine. Bernardino Ochino, for example, identifies the "I" in Romans 7 with unregenerate sinners, who are subject to the law of God, but incapable by their own power of loving, trusting, and hoping in him.[6] As children of Adam, they are so vitiated by sin that they cannot do what the law commands. Unless reborn through Christ, human nature spontaneously inclines toward what is evil.

Although Ochino speaks eloquently of human wickedness, he nevertheless concedes that sinners under the law are not bereft of every good.[7] They have some knowledge of the will of God and some desire to do it. Such knowledge is not saving because it does not free those who have it from their sin or empower them to do God's will. In Ochino's opinion, the inner conflict described by Paul arises from a knowledge of the law of God divorced from the ability to obey it. Ochino therefore aligns himself with the Pauline exegesis of the young Augustine. Romans 7:14–25 does not refer to the experience of Christian believers but to pre-Christian existence under the law.

Ochino's interpretation is supported by Fausto Sozzini, who agrees that Paul is describing life under the law of Moses and before the advent of the grace of Christ.[8] Sozzini rejects the notion that Paul is speaking autobiographically, at least whenever he is speaking of himself as "reformed by the Spirit of Christ." What Paul is describing is the miserable condition of humankind under the law.[9]

This characterization, argues Sozzini, stands in sharp contrast to Paul's characterization of life in the Spirit. Romans 7 describes a person who is covetous (7:8), dead in sin (7:9–11), carnal (7:14), sold under sin (7:14), incapable of doing the good he wills (7:19), captive to the law of sin (7:23), and oppressed by death (7:24). Paul characterizes Christians, on the other hand, as people who have crucified the flesh with its passions and desires (Gal. 5:24), are not subject to the dominion of sin (6:2, 6, 11–12, 14), are no longer in the flesh (7:5; 8:8–9), have been set free from sin (6:18, 22), walk according to the Spirit (8:1, 4, 13), and have been liberated from the law of sin and death (8:2).[10] In Sozzini's opinion, these points of contrast, which are absolute and admit of no mitigation, make it impossible for anyone to maintain that Romans 7 describes the experience of Christian believers.

II

Nevertheless, a substantial number of Catholic commentators on Paul (a notable exception is Jacopo Sadoleto)[11] do exactly that—namely, accept Romans 7 as a description of life under grace. These commentators include such important theologians and churchmen as Thomas de Vio (Cajetan),[12] Ambrosius Catherinus Politus,[13] Domingo de Soto,[14] and Girolamo Seripando.[15] If Paul is speaking of Christian rather than pre-Christian experience (and these theologians are convinced that he is), then some hypothesis must be proposed to account for the contrary evidence offered by Ochino and Sozzini. How is it possible for a Catholic theologian to regard Christians as simultaneously spiritual and carnal without falling into self-contradiction on the one hand or Lutheranism on the other?

The solution proposed by the four commentators is presented somewhat differently by each, but contains three main elements: (1) a distinction between higher and lower human faculties, (2) an emphasis on concupiscence as a punishment for sin rather than as sinful, and (3) a recognition of the difference between the perfection possible in this life and in the final kingdom of God.

Each of the commentators presupposes a hierarchically ordered human being, in whom the soul is superior to the body, and reason (or in the case of Seripando, the will) superior to the other faculties of the soul.[16] The fall of Adam and Eve into sin so disordered the relationship between these higher and lower human faculties that what is inferior no longer necessarily obeys what is superior to it. Grace has, of course, begun to restore what was lost in the fall, starting with the higher powers of the soul (the mind or will). But the work is not completed in this life. Christian existence is marked by a constant struggle between higher powers that have been renewed by the Holy Spirit and lower powers, in which the work of renewal has scarcely begun.

Morever, while baptism washed away the guilt of original sin, it did not remove concupiscence, which was left in the human soul as a punishment for sin.[17] Concupiscence is an unholy longing for whatever stands in opposition to the will of God, but it is not sinful in itself. Concupiscence is only sinful when Christians cease to resist it and freely consent to its illicit suggestions. Sin dwells in Christians, Seripando admits (citing Augustine), but it does not reign in them.[18] As long as they resist it, they are not its servants.

De Soto, Seripando, and Catherinus Politus remind their readers that the righteousness attainable in this life (*perfectio viae*) falls short of the righteousness that will be realized after death (*perfectio coelestis patriae*).[19] Christian existence is marked by constant warfare against concupiscence and the instincts of one's lower nature. Christians are spiritual to the extent they have been renewed by the Spirit; they are carnal to the extent they are oppressed by the longings of their own flesh. Justice and holiness are compatible in this life with weakness and failure but not with the loss of the will to resist.

The problem with the exegesis of the heretics, especially Lutheran heretics, is that they regard any stirring of concupiscence as sinful in itself apart from the will's consent.[20] Against such heretics, Catherinus Politus insists that Christians can perform good works, even if they cannot do the absolute good willed by the Spirit.[21] They are unhappy and cry out for deliverance ("O wretched man that I am!"), not because they are still in a state of mortal sin, but because they cannot yet do in this life the perfect and absolute good that was possible for human beings in an unfallen state of nature.

III

Luther's quarrel is not with Catholic commentators who accept the priority of the older Augustine, but with commentators who do not.[22] Luther has in mind medieval interpreters like Peter Lombard, Nicholas of Lyra, and Denis the Carthusian (though not Thomas Aquinas), who identified the "I" in Romans 7 with someone living under the law.[23] Such an interpretation has, from Luther's perspective, one fatal flaw: hatred of sin and a longing to do the will of God is not characteristic of the genuinely wicked.[24] Only spiritual men and women know the extent to which they are still carnal. "Certainly," Luther remarks, "no one will declare himself wretched except one who is a spiritual man."[25]

On several points, Luther's exegesis of 7:14–25 sounds remarkably like the exegesis of his Catholic contemporaries. For example, while he calls concupiscence sinful in itself, he nevertheless admits that no believer is guilty apart from the consent of his or her own will.[26] Moreover, to the objection that Paul could be understood to teach that a Christian can only do the evil he hates and never the good he desires, Luther responds that Paul wants only to say "that he does not do the good as often and to such an extent and as readily as he would like."[27]

But on the issue how one is to understand the claim that believers are simultaneously just and carnal, Luther and the Catholic interpreters part company. Catholic interpreters are willing to admit how weak even the saintliest Christians are and how buffeted by the world, the flesh, and the devil. What they are unwilling to concede is that grace has left justified sinners in a state of mortal sin. To be in a state of grace is to have crossed an invisible boundary, to have abandoned captivity in order to return to one's homeland, and to have traded one condition for its opposite. It is possible to have committed venial sins and still be in a state of grace. It is possible to fall short of one's aspirations in the performance of God's will and still be in a state of grace. It is even possible to commit mortal sin and be restored to a state of grace through the penitential disciplines of the Church. It is not possible, however, to be carnal, in the sense of unrenewed by the Spirit, and just. In this sense, a state of sin and a state of grace are mutually exclusive.[28]

Luther has, of course, no intention of arguing that Christians are unrenewed by the Spirit or that the carnal "I" of Romans 7 is not at the same time profoundly spiritual. The question is not whether Christians are renewed by the Spirit but whether that renewal forms any basis for their acceptance by God. Luther is convinced that Paul teaches a doctrine of justification very different from the doctrine taught by the late medieval church. The basis for the sinner's acceptance by God is the righteousness of Christ imputed to the sinner and received by faith.[29] This righteousness is absolute and admits of no diminution or increase.

Renewal, on the other hand, is not absolute but relative and can be encouraged or retarded. When the issue is justification, Christians are already righteous because of the righteousness of Christ and need no longer fear God's judgment. When the issue is renewal, Christians are like convalescents in a hospital, still seriously ill but living in the hope of a full recovery.[30] Renewal is the effect of justification rather than its cause. The "wretched man" of 7:24 is already just, but not yet fully renewed. Indeed, Romans 7 provides an exemplary illustration of the fundamental theological truth that the Christian man or woman is always *iustus et peccator simul*, never in this life simply one or the other. In that sense, a state of sin and a state of grace are never mutually exclusive but coinhere in the person of the believer.

Other early Protestant commentators agree in the main with Luther's reading of the text. Like Luther, Oecolampadius and Bullinger believe that Paul is talking autobiographically about his own experience as a Christian.[31] Although he has been justified, he still finds in himself a desire to commit sin. Even the good he does, he fails to do as well as he would like. Zwingli and Bucer concur that Paul is describing a conflict in believers,[32] whereas Melanchthon brings the discussion back to the central issue by repeating the point first made by Augustine and forcefully restated by Luther: Paul must be speaking of his postconversion experience because no ungodly man or woman ever wills from the heart what the law commands.[33]

IV

There were, then, in Calvin's day defenders of at least three positions on the question of the proper interpretation of Romans 7: (1) that this passage describes pre-Christian existence under the law; (2) that it describes the experience of a believing, but imperfectly just human being; or (3) that it describes the experience of a justified, but imperfectly renewed believer. Defenders of the first position agree with the exegesis of the younger Augustine, while defenders of two and three prefer the exegesis of the older. This agreement can be implicit, as in the case of Bernardino Ochino, or explicit, as in the case of Martin Luther and Domingo de Soto.[34] Some theologians, like Luther, Oecolampadius, Bullinger, and Calvin, feel that Paul is speaking autobiographically, whereas others, like Sozzini and Sadoleto, deny it.

In Calvin's view, the main thrust of Romans 7 is to illustrate "the great difference which exists between the law of God and the nature of man" and to demonstrate "the impossibility of the law itself producing death."[35] The law is not and can never be anything but good. If sinners have disobeyed the law, the difficulty is not with the law itself, but with fallen human nature. Indeed, the contrast between the goodness of the law and the wickedness of human nature is better exemplified in the experience of a Christian than in the experience of an unregenerate man or woman.

An unregenerate human being is "so completely driven by the power of sin" that his or her whole mind, heart, and actions are inclined toward it.[36] Calvin does not, of course, mean to suggest that human beings are compelled to sin, since sin by its very nature is voluntary, or that sinners have lost the distinction between right and wrong. "Sometimes," he admits, "they are struck with horror on account of a sense of their sin, so that they bear a kind of condemnation even in this life. Nevertheless, they approve of sin with all their heart, and therefore yield to it without any feeling of genuine repugnance."[37] The pangs of conscience that they suffer arise "from a contradiction of judgment rather than from the contrary affection of the will."[38]

There is, therefore, a perverse sense in which sinners may be regarded as integrated personalities, at least on the level of the will's affections. If the ungodly are not free from a sometimes troubled conscience, they are at least free from the inner conflict that marks the life of faith. "Since the carnal man rushes into the lust of sinning with the whole inclination of his mind," Calvin notes, "he appears to be sinning with as free a choice as if it were in his power to govern himself."[39] But this freedom is deceptive, a mark of a subtler and deeper bondage.

Christians, on the other hand, love the will of God contained in the law, but are hindered from performing it by the depravity of their old nature "which obstinately resists and strives against what is opposed to it."[40] Because the law is good, believers hate the vices the law condemns and attempt to pattern their lives on what it commands. Through the activity of the Holy Spirit, the law ceases to be an instrument of death for them and becomes an active principle of their sanctification. The godly are aware of and deplore the difference that still remains between the demands of the law and the achievement of their redeemed, but not yet wholly renewed, natures. Unlike the unregenerate, whose personalities are focused in their wicked rejection of God's will, Christians are conflicted personalities, caught in a struggle between the good of which they approve and the sin that they abhor but have not overcome.[41]

Like Luther, Calvin believes Paul ought not to be misunderstood to teach that Christians are utterly incapable of doing good or that they have "nothing but an ineffectual desire."[42] Men and women renewed by the Spirit are certainly capable of obeying God's will, even if imperfectly. Paul "merely complains of his inability to do what he desired—to pursue goodness with due alacrity—because he was to some extent held back."[43] The problem is not so much inability as an ability unequal to what it desires.[44]

Rather than talk about concupiscence, as Catholic commentators prefer to do, Calvin talks about the "remnants of the flesh."[45] By the term *flesh*, Calvin includes "all the endowments of human nature" unsanctified by the Holy Spirit.[46] By the term *spirit*, he refers to "that part of the soul" in which the Holy Spirit has restored the image of God.[47] Both terms apply to the human soul: spirit—to the part of the soul that has been regenerated, flesh—to the part that has not. Calvin believes that Paul makes the same point by referring to the inward man ("the spiritual part of the soul which has been regenerated by God") and the members ("the other remaining part").[48] The struggle of the godly with the flesh should therefore not be misinterpreted as warfare between the soul and the body, but as a conflict between the renewed and unrenewed parts of the human soul. This conflict continues unremittingly until death. As Calvin ruefully remarks, "regeneration only begins in this life."[49] Perfect renewal remains an eschatological goal of the life of faith.

Although, unlike Luther, Calvin does not spend time in his exegesis of Rom. 7:14–25 outlining his understanding of Paul's doctrine of justification, he nevertheless agrees with the distinction Luther draws between justification and renewal. Christians have been "received into the protection of God, so that they may never perish" and have been "given the first fruits of the Spirit, which make certain their hope of the eternal inheritance."[50] Contemplation of these benefits ought to "check impatience" and give believers "a reason for joy" in the midst of their conflict with the flesh.[51] Although they have not been fully renewed and so "lament and bewail" their "unhappy condition," they nonetheless have learned to be "content with the measure which they have obtained."[52] Paul's cry, "O wretched man that I am," is not—and can never be—the last word, not even in this life.

V

What this brief history of the exegesis of Rom. 7:14–25 in the sixteenth century makes clear is that the division between exegetical schools does not correspond in any simple way to the division between the competing confessional families. Bernardino Ochino was a Reformed theologian, who later developed Anabaptist sympathies. Fausto Sozzini was a radical Protestant and Jacopo Sadoleto a Catholic prelate. Yet all three defended the exegesis of the younger Augustine.

The twelve remaining theologians—four Catholic, three Lutheran, and five Reformed—declared themselves just as strongly for the exegesis of the older Augustine. Confessional differences did not prevent the formation of a consensus over the identity of the speaker in 7:15. At the same time, Catholic interpreters who rejected the position of the young Augustine differed as a group with the eight Protestant interpreters who shared their fundamental orientation to the text. The Catholic interpreters identified that difference as a disagreement over the nature of concupiscence and the degree of perfection possible in this life. If concupiscence is sinful in itself, as the Protestants teach, then baptized and penitent Christians remain in a state of mortal sin and are hindered from attaining even the relative justice possible in this life—a position incompatible with traditonal Catholic teaching. Luther identified the source of the quarrel as a disagreement over the nature of justification.

From Luther's perspective, Paul speaks of a human being who has already been justified by faith and to whom the righteousness of Christ has been imputed. The imperfection Paul so graphically describes from his own spiritual experience is not an imperfection in justification, but in the renewal that flows from God's justifying act. Romans 7:14–25 illustrates for Luther what it means in practice to claim that the sinner is both just before God by faith and sinful in his old, as yet unrenewed, self.

Calvin regards Romans 7 less as an opportunity to talk about justification (though he agrees with Luther against his Catholic critics) than as an occasion to discuss anthropology. Human wickedness is made all the more vivid for Calvin when he considers its force and staying power in the lives of the redeemed. Even the apostle Paul was oppressed by the "remnants of the flesh," the unrenewed compartments of his soul that still resisted the will of God. In spite of renewal by the Holy Spirit, Christian existence is marked by an ability unequal to the good it desires.

When Calvin rejected the exegesis of the younger Augustine, he made an exegetical decision that was supported by a broad consensus of Catholic, Lutheran, and Reformed theologians. Not everyone who agreed with Calvin understood Paul in the same way. Yet the disagreements among Pauline interpreters in the sixteenth century ought not to be allowed to obscure either their common commitments or their sometimes surprising agreement in detail. For a significant number of Calvin's contemporaries, both Catholic and Protestant, the medieval tradition that accepted Romans 7 as a description of life under the law was no longer convincing. For them, the self that is divided is the believing self. On that point Cajetan and Calvin made common cause.

NOTES

1. T. H. L. Parker, ed., *Iohannis Calvini Commentarius in Epistolam ad Romanos* (Leiden: E.J. Brill, 1981), p. 149, abbreviated as Calvin, *Commentarius*. Quotations in the text are from the English translation by Ross MacKenzie, John Calvin, *The Epistles of Paul the Apostle to the Romans and to the Thessalonians* (Grand Rapids, Mich.: Wm. B. Eerdmans, 1961).

2. Still valuable is the study of Augustine's exegesis by A. F. N. Lekkerkerker, *Römer 7 und Römer 9 bei Augustin* (Amsterdam: H. J. Paris, 1942).

3. Tilemann Hesshusen, *Explicatio Epistolae Pauli ad Romanos* (Jena: Gunther Huttichius, 1571), p. 216: "Hunc locum Origenes, Pelagius, Monachii, et infiniti alii corruperunt, dum fixerunt Paulum loqui de homine sub lege et sub peccato constitutum: et in se transfigurasse peccatorem. Ac Augustinus multis locis fatetur se aliquandiu ita sensisse: sed manifestissimum est Paulum loqui de se ipso, et quidem de se renato et converso: vult enim suo exemplo ostendere homini esse impossibile, ut impleat legis spiritualem obedientiam."

4. Calvin, *Commentarius*, p. 148: "Quo igitur tota haec disputatio fidelius ac certius intelligatur, notandum est, hoc certamen de quo loquitur Apostolus, non prius extare in homine, quam Spiritu Dei fuerit sanctificatus."

5. Ibid., p. 149: "Ita Sophistae, quum liberum arbitrium definire volunt, vel aestimare quid valeat naturae facultas, in hunc locum insistunt. Atqui Paulus, ut iam dixi, non hic proponit nudam hominis naturam: verum qualis et quanta sit fidelium infirmitas, sub persona sua describit."

6. Bernardino Ochino, *Expositio Epistolae divi Pauli ad Romanos de Italico in Latinum translata* (Augsburg: Philippus Ulhardus, 1545), p. 56: "Nam quod ago, non novi (ut de me, tanquam de homine terrestri, nondum per Christum renato, loquar, in quo vivat lex, et officio suo fungatur, ipso mortuo, neque adhuc in vitam per beneficium revocato)."

7. Ibid., p. 56v: "In homine corporali, in quo lex suo fungitur officio, cuius in persona loquitur Paulus, inest tamen aliquid boni: inest enim illa dei voluntatis cognitio: insunt etiamnum certe laudabilium cupitatum, et voluntatum scintillae."

8. Fausto Sozzini, *De Loco Pauli Apostoli in Epistola ad Rom. Cap. Septimo. Disputatio* (Rakow: Sebastian Sternacius, 1612), p. 7: ". . . Paulum sub sua ipsius persona non de seipso, aut certe, non de se, tamquam Christi Spiritu reformato, locutum fuisse ostenderem."

9. Ibid., p. 8: ". . . ostendens potissimum inter caetera, miserum esse statum hominis sub ipsa lege."

10. Ibid., p. 16.

11. Jacopo Sadoleto, *Liber Secundus commentariorum in Pauli epistolam ad Romanos*, Opera omnia, tomus IV (Verona: Joannes Albertus Tumermanus, 1738), p. 173: "Quarum duarum partium inter se contentionem, atque pugnam exponere conatur, hominem illum exprimens, qui ante adventum gratiae Dei, et Christi, in lege Moysis fuit, is enim maxime his certaminibus et praeliis carnis adversus mentem erat expositus."

12. Thomas de Vio (Cajetan), *Epistolae Pauli et aliorum Apostolorum ad Graecam veritatem castigatae, et iuxta sensum literalem enarratae* (Paris: Carola Guillard et Jean de Roigny, 1540).

13. Ambrosius Catherinus Politus, *Commentarius in omnes divi Pauli et alias septem canonicas Epistolas* (Venice: Vincent Valgrisius, 1551).

14. Domingo de Soto, *In Epistolam divi Pauli ad Romanos Commentarii* (Antwerp: Jan Steelsius, 1550).

15. Girolamo Seripando, *In d. Pauli Epistolas ad Romanos, et Galatas Commentaria* (Naples, 1601; rpt. Gregg, 1971).

16. Politus, *Commentarius*, p. 69; Cajetan, *Epistolae Pauli*, pp. 37–38; De Soto, *Commentarii*, p. 196; Seripando, *Commentaria*, p. 116.

17. Politus, *Commentarius*, pp. 69–70; Cajetan, *Epistolae Pauli*, p. 37; Seripando, *Commentaria*, p. 118.

18. Seripando, *Commentaria*, pp. 119–20.

19. Politus, *Commentarius*, p. 72; De Soto, *Commentarii*, p. 198; Seripando, *Commentaria*, p. 113.

20. De Soto, *Commentarii*, p. 202.

21. Politus, *Commentarius*, p. 70.

22. Two important studies of Luther's exegesis of Romans 7 are Paul Althaus, *Paulus und Luther über den Menschen*, 2d ed. (Gütersloh: Gerd Mohn, 1951), pp. 31–67, and Leif Grane, *Modus Loquendi Theologicus, Luthers Kampf um die Erneuerung der Theologie (1515–1518)* (Leiden: E.J. Brill, 1975), pp. 94–100.

23. For the opinion of Denis the Carthusian, see Denis, *In Omnes Beati Pauli Epistolas Commentaria* (Cologne: Peter Quentel, 1533), p. 17r: "Loquitur autem Apostolus (sicut iam dictum est) in persona hominis generalitur." Against that opinion see Thomas Aquinas, *Expositio in omnes Sancti Pauli Epistolas*, Sancti Thomae Aquinatis Opera Omnia XIII (Parma, 1872), p. 70. Thomas shows how the text could describe the human condition under the law or under grace, but pronounces the second exposition—that is, of *homo sub gratia*—as "melior."

24. WA 56.340.6.

25. WA 56.346.18.

26. WA 56.351.9: "Ex ista pulchra authoritate patet, Quomodo Concupiscentia sit ista infirmitas nostra ad bonum, qui in se quidem rea est, Sed tamen reos nos non facit nisi consentientes et operantes."

27. WA 56.341.30: "Sed vult, quod non tot et tantum bonum nec tanta facilitate faciat, quantum et quanta vult."

28. See, for example, Politus, *Commentarius*, p. 70: "Itaque anathematizandum est dogma illud, quod novi haeretici suscitarunt, esse in homine peccatore et criminoso gratiam Dei: contra quos Dilectus clarissime ait. Si quis diligit mundum, non est charitas Dei in eo: quia nec diligit Deum, nec diligitur a Deo."

29. WA 56.347.9: "Quod simul Sancti, dum sunt Iusti, sunt peccatores; Iusti, quia credunt in Christum, cuius Iustitia eos tegit et eis imputatur, peccatores autem, quia non implent legem, non sunt sine concupiscentia."

30. WA 56.347.11: "Sed sicut egrotantes sub cura medici, qui sunt re vera egroti, Sed inchoative et in spe sani seu potius sanctificati i.e. sani fientes, quibus nocentissima est sanitatis presumptio, quia peius recidivant."

31. WA 56.339.5: "Quod Apostolus ab hoc textu usque in finem loquatur in persona sua et spiritualis hominis et nequaquam in persona tantum Carnalis, primum b. Augustinus locupletissime et constanter asserit in libro contra Pelagianos." Johannes Oecolampadius, *In Epistolam b. Pauli Apostoli ad Rhomanos Adnotationes* (Basel: Andreas Cratander, 1525), p. 62v: "Ex hoc loco manifestum est Paulum haec in sua persona dixisse, quamvis esset iusticans. Non enim delectat

lex Dei, nisi iustificatos." Heinrich Bullinger, *In sanctissimam Pauli ad Romanos Epistolam Commentarius* (Zurich: Christophor Froschouer, 1533), p. 99v.

32. Huldrych Zwingli, *In evangelicam Historiam de Domino nostro Iesu Christo, Matthaeum, Marcum, Lucam et Ioannem conscriptam, Epistolas aliquot Pauli, Annotationes D. Huldrychii Zvinglii per Leonem Iudae exceptae et editae* (Zurich: Christophor Froschouer, 1539), p. 424: "Iam incipit describere pugnam carnis et spiritus, quae in fidelibus est." Martin Bucer, *Metaphrases et Enarrationes perpetuae Epistolarum d. Pauli Apostoli* (Strasbourg: Wendelin Rihel, 1536), p. 96. On this question see Peter Stephens, *The Holy Spirit in the Theology of Martin Bucer* (Cambridge: Cambridge University Press, 1970), p. 82.

33. Philip Melanchthon, *Römerbrief-Kommentar 1532*, ed. Rolf Schäfer, in *Melanchthons Werke in Auswahl* 5 (Gütersloh: Gerd Mohn, 1965), p. 224.

34. WA 56.339.7; De Soto, *Commentarii*, p. 196.

35. Calvin, *Commentarius*, p. 147.

36. Ibid., p. 147.

37. Ibid., p. 148.

38. Ibid., p. 148.

39. Ibid., p. 147.

40. Ibid., p. 147.

41. Ibid., p. 148.

42. Ibid., p. 151.

43. Ibid., p. 149.

44. Ibid., p. 151.

45. Ibid., p. 151.

46. Ibid., p. 151.

47. Ibid., p. 151.

48. Ibid., p. 153.

49. Ibid., p. 148.

50. Ibid., p. 155.

51. Ibid., p. 155.

52. Ibid., pp. 153, 155.

9

Calvin and Patristic Exegesis

T. H. L. Parker in his book, *Calvin's New Testament Commentaries*, observed that Calvin appears to rely chiefly on the Fathers and certain of his contemporaries in the development of his own exegesis.[1] While Parker himself made no attempt to explore the question of Calvin's use of Patristic sources (apart from noting that Calvin especially favored Chrysostom, Augustine, Jerome, Origen, and Ambrose), he did suggest that the subject merited further independent study. Aside from the earlier monograph on Calvin and Augustine by Luchesius Smits[2] and the more recent essays by Walchenbach[3] and Meijering,[4] very little has been done to illuminate the relationship of Calvin to the exegetical tradition of the early church.

In the dedicatory letter to Simon Grynaeus (1539) that serves as a preface to his commentary on Romans, Calvin indicates that he has been particularly helped in his understanding of Paul by the "ancient commentators, whose godliness, learning, sanctity and age have secured them such great authority that we should not despise anything they have produced."[5] While he does not mention any ancient commentators by name, he does refer in the course of his exposition to Ambrose (though it is probably Ambrosiaster that he has before him), Augustine, Chrysostom, Eusebius, Jerome (very likely Pelagius masquerading in his guise as Pseudo-Jerome), Lactantius, and Origen. Of medieval commentators from Sedulius Scotus to Denis the Carthusian there is no mention, though Erasmus, omitted from the preface, is frequently cited in the text. Of course, Calvin may know some of the more famous opinions of the Fathers through canon law or through references to them in the writings of other commentators. It seems likely, however, that Calvin has, whenever possible, consulted the writings of the Fathers themselves. This is certainly the case with Chrysostom and probably the case with Origen as well.[6]

The reliability of the Fathers as interpreters of the writings of Paul has been the subject of some debate among modern historians. Judgments have ranged from the almost rhapsodic evaluation of Chrysostom by M. J. Lagrange, who regarded Chrysostom's commentaries on Romans and Galatians as revelations not easily surpassed of the mind and soul of Paul, to the wry dictum of Adolf von Harnack that Marcion alone of the second-century theologians avoided the common fate of failing to understand Paul by embracing the more imaginative alternative of simply misunderstanding him. Even historians who stood between the two extremes were inclined to concede that the early church, while remarkably sensitive to certain themes in Paul, was curiously dense about others. It was not only the heretics but even the orthodox Fathers who from time to time made heavy weather of Paul.

The more recent critical essays on Patristic exegesis by Karl Hermann Schelkle[7] and Maurice Wiles[8] have given us a more satisfying and complete picture of Pauline studies in the early Christian era. The Fathers stressed what they regarded as the anti-Marcionite and anti-Gnostic features of Paul's theology. They emphasized against Marcion that the law was a schoolmaster to bring men and women to Christ (though they gave this genuinely Pauline theme more prominence than Paul himself had done), and they explained away Paul's apparent hostility to the law by drawing an un-Pauline distinction between moral and ceremonial law. They interpreted Paul's teaching on grace in such a way as to strike a balance between divine sovereignty and free human response and to minimize those predestinarian elements in Paul that smacked of Gnostic or Manichean determinism.

The Fathers were also anti-Gnostic in their resolve to interpret "flesh," whenever possible, as a moral or theological category for Paul and to suppress any notion that Paul was hostile to the physical body as such. Christological passages were given a precision more appropriate to the theological debates of the third and fourth centuries than to the theological world of the first-century church, though one may argue that such precision, however anachronistic, was not necessarily a distortion of the thrust of Pauline thought. Only in their discussion of faith do the Fathers seem to have faltered and seriously misrepresented Paul. They tend, on the whole, to reduce faith to intellectual assent to the dogmatic truths summarized in the creeds, a reductionism, one must hasten to add, not found in the Pauline exegesis of the great third-century commentator Origen.

In short, the Fathers were concerned to present the teaching of Paul as a well-rounded and philosophically consistent system rather than as an occasionally fragmentary, pastoral response to a cluster of disparate and specific problems in the past. Paul was less a prophet to them than a teacher of orthodox theology and a guide to proper Christian practice. What such an exegesis lost in the way of religious vitality, it gained in the way of pedagogic utility.

In order to test the influence of this vision of Paul on Calvin's own Pauline exegesis, I propose to compare Calvin's exegesis of Rom. 8:1–11 with Patristic exegesis of the same passage. Although allusions to Pauline writings are widespread in the theological literature of the Patristic age, the number of complete commentaries on Paul's letter to the Romans is relatively small.[9] Among the Greek commentators only Origen and Chrysostom have left substantial commentaries on Romans and, in the case of Origen—apart from some Greek fragments unknown to Calvin—the complete commentary exists only in the Latin translation of Rufinus. It is therefore clearly a bowdlerized and amended version. Augustine, whose discussion of Pauline themes is scattered throughout the entire corpus of his writings, never completed his commentary on Romans, though he did make a start when he was a presbyter in Hippo Regius. Most of his comments were gathered together in one remarkable volume by Florus of Lyons in the ninth century, a book very popular in the twelfth century but probably unknown to Calvin in the sixteenth. Latin exegesis of Romans is represented by an interesting series of expositions of Paul written by Pelagius before his great controversy with Augustine and an anonymous commentary once ascribed to Ambrose and now known by the curious name of the Ambrosiaster.[10]

I want to use as the principal basis of comparison with Calvin two of the longer Patristic commentaries on Romans 8: the homily on this passage that John Chrysostom[11] preached in Antioch sometime before 397 and the exegesis that Ambrosiaster[12] wrote, probably in Rome and certainly no later than 384. Both were composed at roughly the same time; namely, after the Council of Nicaea and before the great Latin controversy over grace and free will precipitated by the teaching of Pelagius. They reflect the theological situation in two of the principal theological centers of fourth-century Christianity, one Greek, the other Latin. They are less well-known than the commentaries of Origen, Pelagius, and Augustine, but are, without a doubt, two of the most remarkable commentaries on Paul written in any language at any time.

Chrysostom and Ambrosiaster deal with four interrelated problems in the course of their exegesis of Romans 8: (1) what does Paul mean by the law and how are the various kinds of law to be distinguished from one other; (2) what is the significance of the anthropological terms, *soul, spirit, flesh, body*, and how do they function in Paul's argument; (3) how should one understand the person and work of Jesus Christ, who came "in the likeness of sinful flesh," who "condemned sin in the flesh," and who works in believers by his Spirit; (4) and, finally, what is the relationship of the gift of salvation to the moral obligations of the Christian, particularly now that the Christian stands under grace rather than under the law? These exegetical questions are perennial ones, and Chrysostom and the Ambrosiaster tackle them with considerable verve and imagination.

THE AMBROSIASTER

The Meaning of Law

Ambrosiaster's understanding of the meaning of the word, *law*, is not altogether transparent to the reader. Some things, however, are clear. The law of Moses, while it is spiritual in the sense of having been given by the Holy Spirit, is not the law of the Spirit of life because it does not remit sin or bring sinners, who stand under the sentence of death, back to life.[13] Indeed, the law of Moses can simply be identified with the "law of death" in the sense that it condemns and slays sinners.[14] The Mosaic law, while undoubtedly given by God, serves to intensify the predicament of the non-Christian.

Ranged against the Mosaic law is the "law of the Spirit of life." The word "law" is used here, not in the sense of a legal code, but rather in the sense of a general principle of universal applicability. Paul uses law in just this sense when he affirms that the Spirit, by remitting sin, delivers Christians from what Ambrosiaster calls "the second death." Because the Spirit does this work and is, finally, the object toward which the Christian faith is directed, the principle of the Spirit's operation is called the "law" of the Spirit of life. Furthermore, because the Spirit only delivers from second death those persons who believe the gospel, the "law" of the Spirit is simultaneously a "law" of faith.[15]

The Mosaic law is a "law" of death, not because of any defect in its essential nature, but because of the "law" of sin.[16] There is a principle at work in unbelievers, persuading them to deny the fundamental tenets of the Christian faith and to embrace things that run contrary to the "law" of the Spirit. (Ambrosiaster has particularly in mind the fascination of pagans with astrology.)[17] The justified are made friends of the Mosaic law, not through the law itself (the law code as code being no match for the awesome power of sin), but through the activity of the Spirit.[18] The righteousness that was the aim of the law of Moses is only attained in human life by the power of the Spirit through the remission of sins.

The Anthropological Terminology

The most striking feature of Ambrosiaster's discussion of the anthropological terminology of Paul is his perception that each of these terms—*spirit, soul, body,* and *flesh*—is a designation, not for a faculty or portion of the human personality, but for the whole person considered from some special angle or in some particular relationship. Ambrosiaster is full of little sayings that turn on the recognition of the holistic character of Pauline anthropology: for example, the baptized person when given the Holy Spirit is called spirit;[19] the soul when it sins is called flesh;[20] the resurrection of the body is a synonym for the resurrection of the whole human being;[21] to talk about weak flesh is really to talk about human weakness;[22] even the whole world, that is to say, everything that is visible, can be identified as flesh.[23]

In all this terminology, however, it is the word, *flesh,* that is the most worrisome. Ambrosiaster is clearly concerned to avoid any Gnostic identification of "flesh" as physical reality with evil and hastens to affirm in the strongest possible language that the substance of the flesh (in the sense of physical matter) is not the enemy of God.[24] God is opposed to the prudence of the flesh, an anti-God state of mind that is implacably hostile to invisible realities as both morally inconvenient and logically improbable.[25] Indeed, so eager is Ambrosiaster to avoid the pitfalls of Manichaean dualism that he sounds at times almost like Martin Luther, especially in his discussion of the Pauline phrase, "prudence of the flesh."

Prudence is that virtue of the mind which enables it to distinguish what is sensible from what is stupid.[26] Like any human virtue, prudence can be turned to unworthy objects and can evaluate the human situation from a distorted perspective. When prudence is rightly ordered, it is called wisdom or prudence of the spirit.[27] Prudence of the spirit gains peace for the human soul by pursuing invisible and spiritual objects.

Prudence of the flesh, however, leads to death because it regards the visible world and the realm governed by human reason as the only trustworthy reality.[28] People submissive to the prudence of the flesh deny the wonderful works of God in the miraculous birth of Isaac by Sarah, in the virgin birth of Jesus, and in the event of the resurrection.[29] They are easily swayed by the predictions of astrologers, whose tables make creatures (namely, the stars) coequal with God.[30] The prudence of the flesh regards as self-evident the conviction that nothing can happen in the world that sinful reason regards as unlikely. What matters to the flesh is what can be seen, touched, cataloged, and statistically evaluated. The prudence of the flesh is not subject to the law of God because it repudiates the acts of God.[31] The visible world defines for it the limits of reality. Therefore there is no salvation for the worldly wise who, out of respect for the world and its ephemeral values, resist spiritual wisdom.[32]

Christology

When Paul claimed that Jesus came in the likeness of sinful flesh, he was not, so far as Ambrosiaster is concerned, suggesting a docetic christology. The humanity of the Redeemer is true humanity. His flesh differs from ours only in the sense that it was sanctified in the womb of Mary and born without sin.[33] In short, although Jesus bears the same substance of flesh as we do, he did not have the same birth.[34] A virgin womb was chosen for his birth so that his flesh might differ from ours in sanctity.[35] Physically we are one; morally we are distinct.

Ambrosiaster's doctrine of the atonement turns upon his understanding of the sinlessness of Jesus. Jesus was as innocent of sin as Adam was before the Fall.[36] Therefore, the devil did not have the same legitimate claim to him as it had to Adam and Adam's progeny. When, however, Satan lost patience with the sinless Jesus and set in motion the forces that crucified him, he acted unjustly and committed homicide against a completely innocent man.[37] By the act of homicide, Satan lost the last shred of any legitimate claim to Adam's children.[38] On the contrary, his contempt for the question of guilt gave Jesus the right to act against him in justice and not merely in sheer naked, sovereign power. The murder of a just man is central to Ambrosiaster's doctrine of the atonement.

Jesus condemned "sin in the flesh" in three ways: (1) he refused to sin himself; (2) he atoned for sin through the cross; and (3) as an effect of his death and resurrection, he remits the sins of the faithful.[39] If we follow the example of our Savior, we do not commit sins ourselves and we condemn sin wherever it appears.[40] In this way we imitate the action of Jesus who broke the lordship of Satan over the souls in captivity. Satan has been so weakened through the atoning act of Christ that he can no longer hold in second death any souls sealed with the sign of the cross.[41]

Ambrosiaster feels it is important at this point to introduce what sounds suspiciously like the later doctrine of the *filioque*. He does not regard this as an alien imposition on the theology of Paul but rather as a logical conclusion from it. When Paul speaks of the Spirit of Christ, he is speaking of the Spirit of the Father as well as of the Son.[42] The Spirit who is active in the church is as much a Spirit of the Son as of the Father.

Ethics and Redemption

Ambrosiaster does not have a great deal to say on this subject. Still, the thrust of his argument is plain enough. Romans 8:1–11 is an admonition to good behavior.[43] Christians should not appear to be unworthy of the name by which they are called.[44] Christians are not saved by their morally responsible activity. Nevertheless, morally responsible action is a necessary response to the proclamation of salvation in Christ. The Spirit deserts human beings who devote themselves to the prudence of the flesh.[45] But the baptized, the friends of the law, the faithful, who devote themselves to the prudence of the Spirit, find salvation in Christ is a secure status.[46] Christians are not in the flesh—that is, they do not love the visible world and its tangible benefits—but are in the Spirit—that is, they risk their lives on a reality they cannot see, touch, or empirically verify.[47] As Ambrosiaster understands Paul, faith is both dangerous and exciting.

JOHN CHRYSOSTOM

The Meaning of Law

Chrysostom's homily begins with the fourteenth verse of chapter seven and, therefore, Rom. 8:1–11 cannot be treated in isolation from Chrysostom's comments on the verses immediately preceding. Chrysostom believes that Paul is eager to clear the law of any suspicion that it is the root of the human predicament.[48] The law is spiritual in the sense that it is a teacher of virtue and hostile to vice.[49] It points unfailingly to what is right and attempts to lead us away from sin of every kind. If the law fails to achieve its objective, the fault cannot be lodged in the law itself but must be attributed to some other source.

Chrysostom distinguishes natural law from the law of Moses. The knowledge of good and evil is an original and fundamental part of human nature.[50] The law of Moses confirms the conclusions of natural law, accusing more intensely what natural law already recognizes as evil and heaping lavish praise on what natural law already confesses to be good.[51] However, while the Mosaic law confirms the conclusions of natural law, it is unable to abolish the agency of evil in the sinner.[52]

Sin overcomes even a mind that delights in the law.[53] When Paul talks of the law of sin, he is not referring to sin as a law code or even as a principle. Sin is a law in the sense that it compels strict obedience from everyone who complies with it.[54] In other words, sin exercises power and places its adherents in thralldom. The Spirit is the only law or power that can deliver sinners from the law and power of sin.[55] The law of the Spirit of life furnishes everyone who believes in Christ with a large measure of the Spirit. The Spirit frees believers from the law of Moses. Freedom in the Spirit is not freedom from moral obligation but freedom to discharge it.[56] Chrysostom draws no antinomian conclusions from the Pauline doctrine of freedom.

The Anthropological Terminology

Chrysostom agrees with the Ambrosiaster in interpreting the anthropological terminology of Paul holistically, particularly the word *flesh*, but does so somewhat more cautiously than the Ambrosiaster. Flesh is, of course, a metaphor for a life that is worldly and thoroughly self-indulgent.[57] As a physical reality, flesh is morally neutral and Paul has no intention of disparaging it.[58] But if the flesh, which does not have a reasoning power of its own, is allowed to transgress its proper bounds, it devotes itself to the pursuit of the things of this life and debases the mind that should have governed it.[59] Paul calls the whole person, body and soul, "flesh," giving the mind a name from its inferior part.[60] Similarly, while the "mind of the flesh" is always wicked, since it is unreservedly committed to worldly goals, Christ can through grace give the morally neutral flesh wings so that the redeemed person may be regarded as wholly spiritual.[61] At any rate, the clash between flesh and spirit in Pauline thought is not interpreted as a clash between material and immaterial realities. As Chrysostom understands Paul, the flesh can be spiritual and the soul carnal.

Christology

Chrysostom does not elaborate a doctrine of the atonement in his exegesis of Romans 8, but he does make some important christological and trinitarian observations. On the one hand, Chrysostom wants to stress the unity of the Trinity and takes the argument of Paul in 8:9–10, which juxtaposes "Spirit," "Spirit of God," "Spirit of Christ," and "Christ," as an occasion for remarking that where one Person of the Trinity is present, there the whole Trinity is present as well.[62] On the other hand, Chrysostom wants to emphasize the unique thing that marks off the Second Person of the Trinity from the other two—namely, the assumption of real humanity. Therefore, like Ambrosiaster, Chrysostom interprets the phrase, "in the likeness of sinful flesh," to mean that Christ shares a common nature with us, except that his humanity is untainted by sin.[63] So far as the substance of the flesh is concerned, there is no difference between his humanity and ours.

Yet, while Christ did not come "in sinful flesh" but only in its "likeness," he did identify himself fully with the weakness and frailty of our flesh. Christ assumed a flesh that was, to say the least, in grave difficulty, threatened on every hand by sin and death.[64] It was entirely appropriate that Christ should gain a marvelous victory over sin and death by means of the very flesh that had been defeated times without number.[65] As Chrysostom understands the thrust of the gospel, Christ condemns sin and not the substance of poor human flesh.[66]

Ethics and Redemption

Romans 8:1–11 addresses the problem of sin after baptism.[67] Christians now have the power through the Spirit of not "walking after the flesh."[68] They are now able to achieve the righteousness, the end, the scope, the well-doing which the Mosaic law intended.[69] Indeed, Christ makes believers able to do more than the law commands.[70] The power of sin cannot be broken by weak human flesh, but the Spirit can achieve what the flesh cannot. While Chrysostom ends his homily with a stirring summons to ethical action, he is quite clear it is the gift of grace, particularly the gift of the Spirit, that gives such exhortation any force or point.[71] You can do it, not because you should, but because the power of the Spirit at work in you is far greater than the power of sin.[72]

While there are differences between Ambrosiaster and Chrysostom in their treatment of Romans 8, those differences highlight a far more fundamental unity in their approach to the text and in their exegetical results. Although at times they treat Pauline themes anachronistically by speaking about matters more precisely than Paul himself had spoken, still the overwhelming impression which they create is that they have written sound, relevant, imaginative exegesis that casts fresh light on the mind of Paul. They are remarkably shrewd in identifying the crucial problems in the Pauline text and reflect faithfully the unresolved tensions in Paul's thought about the nature of the flesh and the role of the law. It is easy to understand why Calvin admired their exegesis, even if he did not follow it in all details.

JOHN CALVIN

There is a reciprocal relationship in Calvin's exegetical work between his struggle with the biblical text and the continuous revisions of his systematic position in successive editions of the *Institutes of the Christian Religion*. In the 1536 edition of the *Institutes*, Calvin alludes to Rom. 8:1–11 eight times.[73] If we keep to the categories emphasized by the Fathers—namely, law, anthropology, christology, and ethics—we find very little evidence that Calvin in 1536 was particularly concerned with the exegetical traditions of the early church. While he cites Ambrose (not Ambrosiaster) to support his contention that the "prudence of the flesh" seeks to penetrate God's hidden judgments apart from his Word[74] and agrees with the Fathers that 8:9–11 teaches the unity of the Trinity (since the Holy Spirit is the Spirit of both the Father and the Son),[75] he is not terribly interested in Patristic themes. Calvin does not cite Romans 8 to support the holistic character of human nature or to highlight the ambiguity of the word *law*. He does not explain the puzzling phrase "likeness of sinful flesh" or react to the Patristic notion that the death of Christ rendered Satan culpable. Calvin's interest lay elsewhere, in a Protestant polemic against such medieval Catholic commonplaces as the distinction between commands and counsels[76] or the sacramental obligation of the penitent to do works of satisfaction.[77] The death of Christ put a decisive end to all penitential works of satisfaction.[78]

In the final Latin edition of the *Institutes* (1559), the situation has noticeably altered. That is not to say that the thirty-three allusions Calvin makes to Rom. 8:1–11 are altogether new. Calvin still scores polemical points against the Catholic church and even embellishes one or two older charges with further details. For example, the "prudence of the flesh," which was earlier condemned for its vain curiosity, is now excoriated for its empty speculations about the intercessory activity of departed saints.[79]

On the other hand, one catches repeated glimpses of the Patristic reading of Paul. Like Ambrosiaster and Chrysostom, Calvin interprets the anthropological terminology of Paul holistically: the whole person is involved in sin,[80] the whole person is flesh,[81] and all the emotions of the flesh are implacably hostile to God.[82] In his christology, however, Calvin goes beyond the Fathers. He agrees with them that Christ was truly human, though sinless (hence "in the likeness of sinful flesh"),[83] and that he expiated human sin in his flesh.[84] But Calvin also had a sixteenth-century agenda. He contended against Osiander that the sole purpose of the incarnation was redemption[85] and explained the relationship between Christ and the Holy Spirit in such a way as to exclude both Catholic and Lutheran understandings of real presence.[86] More than the Fathers, though not in contradiction to them, Calvin read Rom. 8:1–11 as a celebration of the activity of the Spirit in regeneration, sanctification, assurance, and resurrection.[87]

The commentaries on Romans also give evidence of a development in Calvin's use of his Patristic sources. John R. Walchenbach argues that, although Calvin knew the writings of Chrysostom before 1536, he did not become intensely interested in Chrysostom as an exegete until the period 1539–1546.[88] In any event, it is certainly true that no Fathers are cited by name in the 1540 commentary on Rom. 8:1–11. Although three opinions are cited anonymously, none of the three is, so far as I can determine, a reference to a Patristic author.

In the 1556 commentary, Calvin cites Chrysostom once, though the position he attributes to Chrysostom is held by Ambrosiaster instead. Eight opinions mentioned by Calvin are held by Calvin's contemporaries and so can be set aside: Erasmus, who is cited by name on four technical points (vv. 2, 3, 6); the Libertines, who despise the law of God (v. 7); the Sophists (read: Scholastics), who defend the freedom of the human will (v. 7); the "advocates of free will," who equate the Spirit in chapter 8 with the mind or superior part of the soul (v. 9); and the "Papists"—probably Catholic

controversialists like Latomus or Cochlaeus[89]—who deny the claim that
Protestants are indwelt by the Holy Spirit, though Calvin does not make
clear the grounds for this denial (v.9). Calvin also alludes to Pseudo-
Oecumenius, an eighth-century Byzantine commentator who was first published in the West by Donatus of Verona.[90] The allusion to Oecumenius
hangs on a small grammatical point that Calvin does not accept but which
he is also not prepared to reject absolutely.

The three remaining anonymous attributions are to ancient authors—
namely, Origen, Ambrosiaster, and Augustine. Together with the misplaced
allusion to Chrysostom (though Chrysostom is reflected elsewhere in
Calvin's exegesis), Calvin believes he has taken into account the opinions
of four of the most important early commentators. Interestingly enough,
he rejects the opinions of all four. In fact, of the thirteen opinions he cites,
he cheerfully dismisses twelve.

Some interpreters, according to Calvin, believe that when Paul spoke of
the weakness of the law (v.3), he was "depriving only ceremonies of the
power to justify." Calvin may be alluding to a much more finely nuanced
argument in Origen[91] (though the point is repeated by Lanfranc[92] and Haymo
of Auxerre[93] as well), which plays spirit against letter and Old Testament
against New. What cannot justify is law understood according to the letter. What Origen cites to substantiate this point are two ceremonies of the
old covenant: Sabbath-keeping and temple sacrifices.

Other interpreters equate the law of sin and death with the law of Moses
(v.2). This position, as we have seen, is held by Ambrosiaster,[94] though not
by Chrysostom (or, for that matter, Augustine[95] or Pelagius[96] either). Calvin
finds this equation too harsh, even invidious. He tries an even more radical
demythologizing of the "law" than the Fathers attempted. The "law of the
Spirit of life" is simply an inept and inappropriate way to refer to the Holy
Spirit.[97] The "law of sin and death" refers to the "dominion of the flesh and
the tyranny of death which follows from it."[98] The law of God stands in the
middle between two conflicting powers. It teaches righteousness, but it
cannot confer it. Rather, as Calvin laments, it "binds us in bondage to sin
and death by still stronger bonds."[99] While Calvin portrays his objection
to the position of Ambrosiaster in severe language, it is difficult to see that
there is a substantial difference between them on the main issue.

Calvin also rejects the "opinion of those who explain *the law of sin* to mean
the lust of the flesh, as if Paul had said that he had conquered it" (v.2).[100]
This objection appears to be directed against Augustine and the Augustinian tradition of biblical interpretation. To be sure, Augustine does not use
the phrase *concupiscentia carnis* in his comment on 8:1–2 or the related terms
fomes peccati and *consuetudo peccandi*.[101] Those terms are, of course, used by
Peter Abelard,[102] Hervaeus of Bourg-Dieu,[103] William of St. Thierry,[104]

Pseudo-Bruno the Carthusian,[105] Hugh of St. Cher,[106] and Thomas Aquinas[107] in their comments on these verses. Augustine speaks rather of *carnalia desideria* and of life *sub lege* and *sub gratia*. Fleshly desires remain in Christians even after baptism. Nevertheless, they are not a source of condemnation for Christians because Christians do not obey them. This victory over sin marks life under grace rather than the old life under the law. Life *sub lege* was life in subjection to the flesh. Concupiscence in believers, in other words, is not sinful unless it is freely consented to by an act of the human will. The Augustinian tradition is clear on that point and it is a tradition Calvin rejects.

The one really puzzling note struck by Calvin in his discussion of 8:1–11 is his ascription to Chrysostom of an opinion found in Ambrosiaster. Ambrosiaster argued that "sin had been condemned on account of sin (*de peccato*), because it assailed Christ unjustly and contrary to what he deserved" (v.3), not Chrysostom. Clearly Calvin has made a mistake. He may have been misled by Bucer, who, while properly ascribing this exegetical comment to Ambrose (Ambrosiaster), nevertheless adds, "with whom Chrysostom agrees."[108] Or he may simply have suffered a lapse of memory. Walchenbach has already demonstrated that many of the references Calvin makes to Chrysostom in his commentary on 1 Corinthians are made from memory. They are inexact, sometimes prejudiced, rarely up to the rigorous standards that govern modern research. Under the circumstances it is hardly astonishing that Calvin has from time to time made an inexact ascription. On the whole, it would be far more astonishing if he had not.

Calvin's exegesis of Rom. 8:1–11 can be summarized very quickly, particularly if we use the four categories—law, anthropology, christology, and ethics—under which we discussed the Pauline exegesis of Ambrosiaster and Chrysostom.

Law

Unlike Chrysostom, Calvin does not find any reference in this passage to natural law. The only "law" in the proper sense of the term Calvin finds in these verses is the Mosaic law. The "law of the Spirit of life" and the "law of sin and death" are only loose and inexact expressions for the two powers that confront the Mosaic law: the Holy Spirit, on the one hand, and the dominion of sin and death, on the other.[109] The Mosaic law teaches a righteousness it cannot confer and thereby intensifies the human predicament.[110] The fault lies in human corruption and not in the law itself. Indeed, far from blaming the law, Calvin lashes out against the Libertines, who argue that since everything in nature and history happens by the will of God (a point Calvin is not prepared to dispute), everything that happens is by that very fact morally good (an opinion Calvin categorizes as blasphemy).[111] That something happens is not in and of itself a sufficient moral sanction. The law of God is the standard according to which actions and events must be judged. The law is a reliable guide to the will of God, even if it is "impotent" (Calvin believes that no weaker term will do justice to Paul's argument) to effect the good it teaches.[112] Paul's discussion of the law, therefore, resolves itself very rapidly into a discussion of anthropology.

Anthropology

Calvin combines a very clear emphasis on the unity of human nature with a very strong suggestion that there are higher and lower faculties in the human personality. On the one hand, he will define flesh as "all the endowments of human nature, and everything that is in man, except the sanctification of the Spirit."[113] On the other hand, he will talk about the body in deprecating terms as that "stolid mass" as yet unpurified by the Holy Spirit[114] or refer to the human spirit as that "part of the soul" which the Holy Spirit has purified from evil.[115] But it is the holistic language that predominates. Paul uses flesh and spirit to refer to the soul.[116] He neither blames the poor human body as the source of sin and death nor celebrates the human soul as a source of continual life.[117] When Paul uses the term *mortal bodies*, he is referring to everything in human nature subject to death.[118] Even though body and soul can be distinguished and there are some senses in which the soul is superior to the body, the human predicament embraces the whole human person in its relationship to God. Flesh is not a faculty but the *totus homo* in opposition and rebellion against God. Calvin rejects the doctrine of free will. The "mind of the flesh" (Calvin prefers this translation to the "prudence" of the Vulgate or the "affection" of Erasmus) "includes all the feelings of the soul from the reason and understanding to the affections."[119] This mind is not only not subject to the law of God; it cannot be (a declaration that puts an end to the arguments of the "Sophists" and their "non-Christian philosophy" of the freedom of the will).[120]

Christology

Calvin agrees with the main Patristic point that the phrase, "likeness of sinful flesh," means that there is no substantial difference between Christ's humanity and ours, except for his freedom from sin.[121] "Likeness" refers to the word *sinful* and not to the word *flesh*, as though Christ were a docetic apparition. Christ's flesh had the appearance of sinful flesh because it sustained the punishment due our sins and also because Christ learned sympathy with us by bearing our infirmities.[122] While Calvin rejects Ambrosiaster's interpretation of v.3 that "sin had been condemned on account of sin (*de peccato*), because it assailed Christ unjustly and contrary to what he deserved," he does not doubt that Christ was unjustly condemned or that he was an innocent expiatory victim. He agrees with the point that goes back to Origen that *peccatum* is a sacrifice on which a curse has been laid.[123] Calvin also spends some time repeating the axiom that the Spirit of the Father is the Spirit of the Son[124] and attempting to reconcile the Pauline perspective that "ascribes to the Father the glory of having raised up Christ" (v.11) with the Johannine claim that "Christ certainly rose of himself and through his own power" (John 10:18).[125]

Ethics

Calvin observes that the children of God are spiritual, not because they are perfect, but because the beginnings of new life are stirring in them.[126] Although they are always imperfect, they are always subjects of the mercy that pardons their sins and the power of the Spirit who regenerates them.[127] Free remission of sins is offered to believers who "join repentance to faith, and do not misuse the mercy of God by indulging the flesh."[128] Calvin regards this passage as an important consolation for the "trembling consciences" of the godly.[129] Christians are beyond "every danger of condemnation" if they struggle against the flesh.[130] Perfect consolation is not a reward for perfect obedience. Freedom from condemnation does not mean that there is nothing blameworthy in the Christian or that the Christian has "completely put off all the feelings of the flesh."[131] What it does mean is that divine mercy comforts the godly as though the struggle itself were already the final victory.

CONCLUSION

It would be a mistake to judge Calvin's relationship to the Fathers solely on the basis of his explicit references to them. If, for example, one relied only upon the index of the *Corpus Reformatorum* as a guide to Calvin's knowledge of the Fathers, one would conclude that Calvin referred in his commentaries on the New Testament to Chrysostom 105 times, to Augustine 101, to Jerome 38, to Ambrose 23, and to Ambrosiaster not at all. Careful examination of Rom. 8:1–11 has shown that the relationship of Calvin to the Fathers is far more complicated and cannot be unraveled without paying careful attention to the anonymous attributions scattered throughout his commentaries. When Calvin refers to "some commentators" or "the opinion of those who hold," he may very well have in mind the exegetical comment of some unnamed Father. One can also not exclude the possibility that, when Calvin refers explicitly to an author, he may from time to time suffer a lapse of memory.

Calvin's attitude toward the Fathers changes in the period between his earliest and latest works. Walchenbach noted this development in his study of Calvin on 1 Corinthians and our examination of Romans 8 tends to confirm his conclusions. In the period between the 1540 commentary on Rom. 8:1–11 (in which Calvin cites no Fathers) and the 1556 commentary (in which he cites four), Calvin accepts the Fathers as commentators whose views must be taken into account as he writes his own exegesis. He does not appear to develop such respect for medieval exegetical literature and there is some reason to believe that he does not know that literature in the same depth. But the Fathers clearly form part of his working library as he attempts to understand the mind of Paul.

Calvin does not use the Fathers in the way a medieval commentator used his ancient authorities. The Fathers are not cited by Calvin in his exegesis of Romans 8 because he agrees with them and needs their authority to strengthen his argument. Nor does he cite them because their teaching is binding on him and forecloses in advance the range of his exegetical options. He does not attempt to harmonize the teaching of the Fathers or to reconcile differences between them, though he does feel obliged to reconcile what appears to be a disagreement between Paul and John. In every case, explicit and anonymous, in which Calvin has referred to Patristic exegesis, he has quarreled with it.

One ought not to make too much of this quarrel. After all, as we have already seen, there is a wide range of issues on which Calvin is in complete agreement with the Fathers. Disagreements over smaller points of exegesis ought not to obscure that larger consensus on anthropological and christological issues. Still it is true to say that Calvin treats the Fathers as partners in conversation rather than as authorities in the medieval sense of the term. They stimulate Calvin in his reflections on the text. They present him with ideas and suggestions he does not find in the writings of his contemporaries. Nevertheless, they do not have the last word. Paul does. A commentary is useful to the extent that it illuminates the mind of Paul. *Medicus non est qui non medetur*. But the text of Paul takes precedence over even the best of the commentators, ancient and modern.

Calvin, after all, is writing a commentary on Paul, not on Origen or Chrysostom or Augustine or Ambrosiaster. Calvin keeps his pages as uncluttered as possible because it is Paul himself and not the commentators he wants to interpret. To cite too many of the Fathers, too often, or in an unassimilated fashion, would conflict with Calvin's exegetical ideal of lucid brevity. But the fact that Calvin does not clutter his pages with citations does not mean that the Fathers are not constant companions in his study.

Calvin regards the interpretation of Paul as a work carried on, not only in association with his contemporaries, but also in conversation with the greatest interpreters of Christian antiquity.

NOTES

1. T. H. L. Parker, *Calvin's New Testament Commentaries* (Grand Rapids, Mich.: Wm. B. Eerdmans, 1971), p. 88.

2. Luchesius Smits, *Saint Augustine dans l'oeuvre de Jean Calvin*, 2 vols. (Assen: Van Gorcum, 1957–58).

3. John R. Walchenbach, "John Calvin as Biblical Commentator: An Investigation into Calvin's Use of John Chrysostom as an Exegetical Tutor," (Ph.D. diss., University of Pittsburgh, 1974).

4. E. P. Meijering, *Calvin wider die Neugierde: Ein Beitrag zum Vergleich zwischen reformatorischem und patristischem Denken* (Nieuwkoop: B. De Graaf, 1980).

5. T. H. L. Parker, ed., *Iohannis Calvini Commentarius in Epistolam Pauli ad Romanos*, Studies in the History of Christian Thought 22 (Leiden: E.J. Brill, 1981), p. 2, abbreviated as Calvin, *Commentarius*.

6. In this connection see Alexandre Ganoczy and Klaus Müller, *Calvins Handschriftliche Annotationen zu Chrysostomus: Ein Beitrag zur Hermeneutik Calvins* (Wiesbaden: Steiner Verlag, 1981).

7. Karl Hermann Schelkle, *Paulus, Lehrer der Väter: Die altkirchliche Auslegung von Römer 1–11* (Düsseldorf: Patmos, 1956).

8. Maurice F. Wiles, *The Divine Apostle: The Interpretation of St. Paul's Epistles in the Early Church* (Cambridge: Cambridge University Press, 1967). See, particularly, the summary of Wiles's conclusions on pp. 132–39.

9. For a detailed survey of the commentators of the Latin and Greek churches, see once again Wiles, *Divine Apostle*, pp. 3–13. See also Schelkle, *Paulus*, pp. 11–14.

10. On Ambrosiaster, the older works of Alexander Souter are still important. See A. Souter, *A Study of Ambrosiaster* (Cambridge: Cambridge University Press, 1905) and *The Earliest Latin Commentaries on the Epistles of St. Paul* (Oxford: Oxford University Press, 1927), especially pp. 39–95.

11. Chrysostom is cited in the edition of J. P. Migne, *Patrologia Graeca* 60 (Paris, 1857–1912), abbreviated as PG.

12. Ambrosiaster is cited in the critical edition prepared by H. J. Vogels, *Ambrosiastri qui dicitur Commentarius in Epistulas Paulinas; Pars Prima, In Epistulam ad Romanos*, CSEL 81 (Vienna: Hölder, Pichler, Tempsky, 1966).

13. Ambrosiaster, "Ad Romanos," in Vogels, *Ambrosiastri*, 251.

14. Ibid., 251.

15. Ibid.

16. Ibid., 253, 255.

17. Ibid., 263.

18. Ibid., 257.

19. Ibid., 269.

20. Ibid.

21. Ibid.
22. Ibid.
23. Ibid., 265.
24. Ibid., 261.
25. Ibid.
26. Ibid.
27. Ibid.
28. Ibid., 261, 263.
29. Ibid., 263.
30. Ibid.
31. Ibid.
32. Ibid., 265.
33. Ibid., 255.
34. Ibid.
35. Ibid.
36. Ibid.
37. Ibid.
38. Ibid., 257.
39. Ibid., 259.
40. Ibid.
41. Ibid., 257.
42. Ibid., 265.
43. Ibid., 267.
44. Ibid.
45. Ibid.
46. Ibid., 255.
47. Ibid., 265.
48. Chrysostom, "Homilia 13," PG 60, 507–8.
49. PG 60, 507–8.
50. PG 60, 510–11.
51. Ibid.
52. Ibid.
53. PG 60, 511–12.
54. PG 60, 511.
55. PG 60, 513.
56. PG 60, 515.
57. PG 60, 517.
58. PG 60, 515.
59. Ibid.
60. PG 60, 515–16.
61. PG 60, 517–18.
62. PG 60, 519.
63. PG 60, 513–15.
64. Ibid.
65. Ibid.

66. Ibid.
67. PG 60, 513.
68. Ibid.
69. PG 60, 515.
70. PG 60, 512–13.
71. PG 60, 520–24.
72. PG 60, 513.
73. The 1536 *Institutes* is cited in the edition by Peter Barth and Wilhelm Niesel, *Ioannis Calvini Opera Selecta* 1 (Munich: Christian Kaiser Verlag, 1926), abbreviated as OS 1.
74. OS 1.100.
75. OS 1.71–72.
76. OS 1.54–55.
77. OS 1.194–95.
78. OS 1.192–93.
79. *Inst.* III.xx.24.
80. *Inst.* II.i.9.
81. *Inst.* II.iii.1.
82. *Inst.* III.iii.8.
83. *Inst.* II.xiii.4.
84. *Inst.* II.xiii.1, II.xvi.6, III.iv.27.
85. *Inst.* II.xii.4.
86. *Inst.* IV.xvii.12.
87. *Inst.* II.i.6, II.ii.16, III.i.3, III.ii.39, III.xxv.3, III.xxv.8, IV.xvii.12.
88. Walchenbach, "John Calvin," pp. 148–49.
89. See the footnote to *Inst.* III.ii.39 in the McNeill-Battles translation of the 1559 *Institutes*.
90. Calvin, *Commentarius*, p. 158. Oecumenius (pseudo-), *Commentaria Luculentissima vetustissimorum Graecorum in Omnes D. Pauli Epistolas ab Oecumenio exacte et magna cura ad Compendium Collecta: Interprete vero Johanne Hentenio Nechliniensi Hieronymiano* (Paris: Jean Foucher, 1547). The real Oecumenius lived in the first half of the sixth century.
91. Origen, PG 14.1091–92.
92. Lanfranc, *Patrologia Latina* 150, ed. J. P. Migne (Paris, 1844–1890), p. 130, hereafter abbreviated as PL.
93. Haymo of Auxerre is incorrectly published under the name Haymo of Halberstadt, PL 117.426. Haymo's commentary on Paul was readily available in the early sixteenth century in the edition *Haymonis Episcopi Halberstatten in D. Pauli Epistolas Omnes Interpretatio* (Cologne: Eucharius Cervicornus, 1539).
94. Lanfranc is careful to attribute this view to Ambrose (Ambrosiaster), PL 150.130.
95. Augustine, "Expositio Quarundam Propositionum ex Epistola ad Romanos," CSEL 84 (Vienna: C. Geroldi Filium, 1887), pp. 21–22.
96. *Pelagius's Expositions of the Thirteen Epistles of St. Paul, II*, ed. Alexander Souter, Texts and Studies 9 (Cambridge: Cambridge University Press, 1926), pp. 60–61.

97. Calvin, *Commentarius*, p. 156.

98. Ibid.

99. Ibid.

100. Ibid., p. 157.

101. Augustine, "Expositio," p. 21.

102. *Petri Abelardi Opera Theologica*, Vol. 2, E. M. Buytaert, ed., *Corpus Christianorum*, Continuatio Mediaevalis 12 (Turnhout: Brepols, 1969), pp. 249–51.

103. Hervaeus of Bourg-Dieu, PL 181.697–98.

104. William of St. Thierry, PL 180.624–25.

105. Pseudo-Bruno the Carthusian, PL 153.70–71.

106. Hugh of St. Cher, *Tomus Septimus in Epistolas D. Pauli, Actus Apostolorum, Epist. septem canonicas, Apocalypsim B. Joannis* (Venice: Nicolaus Pezzana, 1732), fol. 45v.

107. St. Thomas Aquinas, *Opera Omnia* 13 (Parma, 1862), 74–75.

108. Martin Bucer, *Metaphrases et Enarrationes perpetuae Epistolarum D. Pauli Apostoli. Tomus Primus continens Metaphrasim et Enarrationem in Epistolam ad Romanos* (Strasbourg: Wendelin Rihel, 1536), p. 331: "Istuc D. Ambrosius legit, Damnavit peccatum de peccato, hoc est, peccatum proprio peccato damnavit. Christus enim cum a peccato crucifigitur, quod est Satanas. Peccatum peccavit in carne corporis Salvatoris. Haec Ambrosius, cum quo consentit Chrysostomus."

109. Calvin, *Commentarius*, p. 156.

110. Ibid.

111. Ibid., p. 163.

112. Ibid., p. 159.

113. Ibid., p. 151.

114. Ibid., p. 166.

115. Ibid., p. 151.

116. Ibid.

117. Ibid., p. 166.

118. Ibid., p. 167.

119. Ibid., p. 162.

120. Ibid., p. 163.

121. Ibid., p. 159.

122. Ibid.

123. Ibid., p. 160.

124. Ibid., pp. 164–65.

125. Ibid., pp. 166–67.

126. Ibid., p. 165.

127. Ibid., p. 156.

128. Ibid., p. 157.

129. Ibid., p. 156.

130. Ibid.

131. Ibid.

10

Calvin among the Thomists

Among Calvin's closest allies and friends in Strasbourg was an ex-Dominican priest, Martin Bucer (1491–1551). Bucer had entered the Dominican Order in 1506 at the age of fifteen. In 1516 he transferred to the Blackfriars cloister in Heidelberg, where in April 1518, he heard Martin Luther preside at a theological disputation sponsored by Luther's own order, the Hermits of St. Augustine. Bucer was so captivated by Luther's thought that he applied for release from the Dominican Order and in 1521 became a simple parish priest in Landstuhl. After brief parochial duty in Landstuhl and Weissenburg, Bucer fled for refuge to the free imperial city of Strasbourg, where he became the pastor in turn of the churches of St. Aurelia (1524–1531) and St. Thomas (1531–1540). From Strasbourg he swiftly rose to prominence as one of the principal leaders of the Reformation in the Holy Roman Empire.

In 1538 Calvin, who had been expelled from Geneva, arrived in Strasbourg to become the pastor of the congregation of French refugees. From 1538 until his return to Geneva in 1541, Calvin and Bucer were frequently in each other's company. Two years earlier, in 1536, while serving as the pastor of the Church of St. Thomas, Bucer had written a lengthy commentary on Romans called the *Metaphrases et Enarrationes Perpetuae . . . in Epistolam ad Romanos,* which he published through the Strasbourg printer, Wendelin Rihel.[1] Four years later, in 1540, using the same Strasbourg printer, Calvin published his own much shorter *Commentarii in Epistolam Pauli ad Romanos* and included in his dedication high praise for Bucer's 1536 commentary:

Finally there comes Bucer, who spoke the last word on the subject with the publication of his writings. In addition to his profound learning, abundant knowledge, keenness of intellect, wide reading, and many other varied excellences in which he is surpassed by hardly anyone at the present day, this scholar, as we know, is equalled by few and is superior to very many. It is to his especial credit that no one in our time has been more precise or diligent in interpreting Scripture than he.[2]

The question has frequently been asked whether Bucer as a former Dominican brought with him to the Reformation theological and exegetical insights shaped by the teaching of the preeminent theologian of his old order, Thomas Aquinas.[3] If so, did Bucer in turn influence the thinking of John Calvin in a Thomistic direction? The issue is, of course, far too broad to be resolved in a single essay. Yet it is possible to pursue in one essay a limited case study that may provide a partial answer to a long and complicated question. What I propose to do in this chapter is to examine the exegesis of Romans 9 by Thomas Aquinas, Martin Bucer, and John Calvin, in order to isolate the agreements and disagreements among them and to determine whether those agreements and disagreements argue for or against the presence of a common school tradition.[4] In order to provide a contemporary context for Bucer's exegesis, I will compare Bucer's interpretation of Paul at several points with the exegesis of two prominent Dominican theologians who did not become Protestants, Thomas de Vio, known as Cajetan (1468–1534), and Ambrosius Catherinus Politus (1484–1553).

I

Thomas Aquinas probably delivered his commentary on Romans 9 as a series of lectures during his second regency at Paris (1270–72).[5] The exposition is divided into five *lectiones*, covering respectively 9:1–5, 6–13, 14–18, 19–23, and 24–33.[6] The central theme that ties the various sections together for Thomas is the question of the origin of grace. Does grace spring from divine election alone or is it based on human merit?[7] Interwoven with this theme is the question of the place of Jews and Gentiles in the history of salvation.

The first *lectio* struggles to explain Paul's astonishing wish to be "accursed and cut off from Christ for the sake of [his] brethren," the unconverted Jews. Such a wish appears to some medieval critics of Paul to contradict the order of charity by which Christians are bound to love God supremely and their own salvation more than the salvation of any other human being. Paul could mean that he hoped to be anathema (i.e., separated from final salvation), at least for a time, if it would contribute to the conversion of the Jews and thus to Christ's honor. At any event, what Thomas is careful to show is that

Paul's seemingly exaggerated sorrow is not irrational. The people whom Paul loves so intensely are a great people. They alone have decended from Jacob and the patriarchs; they alone have been graced with certain spiritual benefits; they alone have provided the stock from which Christ descended according to the flesh (a point, Thomas notes, that undercuts the Manichean, Valentinian, Nestorian, and Arian heresies).[8]

The second *lectio* follows the sudden turn in Paul's argument from a consideration of the greatness of the Jews as a nation descended from Jacob to a narrower consideration of a remnant among the Jews who form a spiritual seed elected by God. Paul contends that not all the natural descendants of Abraham are his spiritual descendants. Abraham's spiritual children are the children of promise. By the grace of God's promise they have been made Abraham's children through faith. Jews who thought they were worthy of the grace of God because of the merit of their ancestors could always get around the example of Abraham. After all, while both Isaac and Ishmael were children of Abraham, they were children by different mothers. Sarah was free; Hagar was a slave. Furthermore, Ishmael was conceived while Abraham was uncircumcised and therefore still a Gentile, Isaac after Abraham's circumcision. Ishmael as the descendant of a Gentile father and an enslaved mother was naturally excluded from the blessings offered only to the Jews.[9]

In order to counteract this kind of subterfuge, Paul appeals to the example of Rebecca. Rebecca's son, Jacob, was elect; her twin son, Esau, was reprobate. Unlike Isaac and Ishmael, Jacob and Esau came not only from the same father but the same mother. They were conceived through the same sexual act and born on the same day at the same time through an identical act of labor. In spite of the identity of their natural circumstances, God nevertheless chose Jacob as the child of his promise and rejected Esau.[10]

On what grounds, however, was God's choice based, if not natural descent from Abraham? Certainly not a difference in astrological charts, as the Manicheans falsely argued, or in foreseen merit, as the Pelagians incorrectly thought! God's choice was made before Jacob and Esau had been born and therefore before they had made any moral choices. Paul also excludes from consideration Origen's fantasy of a pretemporal fall. Neither preexisting works in this life (Pelagius) nor preexisting works in another life (Origen) form the basis for God's choice of Jacob over Esau. According to his own spontaneous will God elects one twin over the other, not because Jacob was already holy but in order to make him so.[11]

Paul's argument has raised for Thomas important theological questions that need to be clarified before he can proceed further with his exposition. To explain what Paul means by election, Thomas distinguishes three important terms (that are, of course, indistinguishable in God): namely, love (*dilectio*), election (*electio*), and predestination (*praedestinatio*). Love wills the good for someone absolutely. Election wills some good for one person rather than another. Predestination directs the preferred object of love to the good willed by the electing agent. Love therefore precedes predestination as the will concerning an end naturally precedes the direction of someone to it.[12]

In other words, the election of Jacob over Esau is rooted in an absolute and mysterious love that cannot be rationalized. God predestines Jacob, i.e., directs him to final salvation because he has loved and chosen him. The choice and direction are based on God's absolute love and on no other cause, however plausible. Whatever good there is in Jacob is the result of God's electing love and not its cause. The notion, therefore, that election is based on foreknowledge, even in part, is rejected by Thomas as absurd. God predestines the elect to merit glory, but merit remains the effect and not the cause of predestination.[13]

The same cannot be said with respect to Esau. The choice of Jacob over Esau can be described as the nonelection, though not reprobation, of Esau. Esau is not reprobated simply because he was not chosen (though the non-choice of Esau is almost as mysterious as the choice of Jacob). Reprobation is based, at least in part, on God's foreknowledge of Esau's demerits. Esau is reprobated, that is, destined for punishment, because he richly deserves it. The wicked deeds that Esau commits during the course of his life provide the partial ground for his reprobation. In short, the election and predestination of Jacob demonstrate God's mercy; the reprobation of Esau, his justice. The relationship to God of Jacob and Esau (and of all the elect and reprobate) is asymmetrical. Works are not the basis for election; they are, however, an incomplete cause of reprobation.[14]

Paul's discussion of predestination, however, poses for Thomas a further question in *lectio* three: What about distributive justice? If God is just, then surely God must distribute benefits to equals equally. Paul had gone to great lengths in Rom. 9:10–13 to show that at the moment of their birth there was no difference between Jacob and Esau, save for the difference interjected by God through the mysterious election of Jacob. If God is just and if Jacob and Esau were, as Paul himself had demonstrated, equal in a way Isaac and Ishmael could never be, then surely the election of Jacob over Esau flies in the face of God's distributive justice. According to distributive justice, God ought to have chosen both or neither as objects of his mercy. *Tertium non datur.*[15]

Paul proposes a solution from Exod. 33:19. He cites a translation of the Septuagint that ascribes all human goods to the mercy of God. Thomas reads this verse to mean that every benefit tending to salvation is an effect of predestination. He therefore rejects the solution found in the Gloss that the distributive justice of God can be preserved by appealing to a foreseen good use of grace by Jacob. According to this solution, God chose Jacob over Esau because he foresaw that Jacob would make a better use of God's grace if grace were offered to him. Thomas finds this solution inadmissible because God is the source both of the infused grace by which sinners are justified and of every subsequent good use of grace. To illustrate his point Thomas draws an analogy between the realms of nature and supernature. Just as in nature God not only causes the forms of things but also their motions and operations, so, too, in redemption the will of God is the sole origin of the habit of grace and every gracious action that flows from it. Jacob's good use of grace is God's gift to Jacob and not Jacob's gift to God.[16]

Distributive justice has a place in *ex debito* relations, that is, in arrangements in which one party is obligated to another because of contractual agreements or overriding moral claims. But no such obligations govern the realm of mercy. It is not a violation of distributive justice to forgive one of two debtors. Since all human beings are sinners, God can mercifully forgive some and justly punish others.[17]

In view of Thomas's heavy emphasis on the causality of God, the question naturally arise whether sinners make any contribution toward their own salvation. As Thomas reads Paul, the primary causality in redemption must always be assigned to divine grace. However, the human will as a secondary agent is moved by God to embrace the good. God moves all things according to the mode of their nature. Therefore, human beings are moved by God to will and run through the mode of free choice. Human beings act freely when they will and run, but they do so only because God as the principal agent moves them toward ends he has chosen.[18]

The example of Pharaoh offers Thomas an opportunity to explain what he has in mind. While God moves human beings toward good and evil by a certain interior instinct, he does not move human beings toward what is good in the same way he moves them toward what is evil. As a principal agent God directly inclines the human will toward what is good. God's relationship to evil, however, is more occasional and indirect. God proposes to the human will something that is good in itself, but that human malice perversely abuses and turns toward evil ends. Pharaoh was aroused by God to defend his realm; he abused this legitimate impulse from God when he repressed the Israelites through gratuitous acts of cruelty.[19]

In his relationship to Pharaoh, God partly ordained and partly permitted what transpired. God ordained that the wickedness of Pharoah should demonstrate God's glory. But though God ordained such wickedness, he did not cause it. Pharaoh, taking the occasion of sin from the various goods God proposed to him, merited the punishment God's justice imposed. God hardened Pharoah, not by prompting him to sin but by interposing no grace. To say anything else would make God the author of evil in a direct and unqualified sense.[20]

The fourth *lectio* begins with Paul's objection to his own solution: Why does God show pity to Jacob and not to Pharaoh? Can any reason be found except the will of God alone? Is the will of God simply irresistible? If so, why does God hold human beings responsible? As Thomas understands Romans 9, Paul wants to assert both that there is no explanation for the electing activity of God except God's will and that the electing will of God can, to a certain limited extent, be explained and defended.[21]

Thomas provides two examples to defend God from the charge of arbitrary injustice. The first example is teleological and appeals from specific cases to the overall plan that directs the whole. A builder who constructs a house out of stone may place some stones in a place of prominence, while relegating other stones, equally durable and attractive, to the lowly task of buttressing the foundation. The artisan is guided by his vision of the end, the perfection of the house he intends to build. So, too, God in his providential care of the universe exercises both mercy and justice, election and reprobation, to achieve the ends his wisdom has ordained.[22]

The second example is anthropological and is built on Paul's image of the potter and the clay. The image seems particularly apt to Thomas because human beings are descendants of Adam, who was created by God from the dust of the earth. Like clay, human beings are vile in their origin. Their natural vileness was made even viler by Adam's fall into sin. If God leaves some human beings in their weakness and sin, he undoubtedly appoints them to ignoble use, but does them no injury about which they could justly complain. God has the free power to make from the corrupt matter of humankind, as from clay, men and women prepared for glory. He has the same freedom to abandon others to the misery they have merited.[23]

The fifth and final *lectio* returns to the second main theme of Romans 9, the relationship of Jews and Gentiles. After Paul shows that the grace of God is given by divine election, he demonstrates that election pertains to Gentiles as well as Jews. Although the Jews received privileges denied the Gentiles, salvation is nevertheless offered to both on the same terms. The true children of the covenant are the children of Abraham by faith. The people of God are constituted, not by circumcision and law-keeping, but by the electing grace of God. The mysterious love and justice that distinguished Ishmael from Isaac, Esau from Jacob, broke down the wall of separation that divided Jew from Greek, Isaac and Jacob from Ampliatus and Urban. While such a message is offensive to unbelieving Jews, it repeats themes that run throughout the whole Bible, Old Testament as well as New. Thomas ends his lecture by amplifying the catena of quotations Paul provides to demonstrate this point.[24]

II

Bucer, like Thomas, divides Romans 9 into five sections, breaking the first two sections at verses 5 and 13.[25] However, unlike Thomas, who divides the chapter at verses 18 and 23, Bucer breaks sections three to five at verses 21 and 29. Furthermore, whereas Thomas separates Romans 9 into five *lectiones* without further subdivisions, Bucer subdivides each of his five *enarrationes* into an *expositio*, an *interpretatio*, and a series of concluding *observationes*.

Bucer uses the word *enarratio* to mark the major subdivisions of his commentary. The *expositio* is a running commentary that summarizes and clarifies the passage as a whole. The *interpretatio* explains individual words and phrases, while the concluding *observationes* repeat theological or devotional themes important for the life of faith. The *enarratio* of section four has five *observationes*, while *enarrationes* of the other sections have four each. In addition, there is one *conciliatio*, in which Bucer tries to harmonize the statement of Paul that God hardens some sinners with the statement that God wills the salvation of every person, and one *quaestio*, in which Bucer explores the role of human free choice.

Aside from differences in form, three things strike the reader of Bucer's commentary: (1) that Bucer is concerned with several questions and themes posed by his contemporaries that do not occur, or occur in the same way, in the earlier *lectiones* of Thomas Aquinas; (2) that Bucer is nevertheless in general agreement with the Augustinian exposition of election by Thomas, if only in the sense that both appeal in similar ways to a common Augustinian source; and (3) that at least on one question, the limited freedom of second causes, Bucer is specifically indebted to Thomas.

For example, Erasmus had raised the question whether verse 5, "of their race, according to the flesh, is the Christ; God who is over all be blessed forever, amen," is, as traditionally understood, an anti-Arian confession that Christ is both God and man; or whether it is simply an ascription of praise to God the Father that follows immediately upon the confession that Christ is descended from the patriarchs. Erasmus inclines toward the latter view without prejudicing the claim that Christ is both divine and human.[26] The Dominican commentators, Cajetan and Politus, disagree with Erasmus. Cajetan simply repeats the traditional view that 9:5 is the first place in Romans where Paul calls Christ God,[27] while Catherinus Politus hints darkly that Erasmus is an enemy of the doctrine of Christ's divinity.[28] Calvin agrees with Cajetan and Politus, deploring the "audacious attempt" of Erasmus and others "to create darkness where there is full light."[29] Bucer, on the other hand, is sympathetic to Erasmus's view. Scripture clearly teaches that Christ is God in so many places that it is not necessary (and probably counterproductive) to try to elicit that teaching from such an ambiguous passage as 9:5.[30] Thomas, who is much less concerned with philological matters than sixteenth-century commentators, finds the passage unproblematic and uses it as a confession of the true humanity and divinity of Christ in order to refute Manichean, Valentinian, Nestorian, and Arian heresies.[31] While Cajetan, Calvin, and Politus agree with Thomas Aquinas against Bucer, who agrees with Erasmus, their disagreement is historically insignificant, since the debate centers on a question that had not been raised in Thomas's own day.

More significant is the agreement of Thomas and Bucer over the doctrine of election. Unlike Thomas, Bucer does not distinguish between love, election, and predestination. However, like Thomas, he rejects the notion that election is based on foreknowledge, an idea he associates with Origen, Chrysostom, and Ambrosiaster.[32] Against the argument that equates election with prevision of the future, Bucer appeals to the authority of Augustine.[33] Everything concerning human salvation depends on the mysterious mercy of God. The faithful remnant in Israel and the church is constituted by God's free election.[34] Bucer discourages speculation concerning God's electing activity or faithless questioning concerning his justice. "The mere will of God," he writes, "is the cause of everything and that will is itself justice."[35]

In other words, there is no cause for what God does beyond God's will. It is impious for human beings to inquire into it, since everyone knows that God always works for the best. At any rate, sinful human beings, who are caught in the web of their own wickedness and deceit, have no right to call God to account, who always wills what is just and good. Rather than question the justice of God, human beings ought to entrust themselves to his Spirit and cling to the self-revelation of God in his Word.[36]

Cajetan is also willing to argue that election and reprobation hang from the mere will of God.[37] However, to avoid the alarming notion that a good and just God wills evil against the reprobate apart from any consideration of their works, Cajetan observes that one must distinguish between reprobation and the execution of reprobation. Apart from any consideration of their works, God withholds his grace from the reprobate and leaves them to cope with temptation without the assistance of grace. In that sense they are reprobated *non ex operibus*, without reference to their moral achievements and failures.[38] But judgment on the reprobate is never executed before the reprobate actually sin.[39] God can therefore never be accused of partiality or injustice, since reprobation involves the punishment of real guilt. Election and reprobation are truths on the part of God that are always associated with human free will and responsibility.[40]

Ambrosius Catherinus Politus approaches the problem of reprobation from a slightly different angle. He notes that there are theologians who correctly and, perhaps, too easily confess that predestination rests on grace, while insisting that reprobation rests on human demerits.[41] Unfortunately, their carefully balanced view of election and reprobation does not respond to the passage in Romans 9 which affirms that Esau was reprobated by God before he had done anything worthy of divine hatred.[42] Perhaps, Politus suggests, the word "hatred" (*odium*) may be a gentler word in the Bible than it seems to us in our common usage.[43] At any rate, Esau demonstrated by his evil works that he was a type of reprobate and worthy of divine judgment.[44]

In the *conciliatio* that deals with the apparent contradiction between God's universal will of salvation and his act of hardening sinners, Bucer appeals to the distinction in Augustine between the *vocatio congrua* and *incongrua* or what later Calvinism calls the distinction between effectual and ineffectual calling. The *vocatio congrua* is the preaching of the gospel to the elect, who are moved by God to embrace it. The *vocatio incongrua* is the preaching of the gospel to the nonelect, who are not assisted by the mercy of God and so are left in their sins. The church is commanded to preach the gospel to all creatures, knowing full well that only the elect will profit from it.[45]

In the *quaestio de libero arbitrio* that is included in the *enarratio* of section three (9:14–21), Bucer cites Thomas's definition of free choice as "the will by which we choose what reason through mature deliberation perceives and judges to be more advantageous."[46] Agents exercise free choice when they act according to their own best judgment. Free choice to be truly free must be in the power of the acting agent.[47] Bucer raises this point in order to make two others.

First of all, the action of a first cause does not exclude the action of second causes.[48] While God is the primary agent who is at work in all human willing and doing, God works in such a way as to make human beings the agents of their own acts. "Through God's act we know things, choose them, embrace them, flee them, [and] direct our bodily energies."[49] What Bucer seems to have in mind is the point also made by Thomas that human beings are moved by God to will and act through the mode of free choice.

Even more important for Bucer is his second point—namely, that human willing and acting can accomplish nothing unless perfected by the mercy of God.[50] In its present condition the human will is so debilitated by sin that it is incapable of doing anything pleasing to God without the assistance of Christ's Spirit.[51] The notion that the action of God as first cause does not exclude the action of human free choice as a second cause is a disquieting rather than comforting thought if it means that human free choice can only elect what displeases God. Unless human free will is redeemed by God's grace, it merits eternal death.[52]

The good news, of course, is that God uses human wickedness as an instrument to achieve his own ends and to illuminate the honor of his own name. Whereas believers should imitate God's great leniency in their dealings with other human beings, they should also realize that God's power is commended to them through the punishment of the wicked.[53] Furthermore, they should understand that God's chastisement of his people (as exemplified by God's punishment of unbelieving Israel) always bears fruit for them in the end.[54]

Although Bucer is indebted, at least to some extent, to Thomas for his understanding of free choice and the role of second causes, his discussion of election shows little direct dependence on Thomas's exegesis. Unlike Thomas, Bucer does not distinguish between election and predestination or attempt to offer a theodicy based on an argument from design. Whereas Thomas emphasizes the justice of God that permits and then punishes the wickedness of the reprobate, Bucer appeals to the wisdom and goodness of God that merits unwavering confidence and trust. Although Bucer sounds some specifically Thomistic themes in his exposition of Paul, it is probably more accurate to say that Bucer, like Thomas, embraces a strongly Augustinian view of election than to say he embraces it in a distinctively Thomistic way.

III

Calvin breaks Romans 9 into eight sections (1–5, 6–9, 10–13, 14–18, 19–21, 22–23, 24–29, and 30–33), agreeing with Thomas in two divisions (1–5, 14–18) and Bucer in only one (1–5). Unlike Bucer, who separated his commentary into *expositio*, *interpretatio*, and *observatio*, Calvin combines running commentary, discussion of individual words and phrases, and the elucidation of theological and devotional themes into one continuous, verse-by-verse exposition.

The list of agreements between Thomas, Bucer, and Calvin is impressive: all three reject predestination based on foreknowledge, insist that human salvation is dependent on God's election alone, confess that there is no reason higher than God's own will for the election of some over others, and affirm the justice of God in the punishment of the reprobate. Furthermore, Calvin shares with Bucer a horror of speculative theology that attempts to probe the mystery of predestination beyond the limits set by God's self-revelation in Scripture.[55] Yet there are differences among the three, some substantial, some simply a matter of nuance.

For example, Calvin distinguishes between two elections: the election of all the descendants of Abraham, Ishmael as well as Isaac, to be God's favored people, the natural children of his covenant; and the second or secret election of a remnant among Abraham's descendants in whom the power and efficacy of God's promise are found.[56] Ishmael and Esau are children of the promise only in the first sense; Isaac and Jacob are elect children in the second sense as well. Moreover, the second election is not restricted to the natural descendants of Abraham but overrules the boundaries established by the first or general election.[57]

Since one could object that the differences between Ishmael and Isaac were natural differences explainable under the terms of the first or general covenant with Abraham, Paul offers the example of Jacob and Esau, who were twins born of the same father (Isaac) and mother (Rebecca).[58] Calvin agrees with Thomas and Bucer that this example undercuts any view of election based on the foreknowledge of human good works. Indeed, God could see nothing in the corrupt nature of Jacob and Esau that would induce him to show favor to either. Neither Jacob nor Esau were "possessed of a single particle of righteousness."[59] The favor God shows to Jacob rests on God's "bare and simple good pleasure."[60] "God has a sufficiently just cause for election and reprobation," writes Calvin, "in his own will."[61]

When the question of God's justice is raised by Paul, Calvin responds by adopting a severely antiapologetic stance. Whereas Thomas offers a limited theodicy and Bucer appeals to God's goodness, Calvin takes the position that to mount a spirited defense of God's justice is to detract from God's honor.[62] God has the rightful power of life and death over his creatures.[63] His authority is not the absolute justice of which the sophists (read: scholastics) teach, who distinguish between God's absolute and ordained power. Such theologians separate God's power from his justice and so turn him into a tyrant.[64] God's power is always united with his justice, even in decisions that seem most offensive to human reason.[65]

Nevertheless, in spite of the fact that Calvin declines to offer more than a sketchy apologetic for God's justice, he does make some attempt to explain how God's electing and reprobating activity should be viewed. The apologetic has three elements: (1) God is debtor to no human being and so may confer his kindness on whomever he will.[66] This argument is strikingly similar to Thomas's contention that distributive justice has no place outside *ex debito* relations. (2) The reprobate are in fact wicked and are therefore justly punished by God. Indeed, the godly praise God all the more when they contemplate the wretchedness of the ungodly, who do not escape God's wrath.[67] (3) Finally, the power that God exercises over his creatures is not an inordinate, but an equitable right, similar in every respect to the power of a potter over his clay.[68] Therefore, both the salvation of the elect and the punishment of the reprobate demonstrate God's "unimpeachable equity," even though there is no reason why God elects except his purpose alone.[69]

Calvin breaks most sharply with Thomas (and, to a more limited extent, with Bucer) over the question of the hardening of Pharaoh. Calvin complains that many interpreters attempt to mitigate the harshness of 9:17–18 by appealing to God's permissive will, which leaves the nonelect to their own devices, or by positing a general impulse from God that is abused by the wicked.[70] The notion that Pharaoh had been aroused by God to defend his realm but abused this impulse when he repressed the Israelites or that equates hardening with the noninterposition of grace is flatly rejected by Calvin. God did not merely move or permit Pharaoh to be hardened; God hardened Pharaoh in order to destroy him. The ruin of the ungodly is not merely foreseen or permitted by God, but ordained.[71] The asymmetrical relationship between election and reprobation so carefully worked out by Thomas is flattened into a harsher symmetry by Calvin.

The good news for Gentiles is that election, since it rests on God's good pleasure alone, "exists wherever God has willed it to be."[72] There is no difference of nationality in election. God has put Gentiles on a level with Jews and now extends his mercy to both. If one asks why Jews, who sought righteousness from God, were rejected, whereas Gentiles, who did not, were shown mercy, Calvin replies that there is no real answer except the secret predestination of God. Perhaps, Calvin suggests, God may have wanted to show that trust in good works (as exemplified by the Jews) is the chief obstacle to attaining a righteousness that is only given to faith.[73]

IV

If the question of reprobation is set aside, it would be difficult to find three more vigorous exponents of an Augustinian reading of Romans 9 than Thomas Aquinas, Martin Bucer, and John Calvin. All three reject predestination based on God's foreknowledge of human merit, insist that human salvation is grounded in divine election alone, acknowledge that there is no reason higher than God's will for the election of Isaac and Jacob over Ishmael and Esau, and assert that God is just in the punishment of the reprobate. While there are differences between them in matters of detail, there are no significant differences between them in matters of substance.

To say that Thomas, Bucer, and Calvin are strongly Augustinian in their understanding of Romans 9, however, is not to say that they are Augustinian in exactly the same way. Neither Bucer nor Calvin repeats Thomas's important distinction between love, election, and predestination, or attempts to justify reprobation by appealing to a grand design in which places of honor must be offset by places of dishonor. Indeed, several of Thomas's most characteristic modifications of the Augustinian tradition find no corresponding echo in the expositions of Bucer and Calvin.

Bucer, who accepts the important role of second causes, is clearly more receptive to Thomas's ideas than Calvin is, who rejects Thomas's notion of a general impulse toward the good and finds no place in his theology for divine permission. This difference between Bucer and Calvin becomes evident when the question on the table is the reprobation of the nonelect. Thomas, Bucer, and Calvin all agree that the final explanation for reprobation, as for election itself, lies in the mystery of the divine will. The nonelection of Esau like the election of Jacob rests on God's free decision and therefore remains a mystery that cannot be rationalized. Yet the response of Thomas and Bucer to this mystery differs from Calvin's response. Thomas defends God's justice, while Bucer recommends God's goodness. Against both, Calvin understands himself to be maintaining God's honor.

The question whether Thomas, Bucer, and Calvin share a common school tradition can be answered in the affirmative only if one means by a common tradition the tradition of the Augustinian exegesis of Romans 9. To be sure, Bucer repeats Thomas's definition of free will and his contention that the motion of a first cause enables rather than excludes the motion of second causes. But even Bucer is far less keen than Thomas to develop an apologetic for God's justice. Bucer urges his readers to trust the kindness and goodness of God and to set aside their doubts concerning God's justice. Only Calvin seems to revel in the affront to human conceptions of justice posed by the doctrine of election. To defend what requires no defense detracts from God's honor.

The thesis that Calvin is the beneficiary of a Thomistic school tradition mediated to him by Martin Bucer finds no support in the admittedly limited context of the interpretation of Romans 9. Although it is true that Calvin agrees with Thomas and Bucer on most exegetical issues and that Bucer adopts some themes from Thomas in his interpretation of Paul, their agreement may be better explained by appealing to a common Augustinian heritage than to a common school tradition. Indeed, on the issue of the justice of God's action, Calvin shows himself unfriendly to what he regards as the misguided attempt of Thomas and others to mitigate the harshness of God's decree. Calvin wants to fix the unwavering attention of all theologians, including Thomas and Bucer, on the "eternal and inexplicable counsel of God, whose righteousness is worthy of our worship rather than our scrutiny."[74]

NOTES

1. Martin Bucer, *Metaphrases et Enarrationes Perpetuae Epistolarum d. Pauli Apostoli. Tomus Primus continens Metaphrasim et Enarrationem in Epistolam ad Romanos* (Strasbourg: Wendelin Rihel, 1536).

2. T. H. L. Parker, ed., *Iohannis Calvini Commentarius in Epistolam Pauli ad Romanos* (Leiden: E.J. Brill, 1981), p. 2, abbreviated as Calvin, *Commentarius*.

3. W. P. Stephens is not inclined to think that Thomism is an important

factor in Bucer's development. See, for example, his comment in *The Holy Spirit in the Theology of Martin Bucer* (Cambridge: Cambridge University Press, 1970), p. 18: "It is not clear how far the influence of Thomism is more than superficial, affecting Bucer's language rather than his fundamental understanding of the Christian faith." See also Karl Koch, *Studium Pietatis: Martin Bucer als Ethiker* (Neukirchen, 1962), pp. 9, 12–13, 19, 70, 80.

4. The commentaries on Paul by Thomas Aquinas were available in printed editions in the early sixteenth century and reprinted three times between 1522 and 1532. On this and related questions, see Denis R. Janz, *Luther on Thomas Aquinas: The Angelic Doctor in the Thought of the Reformer* (Stuttgart: Franz Steiner Verlag, 1989), p. 105.

5. For a discussion of the problems surrounding the dating of Thomas's commentary on Romans, see James A. Weisheipl, O.P., *Friar Thomas D'Aquino: His Life, Thought and Works* (Washington, D.C.: Catholic University of America Press, 1974, 1983), pp. 246–49.

6. For the text of Thomas's exposition, see the "Expositio in Omnes Sancti Pauli Epistolas," in *Sancti Thomae Aquinatis Doctoris Angelici Ordinis Praedicatorum Opera Omnia* 13 (Parma, 1872), 91–102.

7. Ibid., 91.

8. Ibid., 92–94.

9. Ibid., 94.

10. Ibid.

11. Ibid.

12. Ibid., 94–95.

13. Ibid., 95.

14. Ibid.

15. Ibid.

16. Ibid., 96.

17. Ibid.

18. Ibid., 97.

19. Ibid.

20. Ibid.97–98.

21. Ibid., 98.

22. Ibid.

23. Ibid., 99.

24. Ibid., 100–102.

25. Bucer, *Metaphrases*, pp. 381–412.

26. Desiderius Erasmus, *In Novum Testamentum Annotationes* (Basel: Froben, 1535), p. 391.

27. Thomas de Vio (Cajetan), *Epistolae Pauli et Aliorum Apostolorum* (Paris: Carola Guillard et Jean de Roigny, 1540), p. 64.

28. Ambrosius Catherinus Politus, *Commentaria in Omnes divi Pauli et alias septem canonicas Epistolas* (Venice: Vincent Valgrisius, 1551), p. 90.

29. Calvin, *Commentarius*, p. 198.

30. Bucer, *Metaphrases*, p. 285.

31. Thomas Aquinas, "Expositio", 92–93.

32. Bucer, *Metaphrases*, pp. 391–92.

33. Ibid., p. 392.

34. Ibid., p. 410.

35. Ibid., p. 395: "Caussam vero horum ne inquiramus, multo minus inesse aliquid iniquitatis in iudiciis Dei suspicemur. Ipsa Dei voluntas Deo caussa est omnium et ea ipsa est iustitia."

36. Ibid., pp. 399, 404.

37. Cajetan, *Epistolae Pauli*, p. 65: "Nihil enim aliud ex authoritate Paulus intendit, nisi quod hinc apparet, quod non ex operibus nostris, sed ex voluntate Dei eligentis, et vocantis unus eligitur et alter reprobatur."

38. Ibid., p. 65: "Solutio est quod deus ab aeterno vere quosdam eligit et quosdam odio habet: pro quanto quibusdam ab aeterno vult conferre opem gratiae suae et adiuvare illos usque ad gloriam aeternam, quosdam autem ab aeterno quoque vult permittere sibiipsis, nec adiuvare eos gratuito auxilio quod electis decrevit conferre. Et hoc est deum illos odio habere, hoc est deum reprobare illos non ex operibus."

39. Ibid., p. 65: "Cum quo tamen stat quod nullus damnatur nisi ex propriis operibus. Nec sententia siquidem nec executio damnationis fit antequam huiusmodi reprobi peccent."

40. Ibid., p. 67v: "Quocirca ad curiositatem dico illa esse vera ex parte divinae electionis seu reprobationis, sed non esse vera sola, sed associata aliis veritatibus ex parte nostri, scilicet quod sumus liberi arbitrii, quod faciendo quod ex nobis est erimus per divinam gratiam salvi, et quod nostris meritis salvamur aut damnamur nos adulti."

41. Politus, *Commentaria*, p. 96: "Sunt enim qui recte quidem sentiunt de re ipsa, et facile confitentur praedestinationem non esse ex meritis bonis, sed a gratia. Reprobationem autem non posse esse nisi ex meritis malis."

42. Ibid., p. 96: "Sed ipsi interim ad hunc locum non respondent, ubi sicut de Iacob dicitur, illum non quia fecerit aliquid boni, electum fuisse: Ita de Esau, non quia fecerit ipse aliquid mali, esse odio habitum, ac per hoc reprobatum."

43. Ibid, p. 97: "Hic certe odium non accipitur pro odio vero, nisi ut postponatur pater et mater Deo."

44. Ibid, p. 97: "Non me latet alia de causa Esau tenuisse reprobatorum typum: non quidem ex nativitate, sed ex improbitate sua, et pravitate."

45. Bucer, *Metaphrases*, pp. 397–99, 407.

46. Ibid., p. 400: "Recte itaque Thomas Aquinas liberum arbitrium, voluntatem intelligit qua eligimus, quod ratio consultatione conducibilius esse deprehendit et arbitrata est."

47. Ibid., p. 400.

48. Ibid., p. 400: "Atqui caussa prima non excludit actionem caussarum secundarum."

49. Ibid., p. 400: "Qui utique eius actu res cognoscimus, eligimus, amplectimur, fugimus, corporis vires admovemus."

50. Ibid., p. 404. I am in agreement with Stephens, *Holy Spirit*, p. 261, when

he observes Bucer's discussion of free choice: "Similarly, the use of the term will, considered as free, when one speaks of man's psychological co-operation in his salvation, should be distinguished from its use as bound or enslaved, when one speaks of man's inability to do anything for his salvation theologically."

51. Ibid., p. 401.

52. Ibid., p. 410.

53. Ibid., p. 409.

54. Ibid., p. 410.

55. Calvin, *Commentarius*, pp. 204–5. See, especially, p. 205: "Haec ergo sit nobis sancta observatio, nequid de ipsa scire appetamus, nisi quod Scriptura docet: ubi Dominus sacrum os suum claudit, viam quoque ultra pergendi mentibus nostris praecludamus."

56. Ibid., p. 199.

57. Ibid., p. 200.

58. Ibid., p. 201.

59. Ibid., p. 202.

60. Ibid.

61. Ibid., p. 203: ". . . Deum in suo arbitrio satis iustam eligendi et reprobandi habere causam."

62. Ibid., p. 209.

63. Ibid., p. 210.

64. Ibid., p. 208.

65. Ibid., p. 212: "Secunda responsio, qua breviter demonstrat, etiamsi incomprehensibile sit hac parte Dei consilium, elucere tamen inculpatum eius aequitatem, non minus in reproborum interitu, quam salute electorum."

66. Ibid., p. 206: "Hoc autem oraculo declaravit Dominus, se nemini mortalium esse debitorem: gratuitae esse beneficentiae quicquid illis [tribuerit]: deinde hanc beneficentiam liberam esse, ut eam erogaret, cui placeret."

67. Ibid., pp. 212–13.

68. Ibid., pp. 211–12.

69. Ibid., p. 212.

70. Ibid., pp. 208–9. See, for example, p. 209: "Porro nequis imaginetur, quodam universali et confuso motu Divinitus actum fuisse Pharaonem, ut in illum furorem rueret, notatur specialis causa, vel finis."

71. Ibid., p. 209.

72. Ibid., p. 214.

73. Ibid., p. 220.

74. Ibid., p. 213.

11

Calvin and the Baptism of John

In the fourth book of his *Institutes* (IV.xv.7–8, 18), John Calvin defended the proposition that the baptism offered by John the Baptist and the baptism offered by Peter and Paul were exactly the same. While Calvin hinted that there had been disagreements about the status of John's baptism in the early church, he did not mention the substantial body of medieval tradition on this topic or the ferocious controversy over John's baptism conducted by Huldrych Zwingli and Balthasar Hubmaier in 1525. He alluded in passing and without attribution to a point characteristic of Zwingli's position against Hubmaier, but without giving his readers any sense that this issue had figured prominently in an intra-Protestant debate.[1]

Yet the question of the status of John's baptism was an issue of some importance in the sixteenth century. John the Baptist stands between the two testaments and a number of crucial issues intersect in him. How one views the role of John in the gospel narratives affects in important ways how one views the nature of the history of salvation, the character of the sacraments, and the validity of infant baptism.

I

In his commentary on the *Sentences* of Peter Lombard (*Sent.* IV d.2 q.2), the fifteenth-century Catholic theologian, Gabriel Biel, summarized the main lines of medieval tradition on John's baptism.[2] The question Lombard raised and Biel elaborated in three articles is whether people who had been baptized with the baptism of John were required to be rebaptized with the baptism of Christ. Biel's first article was devoted almost wholly to a clarification of terms: What was meant by the baptism of John?[3] Who were the disciples of John who appeared to need rebaptism?[4] Could one draw a distinction between different kinds of rebaptism?[5]

Biel observed that the New Testament was always very careful to label the baptism of John with his own name. That fact is remarkable when one considers that no one would think of calling baptism administered by the apostles by their names. Their baptism is always called the "baptism of Christ." Only John's baptism is singled out for special treatment.

Medieval theologians could think of several reasons why this might be so. First of all were the historical reasons. John was the first promulgator and the sole minister of his baptism.[6] None of his disciples baptized and the ceremony terminated with his death.

More important still were the theological reasons. Nothing finally took place in John's baptism of which John was not the author.[7] John washed the bodies of his disciples as a sign of penitence for sin, but he was unable to wash their sins away. The weakness of John's baptism was traceable to a defect in its form.[8] John did not baptize in the name of the Trinity, but in the unspecified name of one who was to come. Unless the proper form (the name of the Trinity) is joined to the proper matter (water), no sin is remitted *ex opere operato* (on the basis of the performance of the rite).

Biel reported the opinion of Durand of St. Pourçain who thought that John did not use a form at all when he baptized.[9] Durand had argued that since the power of a sacrament depends on its form, the weakness of John's baptism could only be explained by an absence of form. While Biel did not endorse Durand's image of silent splashings in the Jordan, he did not reject it out of hand. However one explained it, defective form or absent form, something was amiss with John's baptism.[10] If John had baptized in the proper form (which he could have learned from the disciples of Jesus), then his baptism would have been called the baptism of Christ and there would have been no problem of two baptisms to resolve.

Peter Lombard had tried to draw a distinction between the two classes of John's disciples.[11] The first group, described in Acts 19, lacked any knowledge of the Trinity and placed their hope for salvation in the baptism administered by John. These people were obviously proper candidates for rebaptism by the apostles. The second group, mentioned in Acts 8, saw the baptism of John in relation to Christ and shared with the apostles a common faith in the Trinity. There was no need to subject this second group to rebaptism and they were given the Holy Spirit by the imposition of hands.

Biel viewed Lombard's distinction with distaste and observed that later theologians had unanimously rejected it.[12] The disciples of John were not divisible into two groups because the baptism of John did not suffice for salvation. Lacking the proper form, it was not a sacrament in the sense of an efficacious sign of grace. The faith of John's disciples was never really at issue. No amount of piety on the part of John's disciples could overcome the unavoidable defect in the essential composition of his baptism. All of John's disciples, whether they professed faith in Christ or not, were fit candidates for rebaptism by the church.

Biel did think, however, that one should distinguish between "rebaptize" and "baptize with a repeated baptism."[13] Since John's baptism was not a true baptism in the sense of its ability to wash away sins, the disciples of John were rebaptized but not with a repeated baptism. Water was applied twice; water joined to the proper form only once.

If it is true that the baptism of John did not contain grace, was not properly a sacrament, and did not absolve the disciples of John from the obligation to be rebaptized with the baptism of Christ, why on earth was it instituted?[14] What conceivable purpose did it serve? The question is more than a little embarrassing, since the New Testament plainly asserts that John was sent by God to preach and baptize.

Biel conceded that the baptism of John was a sacrament in the loose, though not the strict, sense of the term. It was a sign of a sacred thing; it was a figure of the baptism of Christ. But it would probably be more accurate and certainly less confusing to call it sacramental (a sign that depends for its power on the piety of the recipient) rather than a sacrament (a sign that infallibly communicates grace). In this way John's baptism prepared his disciples for the grace offered through the baptism of Christ.[15]

The principal role of the baptism of John was to serve as a transitional step between circumcision in the Old Testament and the baptism of Christ in the New. John recalled the Jews from reliance on circumcision and so signaled the end of the Old Testament. By offering water as a sign of penitence, John prefigured the new sacramental dispensation of the church. Since water was not joined to the proper form in his baptism, it was powerless to absolve sinners from the guilt and punishment of their sins. Nevertheless Biel regarded it as a step forward in the history of salvation to have consecrated and used the matter, if not the form, of the baptism of Christ.[16]

II

The earliest Protestant controversy over the baptism of John was a paper war conducted by Huldrych Zwingli, the principal minister of Zurich, and his former colleague, Dr. Balthasar Hubmaier, an Anabaptist and a onetime student of the Roman Catholic controversialist John Eck. The controversy broke out in May 1525, raged for about six months, and subsided in November 1525, almost as suddenly as it had erupted. Zwingli had provoked the controversy by attacking the medieval tradition on John's baptism in his *Commentarius de vera et falsa religione*.[17]

Zwingli argued that there was no significant difference between the baptism of John and the baptism of Jesus.[18] They were the same not merely in matter (no one was prepared to dispute this claim) but also in form.[19] John, no less than Peter and Paul, taught his disciples to place their hope in Christ and anyone who put on Christ in John's baptism was dedicated and bound to the Trinity. Not only were the disciples of John not rebaptized but even the disciples of Jesus who were sent out to baptize were first baptized with the baptism of John.[20] One must either admit that Peter was baptized with John's baptism and not rebaptized or concede that the chief of the apostles was unbaptized.

Zwingli challenged the traditional reading of Acts 19, which was cited by medieval theologians as a basis for drawing a sharp distinction between the two baptisms. The New Testament draws a different distinction— namely, between baptism as teaching and baptism as the application of water. The disciples of John at Ephesus had received baptism in the sense of water, but they had not received baptism in the sense of adequate teaching. Paul gave them better instruction and so led them into Christ.[21]

The theological foundation on which medieval scholasticism distinguished the baptism of Jesus from the baptism of John—namely, that the former conferred grace *ex opere operato* while the latter did not—was dismissed by Zwingli. Zwingli did not claim that both baptisms were efficacious signs of grace (which would, of course, have been one way to equalize them) but denied that either was. John's baptism did not confer grace *ex opere operato*; but, then, neither did the baptism of Jesus.[22]

The principal meaning of baptism for Zwingli in his *Commentarius* seems to be summed up in its role as the sign of a changed life.[23] Baptism signifies that a Christian is bound to a new life and will confess Christ until death. In that sense Zwingli can accept the medieval definition of baptism as a sign of a sacred thing.

Zwingli continued his attack on the medieval consensus in *Von der Taufe, von der Wiedertaufe und von der Kindertaufe*, though he broadened his attack by opening up a second front against the Zurich Anabaptists, whom he regarded as equally muddled in their treatment of John's baptism.[24] Zwingli's starting-point was his assertion that baptism is a sign, but only a sign. It is a covenant sign or pledge like the white cross of the Swiss confederation.[25] It should never be confused with the thing signified, as the scholastics do when they claim the waters of baptism contain or convey grace. No material or external thing can justify.[26] Grace remains in God's power, who gives it to the faithful by an immediate and invisible act. The flesh (that is, the world of material signs and symbols) profits nothing; it is the Holy Spirit who makes one alive. To place one's confidence in external rites and ceremonies is to lapse, willy-nilly, into idolatry.

Zwingli offered four definitions of baptism. Depending on its context, the word *baptism* could be used to signify "water," "Spirit," "teaching," or "faith," separately or in any combination.[27] In the ordinary course of events, Christians receive baptism in all four senses, though it is not necessary that the four baptisms coincide and, indeed, improbable that they will. One can receive water and teaching before one receives faith and the Spirit. The New Testament does not stipulate that these four baptisms occur in any particular order.[28] Baptism in the sense of water can be given to children before they have faith, as cowls can be given to novices in a monastic order before they learn the full significance of the discipline they have embraced.[29] The New Testament does not require faith before baptism and neither should right-thinking Christians.

The distinction of four possible meanings of baptism was important for Zwingli's interpretation of Acts 19.[30] Unless he could show that the disciples of John were not subjected to rebaptism (and he could do that only if there were some ambiguity in the meaning of the term *baptism*), he would have been hard-pressed to defend his argument that there was no essential difference between the baptism of John and Jesus. Failure here would have resulted in the collapse of his whole argument.

Zwingli was serenely confident that his exegesis of Acts 19 was sound and that his chain of reasoning stood in no immediate danger of refutation. Indeed, he attacked the medieval position even more vigorously and with greater gusto than he exhibited in his *Commentarius*. Zwingli argued that the medieval tradition of the proper form was theologically unsound and rested on very shaky underpinnings. Medieval theology treated the formula of baptism in the name of the Trinity as though it were a kind of white magic, a formula of incantation. One could justly conclude from the arguments of scholastic theologians that they had forgotten that the power of baptism does not reside in human words, however orthodox, but in a transcendent God who is not bound by human speaking and acting.[31]

On the exegetical question whether the baptism of John involved the whole Trinity, Zwingli believed that it did and cited the Johannine account of the baptism of Jesus as proof of the trinitarian character of John's baptism: the Father spoke, the Son was baptized, and the Spirit descended like a dove.[32] Moreover, it was not clear to Zwingli that the disciples of Jesus always baptized their converts with what medieval theologians regarded as the proper form. There is ample evidence that they frequently baptized in the name of Jesus alone.[33] If so, it is very difficult to see how John, who baptized in the name of the Lamb of God who takes away the sins of the world, administered a baptism in any way inferior to the baptism administered by the apostles. It is not enough to claim that John's baptism was merely a baptism of repentance, because, according to the New Testament, so was the baptism of Jesus.

Attempts to plead the obsolescence of John's baptism on the basis of a particular understanding of the history of salvation were also doomed to failure. John was not a type of Christ and should not be reckoned with the Old Testament.[34] He offered a baptism that was not limited to his own lifetime but that continues in the church up to the present day. Whenever the church points to the Lamb of God and administers the covenant sign of water as the pledge of a new life, it celebrates anew the baptism of John. It is not stretching a point to say that to follow Christ at all is to be baptized by John.[35]

Zwingli had by this time managed to challenge every major point made by medieval theological tradition on the baptism of John. He had also, in passing, challenged the emerging Anabaptist theology insofar as early Anabaptists wanted to distinguish sharply between the two baptisms and argue (as medieval theologians did not) for the fixed sequence of teaching, faith, and baptism by the Holy Spirit prior to baptism by water. Even though Zwingli's major target was the medieval theology of baptism, it was the Anabaptist theologian, Balthasar Hubmaier, rather than a conservative Catholic who first felt impelled to respond to him.

Hubmaier's response, *Von der christlichen Taufe der Gläubigen*, was published in the middle of the summer.[36] He struck hardest at what he regarded as the weakest point in Zwingli's argument, his exegesis of Acts 19.[37] From Hubmaier's perspective, the equation of baptism with teaching was an illusion sprung from Zwingli's overfertile imagination. Baptism by water is a public confession and testimony of an inward faith and commitment.[38] As such, it is always preceded by, but never synonymous with, the teaching of the Word of God and the response of faith. Zwingli was wrong to deny such a fixed order in the New Testament. The New Testament invariably moves from teaching and preaching to faith and baptism.[39] Indeed, because faith is always and without exception prior to baptism, the rite should never be administered to children.[40]

Hubmaier identified John with the law and the Old Testament. He was unmoved by Zwingli's argument that John preached the gospel. As Hubmaier understood John the Baptist, his preaching was filled with the curse of the law, sin, death, devil, and hell.[41] Small wonder that John sent his disciples away to follow Christ.[42] Jesus was the physician of souls, not John. John only prepared his listeners for a consolation he did not himself offer.

For Hubmaier water baptism was necessary to salvation as an expression of obedience to Christ.[43] Christ's baptism did not remit sins *ex opere operato*

(Hubmaier agreed with Zwingli in opposing such a claim) but because of the inward yes of the heart to the proclamation of the gospel (*ex fide recipientis*).[44] Hubmaier brushed aside Zwingli's claim that the baptism of John and Jesus were the same. Everyone baptized by John must be rebaptized by Christ. John was a preacher who drove sinners to Christ, not an apostle who administered Christ's baptism.

There was, however, one aspect of John's baptism that Hubmaier regarded rather wistfully as he pushed John's baptism back into the sphere of the Old Testament. John, after all, did not baptize children.[45] His baptism was restricted to adults who felt guilt for their sins and could make an outward public confession of faith. Hubmaier was convinced that such a restriction, characteristic of John's baptism, should be normative for Christ's baptism as well. But he had seriously weakened his case by drawing an absolute contrast between the two baptisms. If analogies were not permissible elsewhere in considering the two baptisms, why should one suddenly be allowed here?

Zwingli was infuriated by Hubmaier's tract and published his own *Antwort über Balthasar Hubmaiers Taufbüchlein* in November 1525. Zwingli regarded Hubmaier's argument about two baptisms as irresponsible chatter that flew in the face of the Pauline assertion that there is one Lord, one faith, one baptism (Eph. 4:5).[46] If Paul was right, then the baptism of Jesus and John were the same. If he was wrong, then Hubmaier faced a Hobson's choice of distasteful alternatives.[47] Either John's baptism was worthier than the church's, since Christ received it rather than the baptism offered by the apostles, or every Christian should be baptized twice, first with John's baptism for repentance and then with Christ's for forgiveness. In the end there cannot be two baptisms for Zwingli because there is an identity between John and the church at a central point—the preaching of the gospel.[48] John stood beside the Jordan and cried: "Behold the Lamb of God who takes away the sins of the world!" What apostle ever preached a better gospel than that?

Hubmaier replied—rather good-humoredly under the circumstances— with his own *Gespräch auf Zwinglis Taufbüchlein*. He was unmoved by Zwingli's arguments and clung to the point he made earlier concerning the distinction between the two baptisms: the baptism of John signified the confession of sins; the baptism of Christ signified their forgiveness.[49] That this was not just a contrast of sufficient and insufficient baptisms became clear when Hubmaier associated the baptism of John with fear, devil, hell, and death, and the baptism of Christ with comfort, Spirit, heaven, and life.[50] Hubmaier was not the least disturbed by Zwingli's angry charge that he had remained bogged down in the traditional views of John.[51] If anything, he took pleasure in claiming support for his position in the writings of Origen, Cyril, Theophylact, Chrysostom, and Jerome.[52]

Hubmaier agreed with Zwingli that the practices of medieval monasticism provided at least one useful analogy to illumine the meaning of baptism. But whereas Zwingli compared baptism with the assumption of a cowl by a novice, Hubmaier focused on the monastic vow.[53] As a monk vows to live according to the rule of Benedict or Francis, so a Christian vows in baptism to live according to the rule of Christ.

In short, Hubmaier wanted to preserve the medieval tradition of two baptisms in the service of a new and untraditional theology of believer's baptism. He refused to accept what he regarded as Zwingli's ingenious, but finally unconvincing, explanation of the four meanings of the verb, "to baptize."[54] John had an important role in the history of salvation, but it was not the role of an apostle. To linger by the baptism of John is to remain in the obsolete world of the old covenant.

III

The first indication of Calvin's attitude toward the controversy over John the Baptist can be found in his 1536 edition of the *Institutes*.[55] Calvin agreed with Zwingli that the ministry of John the Baptist and the apostles was "exactly the same." There was no difference between their baptisms because they taught the same doctrine: "both baptized to repentance, both to the forgiveness of sins, both into the name of Christ, from whom repentance and forgiveness of sins came."[56]

If that is so, then how does one explain the statement of John that he baptizes only with water, while Christ baptizes with the Holy Spirit and fire? The comparison, Calvin replied, was not between two baptisms but between two persons. John was comparing himself to Christ. John was only a minister of water; Christ alone was the minister of the Holy Spirit. The situation of John was exactly analogous to the situation of the apostles. They offered an outward sign, whereas Christ effected an inward grace. Furthermore, what was true of John the Baptist and the apostles remains true of Christian pastors today. The church administers the outward sign, Christ alone the inward grace.[57] When pastors baptize, they do so in unbroken continuity with John the Baptist.

Calvin differed with Zwingli in his approach to Acts 19 and the story of the baptism of the disciples of John. Calvin was aware of Zwingli's argument that John's disciples were not rebaptized with water when they were "baptized in the name of Jesus" but only given "baptism" in the sense of proper instruction in apostolic doctrine.[58] But he was also aware of the force of the argument directed against such a solution. If the baptism of John and Jesus were the same, and if the disciples of John had been wrongly instructed at the time of their baptism, then their baptism without true doctrine counted for nothing.[59] In such circumstances Paul quite properly rebaptized them with water, since their first water baptism was invalid.

Calvin agreed with Zwingli that John's disciples in Ephesus had not been not rebaptized with water but disagreed with his argument that they had merely been instructed in true doctrine. Calvin's solution was to suggest that "baptism in the name of Jesus" referred in that passage to baptism by the Holy Spirit. Luke in his narration of this incident is following a Hebraic rhetorical device of first summarizing and then offering a fuller explanation. The summary statement, "they were baptized in the name of Jesus," is followed by the fuller explanation, "when Paul had laid hands on them, the Holy Spirit descended upon them." (4.22) Baptism refers in this context to "the visible graces of the Spirit given through the laying on of hands."[60]

In his commentaries on John (1553), the Synoptics (1555), and Acts (1552, 1560), Calvin repeated and expanded positions he had taken in his early *Institutes*.[61] In his commentary on John 1:26–31, for example, Calvin argued that John the Baptist claimed Christ as the author of his baptism. John administered the outward sign, but the power of baptism was in the hands of Christ alone. In this respect John was no different from any Christian minister.[62] Calvin believed the same point was made by Matt. 3:11, Mark 1:7, and Luke 3:15.[63]

In his commentary on Acts 19:1–7, Calvin elaborated but did not otherwise modify the position he had taken earlier. Acts 19 is not about regeneration but about the special gifts and charisms God gives for the edification of the church.[64] The disciples of John had been regenerated by the Holy Spirit and validly baptized but were ignorant of the spiritual gifts that Calvin called "the principal glory of the gospel."[65] When they claimed that they knew nothing of the Holy Spirit, they meant (by metonymy) that they knew nothing of the spiritual gifts distributed to the church by the Spirit.[66]

Their ignorance was, of course, quite easy to understand. Although John preached Christ, the graces distributed to Christ's followers were much fewer in John's time than later. After Christ was glorified, gifts of the Spirit were distributed in great profusion to the church.[67] That John's disciples in Ephesus were ignorant of that fact did not mean that they had not been properly baptized with water. The Anabaptists were in error when they claimed that John's disciples had never received the baptism of Christ and required rebaptism at the hands of Paul.[68] What John's disciples lacked was a baptism of gifts from the Spirit through the laying on of hands. The name of baptism was transferred to the gifts of the Spirit.

Calvin added one cautionary note to his interpretation. By shifting emphasis from the external rite of baptism to the external act of laying on of hands, Calvin did not want to give support to the Catholic sacrament of confirmation, which supplements the rite of baptism administered by a priest with a second rite administered by a bishop. While there was a sense in which the laying on of hands was a sacrament, it was a sacrament restricted to the apostolic age.[69]

In the final Latin edition of the *Institutes* (1559), Calvin summed up his teaching on John the Baptist. He reiterated his thesis that the ministry of John was the same as the ministry of the apostles (IV.xv.7). Both baptized to repentance (which Hubmaier conceded) and to the forgiveness of sins (which he denied). Calvin rejected the position of John Chrysostom (cited by Hubmaier against Zwingli) that denied the forgiveness of sins to John's baptism, since in his judgment Luke's Gospel (3:3) clearly affirmed the contrary. Calvin even rejected the "subtle reasoning" of Augustine, who contrasted John's baptism with Christ's as a remission of sins in hope (*in spe*) with a remission in reality (*in re*). The sole difference between John and the apostles was that John baptized in the name of him who was to come, while the apostles baptized in the name of one who had already revealed himself.

Calvin used Acts 8 as the key to unlock the meaning of Acts 19 (IV.xv.8). Acts 8 tells the story of Samaritans who had been baptized in the name of Jesus during Christ's earthly ministry. Yet they did not have a greater abundance of the gifts and graces of the Spirit than did the disciples of John the Baptist. Only after the resurrection and ascension of Christ did they receive a larger measure of the Spirit through the laying on of hands by Peter and John. In the same way the disciples of John in Ephesus received the graces of the Spirit reserved for Christ's disciples when Paul laid hands on them. To be baptized in the name of Jesus meant in the context of Acts 19 to be given the visible graces of the Spirit by the laying on of hands (IV.xv.18).

Although the disciples of John were ignorant of the fuller gifts of the Spirit, their ignorance did not invalidate their baptism. If ignorance vitiates baptism, then the apostle would have had to have been rebaptized, who in three years "had scarcely tasted a tiny fragment of purer doctrine." Indeed, if ignorance vitiates baptism, "what rivers would suffice" to rebaptize Christ's ignorant disciples in the contemporary church (IV.xv.18). Calvin thus ends his argument in 1559 where he began it in 1536, by affirming the substantial identity of the baptism of John and Christ.

IV

Zwingli is not usually studied against the background of late medieval scholasticism. There are good reasons for this neglect, which we need not go into here. But while Zwingli was not so well trained in scholastic theology as Luther or Hubmaier, he was not entirely ignorant of it, as his polemic on the baptism of John clearly demonstrates. Zwingli knew the scholastic tradition on John in intimate detail and rejected it point by point. His rejection was radical, far more radical in fact than Hubmaier's, and utterly unnostalgic. Zwingli resisted vehemently any attempt to drive a wedge between Jesus and John on the question of baptism, even when the purpose of such an attempt was the thoroughly admirable desire to stress the uniqueness of the saving activity of God in Christ.

Hubmaier, on the other hand, preferred to fish in the familiar coastal waters of late medieval religious thought. Zwingli was exactly right when he pointed out this conservative streak in Hubmaier's Anabaptist theology. Hubmaier was radical on the question of John's baptism only in the sense that he intensified tendencies already present in late medieval thought. He sharpened the split between John and Jesus by placing John in the Old Testament as a preacher of the curse of the law. Medieval theology took the gentler position that John was a transitional or intermediate figure between the two testaments.

In one sense and one sense only did Hubmaier concede the superiority of John to the Old Testament prophets. The prophets could only preach Christ as one who was to come, while John could point directly toward him with his finger. Still the difference between them did not make John a preacher of the gospel. John fulfilled the pedagogical function of the law. He was a stern schoolmaster who drove his reluctant pupils to Christ.

Calvin agreed with Zwingli that there was no difference between John's baptism and the baptism of Christ and that John's disciples in Ephesus were not rebaptized by Paul. However, he resisted Zwingli's attempt to divide baptism into four loosely joined parts. For Calvin, baptism by water and baptism by the Holy Spirit were bound tightly together. The gospel proclaims a message that baptism seals. Whoever receives baptism with right faith is grafted into Christ. "Just as the twig draws substance and nourishment from the root to which it is grafted," so baptized men and women experience the effective working of Christ's death and resurrection.[70]

From Calvin's perspective, the disciples of John in Ephesus did not lack knowledge of the gospel, faith, baptism by water, or regeneration by the Holy Spirit. They had already been grafted into Christ by John's baptism. What they lacked was the fuller gifts and charisms of the Spirit. According to Acts 19, those gifts were offered to them through the imposition of Paul's hands.

Nevertheless, the differences between Calvin and Zwingli should not be allowed to obscure their far more important agreements. From the standpoint of medieval theology, Zwingli and Calvin placed the baptism of Jesus and John on the same level, partly by raising the baptism of John and partly by lowering the baptism of Christ. They elevated the baptism of John by insisting that John preached the gospel and offered the same baptism as the apostles. They lowered the baptism of Christ by arguing that it conferred no grace *ex opere operato*.

Calvin, like Zwingli and Hubmaier before him, was forced to deal with John the Baptist because of his redefinition of baptism. Medieval theology, with its settled definitions of the sacraments, had a carefully allotted place for John; Protestant theology, with its new definitions of faith and the sacraments, did not. The new theological definitions had to do more than satisfy the rational test of internal self-consistency; they had to make sense of the exegetical data of the Bible.

It was impossible for Calvin and his contemporaries to talk about John for very long without making clear their vision of the history of salvation and the relationship between the two testaments. Zwingli's tendency was to lessen the distance between the Old Testament and the New in order to justify analogies between circumcision and infant baptism. It was impossible to do this if there was already a sharp division within the New Testament itself between Jesus and John the Baptist. Hubmaier's tendency was to increase the distance between the testaments in order to stress the uniqueness of the saving activity of God in the New Testament and to stifle the arguments for infant baptism at their source. In pressing his case he gladly made use of arguments from his own Catholic past.

Like Zwingli and unlike Hubmaier, Calvin lessened the distance between the testaments. In doing so, he was motivated by a vision of one people of God in an unbroken history stretching from Abraham to the present. In order to defend such a vision he attacked the medieval Catholic tradition of discontinuity on his right and the Anabaptist reaffirmation of it on his left. John was a symbol for Calvin of the continuity of the two testaments and the unity of the people of God in time. The argument over John was passionate because the issue finally at stake was the validity of that vision.

NOTES

1. *Inst.* IV.xv.18: "Quidam interpretantur, tantum sincera doctrina eruditos a Paulo fuisse: . . ."

2. References to Biel's commentary are from the critical edition by Wilfrid Werbeck and Udo Hoffmann, *Collectorium circa quattuor libros Sententiarum*, Vol. IV/1 (Tübingen: J.C.B. Mohr, 1975).

3. Biel, IV *Sent.* d.2 q.2 a.1 nota. 1, pp. 106–9.

4. Biel, IV *Sent.* d.2 q.2 a.1 nota. 2, pp. 109–11.

5. Biel, IV *Sent.* d.2 q.2 a.1 nota. 3, p. 111.

6. Biel, IV *Sent.* d.2 q.2 a.1 nota. 1, p. 106.

7. Biel, IV *Sent.* d.2 q.2 a.1 nota.1, p. 107.

8. Biel, IV *Sent.* d.2 q.2 a.1 nota.1, p. 108.

9. Biel, IV *Sent.* d.2 q.2 a.1 nota.1, p. 108.

10. From Biel's perspective, both opinions were equally probable. See Biel, IV *Sent.* d.2 q.2 a.1 nota.1, p. 109.

11. Biel, IV *Sent.* d.2 q.2 a.1 nota.2, p. 109.

12. Biel, IV *Sent.* d.2 q.2 a.1 nota.2, p. 111.

13. Biel, IV *Sent.* d.2 q.2 a.1 nota.2, p. 111.

14. Biel, IV *Sent.* d.2 q.2 a.3 dub.1, p. 106.

15. Biel, IV *Sent.* d.2 q.2 a.3 dub.1, p. 117.

16. Biel, IV *Sent.* d.2 q.2 a.3 dub.1, p. 117.

17. Christof Windhorst, in his admirable study of Hubmaier's theology, makes a brief attempt to place the controversy between Hubmaier and Zwingli in the context of medieval theology, but restricts his discussion to the teaching of Peter Lombard. See Christof Windhorst, *Täuferisches Taufverständnis, Balthasar Hubmaiers Lehre zwischen traditioneller und reformatorischer Theologie*, Studies in Medieval and Reformation Thought 16 (Leiden: E.J. Brill, 1976), pp. 65–68.

18. Citations from the *Commentarius* are taken from the edition by M. Schuler and J. Schulthess, *Huldrici Zuinglii Opera*, III (Zurich, 1832), abbreviated as SS III. Zwingli says, SS III.234: "Quid vero distent Joannis Baptismus et Christi, multa tum olim tum nunc est quaestio; sed inutilis plane, nam discrimen omnino nullum est, quod ad causam ac finem attinet: quamvis quod ad usum sive formam attinet non nihil discriminis sit."

19. SS III.236: "Quibus adparet, Christum per ministros suos non alia ratione aut forma baptizavisse, quam qua Joannes baptizabat: name si secus baptizavisset, non potuissent hoc omittere Joannis discipuli." Cf. Zwingli, SS III.239.

20. SS III.236.

21. SS III.237–39.

22. SS III.234: "Nihil efficiebat Joannis tinctio: loquimur autem hic de aquae Baptismo, non de irrigatione interna quae per spiritum sanctum fit. Nihil efficit Christi tinctio: nam Christus Baptismo Joannis contentus fuit, tam in se quam in discipulis."

23. SS III.239.

24. The text of this and the remaining Zwingli treatises are found in the edition of Emil Egli et al., *Huldreich Zwinglis Sämtliche Werke* 4, CR 91 (Leipzig, 1927), abbreviated as ZW 4.

25. ZW 4.218.

26. ZW 4.217.

27. ZW 4.219–20.

28. ZW 4.222–25.

29. ZW 4.231: "Für das erst ist der touff ein pflichtig zeichen, das en, er inn nimpt, anzeigt, das er sin leben bessren und Christo nachvolgen welle. Kurtz, es ist ein anhab eines nüwen lebens, und ist also ein anheblich zeichen, ceremonii oder teleta uff griechisch. Glych als wenn die jungen sind in die örden gestossen, hat man inen die kutten angeschroten; noch habend sy die gsatz und statuten nit gewüsset, sunder sy erst erlernet in der kutten."

30. ZW 4.268–77.

31. ZW 4.267. For an illuminating treatment of Zwingli's concept of the freedom of God with respect to the sacraments, see Carl Leth, "Signs and Providence: The Eucharistic Theology of Huldrych Zwingli," (Ph.D. diss., Duke University, 1991).

32. ZW 4.267.

33. ZW 4.236.

34. ZW 4.259–60.

35. ZW 4.266: "So er [Christus] aber imm touff Johansen getoufft ist, so müssen ouch wir im touff Johansen getoufft werden."

36. References to Hubmaier's works are from the critical edition by Gunnar Westin and Torsten Bergsten, *Schriften*, Quellen zur Geschichte der Täufer 9 (Gütersloh: Gerd Mohn, 1962), abbreviated as HS.

37. HS.131–33.

38. HS.121–22.

39. HS.134–39.

40. Hubmaier rejects Zwingli's use of monastic imagery as an analogy for infant baptism, though he later introduces a monastic analogy of his own, HS.138: "Dann wie die angeschroten kutten meyn Münch macht und nicht nütz ist, sonder wider Gott geschicht, also macht der kinder tauff keyn Christen, fahet keyn new leben an, geschicht wider die eynsetzung des tauffs Christi."

41. HS.124, 127.

42. HS.126–27.

43. HS.140–46.

44. HS.137.

45. HS.125: "Da würdt aber gesehen, das Johannes nit junge kinder getäufft hat, sonder die, so sich jrer sünden schuldig gaben und erkanten." Cf. HS.127–34.

46. ZW 4.598.

47. ZW 4.598.

48. ZW 4.598–99.

49. HS.196: "Yetz hörstu, das der Tauff Joannis nichts anders ist, denn ein offenlich zeügknuss vor den Menschen im Wasser, das sich der Mensch bekennt ein Sünder vor Gott. Mat. 3. Herwiderumb so ist der Tauff Christi ein offenliche unnd éusserliche bekandtnus oder Ayd des glaubens (das ist, das der Mensch inwendig glaub verzeyhung seiner Sünden durch Christum), der halb er sich ein schreyben last und eüsserlich verzaichen under die Christen, dz er wöll nach der Regel Christi leben."

50. HS.197.

51. HS.196: "Gott sey gelobt das wir nit allain Saturnich lätzkopff seind, wir du unns nennst, sonder all Theologi met uns, dich ausgenommen."

52. HS.197.

53. See, for example, n. 49 above.

54. HS.197: "Jch waiss doch nit ainen leerer jung oder alt auf erden, der dir in disem schweren, mercklichen unnd verfierischen Jrsal bey gsteende, das du redst, predigest und schreibst, Joannis tauff und der Tauff Christi sey ain tauf."

55. Citations from the 1536 edition of the *Christianae Religionis Institutio* are from the critical edition of Peter Barth and Wilhelm Niesel, *Ioannis Calvini Opera Selecta* 1 (Munich: Christian Kaiser Verlag, 1926), abbreviated as OS 1.

56. OS 1.129: "In unam doctrinam Ioannes et apostoli consensuerunt; utrique in poenitentiam, utrique in remissionem peccatorum, utrique in nomen Christi, a quo poenitentia et peccatorum remissio esset, baptisarunt."

57. OS 1.129.

58. OS 1.135: "Quidam interpretantur, tantum sincera doctrina eruditos a Paulo fuisse; . . ."

59. OS 1.134: ". . . ita baptismus ille, qui sine vera doctrina fuit, pro nihilo reputandus est, et ex integro baptisari debemus in veram religionem, qua nunc primum imbuti sumus."

60. OS 1.135: ". . . sed simplicius intelligere malim, baptismum spiritus sancti, hoc est, gratias spiritus visibiles per manuum impositionem datas, quas baptismi nomine significari non novum est."

61. For the Latin text, see John Calvin, *Commentarius in Evangelium Ioannis*, CO 47 (Braunschweig: Schwetschke et Filium, 1892); *Commentarius in Harmonium Evangelicum*, CO 45 (Braunschweig, 1891); and *Commentarius in Acta Apostolorum*, CO 48 (Braunschweig, 1892).

62. CO 47.23–24.

63. CO 45.121–24.

64. CO 45.440: "Clausula historiae ostendit non de spiritu regenerationis, sed de specialibus donis, quae Deus initio evangelii in communem ecclesiae aedificationem quibus visum erat varie distribuit, hic a Paulo haberi sermonem."

65. The phrase is "summam evangelii gloriam." *CO* 48.440.

66. CO 48.440–41.

67. CO 48.441.

68. CO 48.442.

69. CO 48.442–43.

70. OS 1.129.

12

Calvin and His Lutheran Critics

Among the non-Lutheran theologians of the sixteenth century, none was more reluctant to disagree with Martin Luther or more eager to find common ground with him than John Calvin. At the colloquy between Roman Catholic and Protestant theologians held at Regensburg in 1541, Calvin, recently accredited as a delegate from Strasbourg, aligned himself with Philip Melanchthon and the Lutheran party by signing the Augsburg Confession, an action that provoked unfavorable comment among some non-Lutheran theologians. As late as 1554, John Haller of Bern criticized Calvin for his excessive partisanship on behalf of Luther and Bucer.[1] It was a reputation that Calvin did very little to dispel.

Calvin's support of Luther, however, was not unqualified. In the first edition of his *Institutes of the Christian Religion* (1536), Calvin, who had modeled his *Institutes* on Luther's *Smaller Catechism*, criticized Luther's doctrine of the Lord's Supper, repudiating especially his doctrine of the ubiquity of Christ's body. Luther taught that the body of the risen Christ was no longer subject to the limitations of space and time and so could be present to believers in, with, and under the consecrated elements of bread and wine. Calvin agreed with Luther's opponent, Huldrych Zwingli, that Christ assumed a finite humanity, which remained finite even after his resurrection and ascension. The body of Christ, like every human body, "has a fixed dimension, is contained in a place, is touched," and "seen."[2]

Calvin's agreement with Zwingli on the finite character of the risen and ascended humanity of Christ did not translate into a general enthusiasm for Zwingli's theology. Calvin regarded Zwingli as a second-rate theologian and ridiculed the esteem in which he was held at Zurich. Though Calvin read and cited Zwingli's important treatise, the *Commentary on True and False Religion*, he confessed that he was put off by Zwingli's reliance on philosophy, his excessive use of paradox, and his confusion of the universal concerns of the gospel with the parochial interests of the Swiss.[3] While Calvin believed that Zwingli was correct to oppose Luther's doctrine of ubiquity, he deplored Zwingli's failure to teach that the eucharistic bread and wine are not bare signs of the absent body of Christ, but signs to which the reality of Christ's saving presence is conjoined.[4] In Calvin's view, Zwingli had avoided one error only to tolerate another.

In the *Consensus Tigurinus*, written in 1549 and published in 1551, Calvin and Zwingli's successor at Zurich, Heinrich Bullinger, attempted to bridge their disagreements by confessing that sacraments are "instruments by which God acts efficaciously when he pleases" and not simply signs of God's invisible and unmediated activity.[5] To be sure, their joint confession is hedged with qualifications intended to quiet Zwinglian fears that too much has been conceded to external rites and ceremonies. For example, the *Consensus* insists that sacraments are powerless to confer grace apart from the action of God, who alone effects what the sacraments figure.[6] Nevertheless, Calvin and Bullinger were able to agree that sacraments are "instruments", "signs," "helps," and "seals" (*organa, signa, adminicula, sigilla*) God uses to offer "Christ with all his gifts . . . to all in common."[7] In careful language that corrects what Calvin had regarded as Zwingli's chief error, the *Consensus* distinguishes between signs and things signified without disjoining the reality offered to faith from the signs that offer it.[8]

Ironically, not every Lutheran theologian read the *Consensus Tigurinus* as a confession that moved Reformed theology away from Zwingli's original position and closer to Luther. The Lutheran pastor at Hamburg, Joachim Westphal (1510–1574), struck by the undeniably Zwinglian elements in the *Consensus*, concluded that Calvin had abandoned Luther entirely in favor of Zwinglianism.[9] Westphal's charges were echoed by Tilemann Hesshusen (1527–1588), a Lutheran pastor and theologian who had opposed the introduction of Reformed theology at Heidelberg.[10]

In 1560 Hesshusen published the first of a series of polemical treatises against Calvin, *De Praesentia Corporis Christi in Coena Domini, contra Sacramentarios* ("On the Presence of the Body of Christ in the Lord's Supper, against the Sacramentarians").[11] The book summarizes what Hesshusen considered the heart of the Lutheran case against Calvin's eucharistic theology. His passionate attack evoked from Calvin a crisp and eloquent response, *Dilucida Explicatio Sanae Doctrinae de Vera Participatione Carnis et Sanguinis Christi in Sacra Coena, ad Discutiendas Heshusii Nebulas* ("The Clear

Explanation of Sound Doctrine concerning the True Partaking of the Flesh and Blood of Christ in the Holy Supper, to Dissipate the Mists of Tilemann Hesshusen").[12] Because this candid exchange comes so late in the controversy between Calvin and his Lutheran critics, it takes the informed reader with refreshing directness to the issues that divided them.

I

Hesshusen alternates his assault on Calvin's position with a spirited defense of Lutheran eucharistic theology against charges leveled against it by a succession of Reformed theologians from Huldrych Zwingli at Zurich to Wilhelm Klebitz at Heidelberg.[13] He dismisses as unfounded their complaint that Lutheran theologians have abandoned the eucharistic teaching of the New Testament and returned to the Roman Catholic doctrine of transubstantiation.[14] Transubstantiation is the doctrine of real presence adopted by the Catholic church at the Fourth Lateran Council in 1215. According to this doctrine, the substance of the eucharistic bread and wine is transformed by priestly consecration into the substance of the body and blood of Christ, while the accidents or sensible qualities of bread and wine remain unchanged. Hesshusen agrees with Luther who rejected transubstantiation and taught that the real presence of Christ in the eucharist did not imply a real absence of the substance of the bread and wine. Christ is present in, with, and under—not in place of—the bread and wine.

No less unacceptable to Hesshusen is the doctrine of consubstantiation, since consubstantiation implies a personal, natural, or formal union of the elements of bread and wine with the body and blood of Christ, on the analogy of the hypostatic union of Christ's divine nature with his human nature.[15] Hesshusen prefers to think of the mode of Christ's presence as extraordinary, divine, and incomprehensible, on the analogy of the presence of the Holy Spirit in the dove who descended on Christ in his baptism. Just as the Holy Spirit once employed the external, visible form of a dove in order to witness to his presence, so Christ repeatedly uses the eucharistic elements in order to represent through visible bread and wine his invisible body.[16]

Since Hesshusen rejects both transubstantiation and consubstantiation, he dismisses the claim of Calvin that Lutherans adore the consecrated bread and wine. It is certainly true that Roman Catholics adore the sacrament after consecration and routinely place the consecrated host in a monstrance, where it serves as an object of private devotion. But Lutherans adore the sacrament neither during the eucharistic service (*in usu*) nor as an object of private veneration after the service is ended (*extra usum*).[17] Because the real presence of Christ in the eucharist implies neither a metabolic change in the bread and wine nor a union of Christ with them, Hesshusen repudiates the adoration of the creaturely elements of bread and wine. The real presence of Christ is not, in the last analysis, a local presence.

To explain what he means by denying that the real presence of Christ in the bread and wine is a local presence, Hesshusen appeals to a distinction in Luther's theology between definitive, repletive, and local (or circumscriptive) presence. According to Luther, an object is locally present when its dimensions correspond exactly to the dimensions of its container, as a liter of wine fills a liter bottle. Luther uses the term *repletive presence* to describe the universal and encompassing presence of God, who fills heaven and earth with his presence without being contained by them or dissolving them into himself.

However, as Luther understands the New Testament, the presence of Christ in the eucharist is neither local nor repletive, but definitive.[18] An object is definitively present when its dimensions, however defined, do not correspond to the dimensions of its container. For example, when the risen Christ passed through a locked door in order to show himself to his disciples, his body was briefly present in the door, though without assuming its proportions. By his momentary and uncircumscribed passage through an alien substance Christ was definitively present.

The risen humanity of Christ has the same relationship to space and time as God does. Just as any attempt to explain the presence of God in our space and time according to geometric rules is doomed to failure, so, too, is any attempt to quantify or measure the risen body of Christ.

> We say that God is no such extended, long, broad, thick, high, deep being. He is a supernatural, inscrutable being who exists at the same time in every little seed, whole and entire, and yet also in all and above all and outside all created things. There is no need to enclose him here, as this spirit dreams, for a body is much, much too wide for the Godhead; it could contain many thousand Godheads. On the other hand, it is also far, far too narrow to contain one Godhead. Nothing is so small but God is still smaller, nothing so large but God is still larger, nothing is so short but God is still shorter, nothing so long but God is still longer, nothing so broad but God is still broader, nothing so narrow but God is still narrower, and so on. He is an inexpressible being, above and beyond all that can be described or imagined.[19]

Luther combined the notion of definitive presence with his doctrine of the ubiquity of the risen body of Christ to show how Christ could be definitively present in the elements of bread and wine. The risen Christ is present (*da*) in all bread and wine, including the—as yet—unconsecrated elements; but Christ is inaccessible (not *dir da*) until the word of promise, joined to the elements, offers Christ to faith. Unlike Calvin, Luther understood the problem of the divine transcendence, not as a problem of distance, but as a problem of inaccessible immanence.

Surprisingly, Hesshusen, who is keen to follow the authority of Luther in all dogmatic questions, denies Luther's doctrine of ubiquity.[20] In fact, what Hesshusen offers as a genuinely Lutheran explanation of the eucharistic presence of Christ appears virtually indistinguishable from Calvin's.

Like Calvin, Hesshusen denies what the doctrine of ubiquity seems to imply; namely, that the risen flesh of Christ has taken on divine attributes.[21] The human nature of Christ remains finitely human even in its union with the divine. While Hesshusen is willing to affirm Christ is omnipresent, he does so by appealing to the union of the two natures in Christ, thus predicating of the whole Christ, including the human nature, what is, strictly speaking, true only of the divine nature.[22] By stressing predication based on personal union (what theologians call the communication of attributes *in concreto*), Hesshusen echoes the position of Calvin.[23]

But there the similarities between them end and the differences begin to multiply. Calvin concludes from his denial of ubiquity that the humanity of Christ cannot exist simultaneously in multiple places, since simultaneous multiplicity is an attribute of divinity alone. Hesshusen, on the other hand, concludes that a denial of the ubiquity of the body of Christ does not imply a denial of the presence of the human nature of Christ wherever and whenever God wills it to be present.[24] The rejection of natural ubiquity does not entail for him the rejection of ubiquity by will. Whereas Luther taught that Christ was present in unconsecrated bread and wine (*da*) but inaccessible (not *dir da*), Hesshusen teaches that Christ is neither present nor accessible until the promise of Christ's presence is claimed and enacted in the eucharistic service. Once that is done, however, there is no limit to the number of places where the body of Christ may be simultaneously present.

On the whole, Hesshusen finds Bullinger and Oecolampadius more palatable than Calvin because he regards them as theologically more candid.[25] Like Zwingli, Bullinger and Oecolampadius teach that Christ cannot be substantially present in the elements of bread and wine because Christ's finite risen humanity is at the right hand of God the Father. While Christ can be present to the church in the power of his divine nature, the elements of bread and wine cannot do more than signify his body and blood. The eucharist is therefore only a symbol of the absent body and blood, which are spatially contained in a specific place in heaven.

Unlike Bullinger and Oecolampadius, Calvin scrambles to show that he dissents from Zwingli's position. To that end he insists on what he calls the spiritual eating of the body of Christ.[26] Unfortunately Calvin's effort to distance himself from Zwingli does not impress Hesshusen, who regards such talk as disingenuous. Whatever differences Calvin may have with the Zwinglians, he agrees with them when they teach that the finite humanity of Christ is seated at the right hand of God the Father and therefore cannot be substantially present in the elements of bread and wine. When Calvin talks about the presence of the body of Christ in the eucharist, he means the efficacy, virtue, power, merit, grace, and spirit of the humanity of Christ.[27] Spiritual eating is participation in those benefits by faith.

Against Calvin and the Calvinist doctrine of spiritual eating, Hesshusen confesses that the substance of the body and blood of Christ is received not only by faith, but bodily by the human mouth, and not only by believers, but even apart from faith by the ungodly and unworthy.[28] This affirmation of the *manducatio infidelium*, participation in the body of Christ by unbelievers, is regarded by Hesshusen as an unavoidable conclusion from the doctrine of the eucharistic real presence of Christ. Unless the body of Christ is really present for both, for unbelievers as well as believers, it is really present for neither. *Manducatio infidelium* marks an essential, ineradicable difference between authentic Lutheran teaching and the crypto-Zwinglian doctrine of Calvin.

When Calvin calls the eucharist the body and blood of Christ, he is speaking figuratively, calling the sign by the name of the thing signified.[29] Calvin uses metonymy and speaks figuratively because any other usage is impossible for him. Since the finite humanity of Christ is at the right hand of God and since this local presence cannot be overcome, even by the omnipotent will of God, the bread and wine are and must remain nothing more than empty signs of an absent body and blood.[30] From Hesshusen's perspective, Calvin rejects the Lutheran *est* and clings to the Zwinglian *significat*.

At several points in his argument, Hesshusen accuses Calvin of advocating theological Epicureanism.[31] The term *Epicureanism* conjures up several images in the sixteenth century, none of them flattering when applied to Christian theology. Epicureans deny the providential involvement of God in the world, are skeptical of assertions not grounded in verifiable sense data, adopt the majority religion as a matter of convenience, and tend to devalue human interest in an afterlife. Although Hesshusen does not explain exactly what he has in mind when he levels this charge, he seems to have primarily in view what he regards as Calvin's faithless rationalism.[32] Calvin and the Zwinglians do not embrace with simple faith the words of Jesus, "this is my body," but like the ancient Epicureans prefer to judge these words on the basis of sense and experience.[33]

Finally, Hesshusen contests the claim of Calvin and the Zwinglians to have Patristic authorization for their eucharistic theology and engages in a battle over the correct interpretation of ancient Christian texts from Tertullian to Augustine.[34] The debate, which ranges over a long catalog of disputed texts, is an important one, but too lengthy and complex to be summarized here.

II

Calvin denies that he ever accused Hesshusen or the Lutheran party of teaching transubstantiation.[35] He is, however, not persuaded by Hesshusen's disclaimer with respect to the adoration of Christ in the eucharist. If Lutherans do not adore the consecrated host, as Hesshusen alleges, they show themselves to be less consistent than Roman Catholics, who correctly perceive that the real presence of Christ in the bread requires worship and adoration by the faithful. To protest that Christ is not hypostatically united to the bread and wine is to draw a theoretical distinction that makes no practical difference. If the body of Christ is present in, with, and under the bread and wine, it should be adored in, with, and under the bread and wine.[36] To say otherwise is to fly in the face of the logic of one's own position.

The heart of the difference between Calvin and Hesshusen, as Calvin sees it, is the quarrel over the mode of Christ's presence in the eucharist.[37] Hesshusen accused Calvin of regarding the eucharist as the sign of an absent body, with the clear implication that no one can hold to the real presence of Christ in the eucharist who agrees with Zwingli that the body of Christ is seated at the right hand of God in heaven. Calvin concedes that the risen, but still finite, body of Christ is locally, though not circumscriptively, present in heaven and therefore withdrawn from our space and time. But he denies that this admission binds him to accept the absence of the body of Christ from the eucharist. Christ is really present, though absent from sight, because the distance between heaven and earth has been surmounted by his boundless power.[38]

Calvin offers four ways in which the distance between the believer and the ascended humanity of Christ can be overcome. The first means for bridging the distance between heaven and earth depends not so much on the descent of Christ as on the ascent of the believer.[39] When Christians participate in the eucharist they ascend in the ecstasy of faith to the right hand of God, where they contemplate the risen Christ, seated at the right hand of God the Father. The spiritual experience of believers, the *sursum corda* of their faith is one, though by no means the most important, ladder linking heaven and earth.

More important for Calvin than the spiritual ecstasy of faith is the threefold descent of Christ by his virtue, Spirit, and divine nature. By *virtue* Calvin means the boundless power of Christ for our salvation.[40] Calvin is willing to concede that the substance of the body of Christ is present in the eucharist, if the word *substance* is properly defined.[41] The substance of the body of Christ is not veins and sinews, but rather the power and effect of Christ's crucified and risen humanity for the redemption of the world. Christ is substantially present in the eucharist when he bridges the chasm between heaven and earth by his boundless redemptive power.

Christ descends from heaven to earth, not only by his boundless power, but also by his Spirit.[42] Since Calvin regards the Holy Spirit as the Spirit of the Son as well as of the Father, he converses readily about the presence of Christ in the church by the Spirit. Because Christ's Spirit is not limited by space and time, as Christ's finite humanity is, it can bridge all distances between heaven and earth, including the distance between the right hand of God and the eucharist. Where the Spirit of the Lord is present, there Christ is present.

However, the presence of Christ's benefits and Spirit, even if conceded by the Lutherans, does not appear to answer the objection of Hesshusen that the risen and ascended body of Christ is still absent from Calvin's eucharist. As Hesshusen sees it, Calvin calls the bread and wine the body and blood of Christ by metonymy, giving the name of the thing signified to the sign that signifies it, because he has no other eucharistic real presence to offer.

Calvin brushes aside Hesshusen's charge as crude and ill-founded. The Holy Spirit appeared at the baptism of Jesus in the form of a dove. One could call the dove by metonymy the Holy Spirit, giving the name of the thing signified to the sign that represents it. To do so, however, does not mean that only a symbolical Spirit was present at Christ's baptism.[43] Just as metonymy does not exclude spiritual real presence at the baptism of Jesus, so, too, it does not exclude spiritual real presence in the Lord's Supper.

Calvin's problem is to explain how the humanity of Christ, though absent from the bread and wine in one sense, is nevertheless present in another. Calvin's explanation involves the invocation of two christological principles. The first principle is one that Tilemann Hesshusen has already invoked—namely, the union of two natures in Christ. The divine nature of Christ is omnipresent; the human nature is not. Nevertheless, wherever Christ's divine nature is present, it is present as a nature indissolubly united to Christ's humanity. To encounter Christ's divine nature is not to encounter a discarnate, disembodied deity. Therefore, wherever Christ is present, both natures are present, even though the finite humanity of Christ is seated at God's right hand. This point can be restated as Calvin's second principle—namely, that the whole Christ can be present even where Christ is not wholly present (*totus Christus sed non totum*).[44]

Though the body and blood of Christ are really offered to the church in the eucharist, they can only be received by faith. Calvin rejects the doctrine of *manducatio infidelium* defended by Hesshusen. It is inconceivable to Calvin that Judas received the body and blood of Christ when he received the elements at the Last Supper.[45] Unbelievers are not united to Christ by the bonds of mystical union nor do they participate in the benefits of his death and resurrection.

By denying the *manducatio infidelium*, Calvin does not mean to deny that Christ is really offered in the eucharist to the entire gathered congregation, believers and unbelievers alike. Christ with all his benefits is offered in the eucharist to men and women without distinction. In that sense Calvin agrees with Hesshusen and the medieval Catholic tradition that the real presence of Christ is not dependent on human faith. On the other hand, Christ, who is offered to all, is authentically received only by believers. Unlike Hesshusen, Calvin draws a sharp distinction in his eucharistic theology between what is offered and what can be received.[46]

Calvin appears mystified by Hesshusen's rejection of spiritual real presence and spiritual eating. The alternative for Calvin to spiritual real presence and spiritual eating is physical real presence and physical eating. As Calvin understands Hesshusen's position, Christ is taken with the mouth, chewed with the teeth, digested by the stomach, and eliminated from the bowels. When Hesshusen angrily replies that he teaches no such thing, Calvin dismisses his response as disingenuous.[47] Christ is either received physically or spiritually. *Tertium non datur.*

From Calvin's perspective, the Lutheran doctrine of the eucharist rests on three absurdities: the distinction of definitive from local presence (which Hesshusen affirms);[48] the doctrine of the ubiquity of the body of Christ (which Hesshusen denies in principle but admits in practice);[49] and the notion of physical reception of the body of Christ (which Hesshusen accepts with certain qualifications).[50] Christ does not pass through the door (as Luther and Hesshusen contend in their defense of definitive presence), but simply appears in the room with his disciples. Christ's body is not ubiquitous, either in Luther's or Hesshusen's sense, unless one wishes to contend that Christ has a monstrous, inhuman body, in no way similar to ours. Christ is not chewed by the teeth (as Westphal, that new Berengarius, proclaims)[51] or even taken by the mouth (as Hesshusen argues),[52] but is offered to the mouth of faith.[53]

Calvin is particularly incensed by Hesshusen's charge that he is an Epicurean.[54] What Hesshusen seems to advocate, from Calvin's perspective, is a cessation of all theological inquiry. Hesshusen wants believers to grasp with simple faith the words of Jesus, "this is my body," and to abandon further theological examination of these words.

The Bible, however, offers repeated accounts of theophanies, manifestations of God under sacramental signs, that cry out for theological explanation. What is meant, for example, by Jacob's vision of the invisible God seated on a ladder or by Moses' vision of God present in a burning bush?

How can the same God be both visible and invisible? Hesshusen, says Calvin, "repudiates examination, and leaves us no other resource than to shut our eyes and acknowledge that God is visible and invisible."[55] Proper theological inquiry, however, demonstrates that "God is never seen as he is, but gives manifest signs of his presence adapted to the capacity of believers."[56]

When Hesshusen attempts to mimic Luther by decrying reason, he only succeeds in revealing his theological confusion. In his general condemnation of human reason, Hesshusen fails to distinguish between three kinds of reason: (1) "reason naturally implanted," which "cannot be condemned without insult to God"; (2) "vitiated reason," which subjects the self-revelation of God to human judgment and arrogance; and (3) "reason . . . derived from the Word of God," which grounds its point of view in the teaching of Scripture.[57] This third form of reason, reason derived from the Word of God, is antithetical to the judgments of vitiated reason, but not to faithful theological inquiry.

Calvin includes in his reply to Hesshusen a brief response to his interpretation of ancient Christian texts from Justin Martyr to Augustine. On the whole, one can say that wherever Hesshusen stresses texts that support the physical real presence of Christ in the eucharist, Calvin counters with a reading or a text that distinguishes spiritual reality from physical sign. While Calvin claims that "it is very well known to the whole world that our doctrine is clearly approved by the consent of the primitive Church"[58] and that it is therefore "intolerable impudence for Heshusius to represent himself as an imitator of the fathers,"[59] he is perfectly willing to correct ancient Christian writers by the still more ancient standard of Holy Scripture and to claim "how much better" his "case is than the case of the fathers."[60]

III

In the short treatise, *Optima ineundae concordiae ratio, si extra contentionem quaeratur Veritas* ("The best method of obtaining concord provided the Truth be sought without contention"), which Calvin appends to his longer essay against Hesshusen, Calvin describes the original controversy over the Lord's Supper as a controversy between Lutherans who alleged "that the grace of the Spirit was tied to external elements" and Zwinglians who contended "that only bare and empty figures like theatrical shows were left."[61] In Calvin's view, "this contention has now ceased."[62] The controversy between Lutherans and non-Lutherans is no longer over the fact of real presence, which is conceded by Calvin and the Zwinglians alike, but over the mode of eating.[63]

Hesshusen's repeated attempt to freeze the debate between Lutherans and non-Lutherans at 1529 and to ascribe to Calvin the positions of Zwingli at the Marburg Colloquy is therefore doomed from the start. The quarrel between Calvin and Hesshusen over the eucharist is not a simple continuation of the disagreement between Luther and Zwingli. While Calvin agrees with many of the points made by Zwingli in 1529, especially Zwingli's insistence on the importance of the ascension of Christ for eucharistic theology, he is opposed to what he regards as Zwingli's devaluation of the bread and wine as a means of grace. Calvin agrees with Luther that the reality offered to faith cannot be disjoined from the signs that offer it. Although he is not prepared to abandon altogether the place of figurative language, he devotes his principal attention in the controversy with Hesshusen to the explication of the reality of Christ's presence. "When I say," writes Calvin,

> that the flesh and blood of Christ are substantially offered and exhibited to us in the Supper, I at the same time explain the mode, namely that the flesh of Christ becomes vivifying to us, inasmuch as Christ, by the incomprehensible virtue of his Spirit, transfuses his own proper life into us from the substance of his flesh, so that he himself lives in us, and his life is common to us. Who will be persuaded by Heshusius that there is any sophistry in this clear statement?[64]

By the same token Hesshusen is not prepared to adopt Luther's eucharistic theology without modification. He finds particularly troubling Luther's doctrine of the ubiquity of the body of Christ, a doctrine that seems to him to endanger the integrity of the two natures of Christ. For Luther, the question is how Christ who is already present, even in unconsecrated bread and wine, can be present for me. For Calvin, as for Hesshusen, the question is how Christ who is absent in his finite humanity can bridge the distance between heaven and earth with his saving presence. Hesshusen differs with Calvin over how this question should be answered but not how it should be framed.

On the other hand, Hesshusen is correct to argue that Calvin's position, whatever else it may be, is not identical with Luther's. Calvin does not mean by the substance of the body of Christ what Luther means. Indeed, he seems at times to imply by his formulations a closer tie to Luther's position than in fact exists. If it is wrong of Hesshusen to characterize Calvin's position as the doctrine of a real absence of the body of Christ, it is equally wrong of Calvin to claim that his formulations of Christ's real presence are unambiguous.

The fact that the dispute between Calvin and Hesshusen is not a repristination of the debate between Luther and Zwingli at Marburg nearly thirty years earlier does not mean that it is entirely irrelevant or that Calvin and Hesshusen failed to identify correctly the questions that separated them. It does mean, however, that historians should not be misled by Hesshusen's attempt to view his debate with Calvin through the narrow lens of Marburg or to identify Calvin's position with the already discredited position of Zwingli. Geneva in 1560 is not Marburg in 1529, as Hesshusen perfectly well knows, and Calvin is not a disingenuous Zwingli.

In the end, it seems to me that Calvin has identified the shift correctly. No one who signed the *Consensus Tigurinus*, certainly not Calvin himself, is willing to defend the thesis that sacraments are "only bare and empty figures." The disagreement between Lutheran and Reformed theologians is not over the fact of the real presence of Christ in the eucharist, but its mode. Westphal and Hesshusen have every right to disagree with Calvin and to reject his interpretation of the real presence of Christ as inadequate. What they have no right to do is to deny that the mode of the real presence is the issue in dispute.

NOTES

1. For a brief treatment of Calvin's relationship to Luther, see François Wendel, *Calvin: Origins and Development of His Religious Thought*, trans. Philip Mairet (Durham, N.C.: Labyrinth Press, 1987), pp. 131–35. See also David C. Steinmetz, *Luther in Context* (Bloomington: Indiana University Press, 1986), pp. 85–97.

2. OS 1.142.

3. Wendel, *Calvin*, pp. 135–37.

4. OS 1.528–29.

5. OS 2.250.

6. See, especially, articles 12–14, 17. OS 2.249–51.

7. See articles 9, 12, 13, 15, 18. OS 2.249–51.

8. OS 2.249.

9. Joachim Westphal, *Apologia Confessionis de Coena Domini contra Corruptelas et Calumnias Ioannis Calvini* (Oberursel: Nicolaus Henricus, 1558).

10. The best study of Hesshusen's early career is Peter F. Barton, *Um Luther's Erbe: Studien und Texte zur Spätreformation*, Untersuchungen zur Kirchengeschichte 6 (Witten: Luther Verlag, 1972). Still important is Johann Georg Leuckfeld, *Historia Heshusiana* (Quedlinburg and Aschersleben: Gottlob Ernst Struntzen, 1716).

11. The first edition was published under this title in 1560. However, I have cited here the Magdeburg edition of 1561 published under the shorter title *De Praesentia Corporis Christi in Coena Domini* (Magdeburg, 1561). The preface was dated at Heidelberg, October 20, 1559. Because *De Praesentia* is less easily accessible than the relevant texts of Calvin, I will give, where appropriate, citations from Hesshusen's Latin text.

12. John Calvin, *Dilucida Explicatio* (Geneva: Conrad Badius, 1561). References to the Latin text are to CO 9.

13. Hesshusen alludes to Wilhelm Klebitz without mentioning him by name in the preface to *De Praesentia*, pp. 10–11. In a later treatise, *Verae et Sanae*

Confessionis: De Praesentia Corporis Christi in Coena Domini, Pia Defensio (Erfurt: Esaias Mechlerus, 1583), Hesshusen attacks Klebitz under the unflattering pseudonym, Kleinwitz. Klebitz himself attacks Hesshusen in the treatise, *Victoria Veritatis ac Ruina Papatus Saxonici* (Freiburg: Daniel Delenus, 1561). For the quarrel between Hesshusen and Klebitz at Heidelberg, see Barton, *Um Luther's Erbe*, pp. 196–225.

14. Hesshusen, *De Praesentia*, pp. 28–29.

15. Ibid., pp. 30–31.

16. Ibid., p. 31: "Ita dicimus, invisibile domini corpus, per visibilem panem repraesentari, sed unionem personalem non fingimus."

17. Ibid., p. 33.

18. Ibid., p. 32.

19. WA 26.339–40.

20. Hesshusen, *De Praesentia*, p. 34: "Cum igitur naturae in Christo maneant distinctae: non dicimus humanum carnem esse ubique, aut divinae essentiae esse parem."

21. Ibid., p. 34.

22. Ibid., p. 35: "Christus est ubique, scilicet communicatio idiomatum, id est, divinitas est ubique, et propter unionem duarum naturarum hypostaticam alterius naturae proprietas toti personae in concreto attribuitur."

23. According to Barton, *Um Luther's Erbe*, p. 231, Hesshusen abandons this position in 1574 in his *Adsertio Sacrosancti Testamenti*, written while he was bishop of Samland against the Calvinizing *Exegesis Perspicua*: "Non tantum in concreto recte dicitur: Christus est omnipotens, vivificus, adorandus—sed etiam in abstracto recte dicitur: humanitas Christi est omnipotens, vivificanda, adoranda."

24. Hesshusen, *De Praesentia*, p. 38: "Non igitur absurdum est, fateri Christum etiam quoad humanam naturam in diversis locis existere posse, ubicunque vult, et se suo verbo alligavit. Ita et de sancta coena adfirmamus, Christi corpus, quod est in coelo, et ad dexteram Dei patris logô unitum sedet, nihilominus in terra locis etiam diversis edendum distribui, non solum quoad efficatiam: sed etiam quoad substantiam. Non movemur, etiamsi philosophia et ratio hic offenduntur.

25. Ibid., p. 26, 46. Hesshusen repeatedly complains that Calvin and the Reformed use misleading language. For example, in *Grundliche Beweisung der waren Gegenwart des Leibs und Bluts Iesu Christi im heiligen Nachtmahl, sampt Widerlegung der furnembsten Behelff und Ungründe der Calvinisten* (Helmstedt: Jacob Lucius, 1586/1587), pp. 10–10v, Hesshusen writes: "Denn wenn sie also sagen, wir werden des waren und wesentlichen Leibs Iesu Christi im heiligen Nachtmahl theilhafftig, das verstehen sie also, das die substantia des Leibs Christi zwar droben im Himel bleibet, und bey uns auff Erden nicht sey, ader seines Verdiensts, das der Leib für uns gestorben ist, seiner Krafft und Wirckung, seines Geists und Lebens werden wir theilhafftig geistlich durch den Glauben. . . . Wer mit Zwinglianern und Calvinisten will reden, der mus stets einen Dolmetscher bey im haben, der im die Wort auslege."

26. Hesshussen, *De Praesentia*, p. 26: "Sacramentum vero illud esse signum et symbolum absentis corporis. Calvinus quidem valde laborat, ut videatur a Cinglio dissentire, et aliquanto plus dicere. Ac multis verbis de spirituali manducatione

declamitando, ita rudem lectorem involuit, ut minus exercitato difficile sit dijudi-
care, utrum probet sententiam, Cinglii ne, an Lutheri. . . . Si quis attendat, evi-
denter deprehendit Calvinum quibuscunque verborum involucris sese occultare
conetur, idem tamen cum Zwinglio docere, videlicet, coenam domini esse symbolum absentis corporis et sanguinis Christi, definito loco in coelo comprehensi."

27. Ibid., p. 27: "Adfirmamus etiam in coena, in et cum pane, vere et substantialiter sumi verum Christi corpus, quod pro nobis in mortem est traditum: non
solum quoad virtutem, efficatiam, potentiam, vigorem, vim, gratiam, spiritum,
seu meritum: sed etiam, quoad essentiam carnis attinet." Cf. ibid., p. 48: "Calvinus
adserit, vere, et substantialiter edi et bibi corpus et sanguinem Christi: sed si
mentem eius respicias, loquitur de praeceptione meriti, fructus, efficatiae, virtutis,
et potentiae e coelo defluentis."

28. Ibid., p. 27: "Nec fide solum a sanctis, sed etiam ore corporaliter, sine fide
ab impiis, et indignis, id est, malis Christianis."

29. Ibid., pp. 173, 175.

30. Ibid., p. 150: "Ergo hoc corpus, quod in coelo certo spacio circumscribitur,
non potest esse in coena domini, quoad substantiam." Cf. ibid., pp. 171–72: "Ergo
in coena non ipsum corpus, sed tantum symbolum absentis corporis Christi
exhibetur."

31. Ibid., pp. 11, 143.

32. Hesshusen may also interpret Calvin's reluctance to embrace the Lutheran
understanding of real presence as an Epicurean reluctance to affirm the active intervention of the omnipotent power of God in nature and history. See, for example,
De Praesentia, p. 71: "Fundamenta quidem huius sententiae nota, et plana sunt,
nimirum, testimonia de immensa Dei potentia, qua eiusmodi praestat, quae non
solum humani ingenii captum, sed omnium quoque angelorum sapientiam, et
acumen longe superant. Deinde, quod scimus, ac credimus Deum veracem esse.
Ac in negotio religionis, cognita voce Dei, nihil amplius quaerendum esse, sed ipsius
verbo simpliciter adsentiendum."

33. Ibid., p. 183: "Quis vero pius animus non abhorreat ab hac petulanti audacia
Epicureorum, qui sciant doctrinam Ecclesiae discrepare prorsus a iudicio humano,
ut suam diffidentiam, et Epicureas cogitationes domestico testimonio prodant:
varias obiiciunt absurditates, quae nos comitentur, si ratione in servitute redacta,
nudo Dei verbo nos adsentiri profiteamur."

34. Ibid., pp. 104–38.

35. CO 9.473.

36. CO 9.473, 516–17.

37. CO 9.519.

38. CO 9.508–9. Calvin refuses to equate local with circumscriptive presence
because the right hand of God is "not a place, but the power which the Father has
bestowed upon Christ to administer the government of heaven and earth." Christ
is therefore present wherever his reign extends. That means his human nature, which
is "withdrawn in respect of bodily presence," is nevertheless present in the eucharist
because of the hypostatic union. The "divine majesty and essence of Christ fills
heaven and earth, and this is extended to the flesh."

39. CO 9.476–77, 523–24.
40. CO 9.508.
41. CO 9.521.
42. CO 9.487.
43. CO 9.472.
44. CO 9.475–76, 507.
45. CO 9.477.
46. CO 9.476–77.
47. CO 9.477–78.
48. CO 9.474.
49. CO 9.475, 520.
50. CO 9.477–78.
51. CO 9.469.
52. CO 9.469–70.
53. CO 9.472.
54. CO 9.468, 515–16.
55. CO 9.471.
56. CO 9.471–72.
57. CO 9.474.
58. CO 9.490.
59. CO 9.480.
60. CO 9.488.
61. CO 9.517.
62. CO 9.517.
63. CO 9.517.
64. CO 9.470.

13

Calvin and the Monastic Ideal

Let my readers accordingly remember that I have spoken rather of monasticism than of monks, and noted not those faults which inhere in the life of a few, but those which cannot be separated from the order of living itself.[1]

With these words Calvin indicates that his criticisms of monasticism are not primarily directed against the failure of individual monks to live up to the ideals they profess, but against the institution and ideology of monasticism as such. That does not mean, of course, that Calvin is reluctant to criticise the faults of individual monks. "No order of men," he complains, "is more polluted by all sorts of foul vices."[2] "You will scarcely find one [monastery] in ten which is not a brothel rather than a sanctuary of chastity."[3] Monks are "ignorant asses," plagued by pharisaical pride and hypocrisy, who lay claim to a learning they do not have.[4] They are false prophets who obscure the clarity of the gospel with specious arguments sprung from the human brain.[5] They are idlers who regard themselves as a regular order, but who are regarded by God as irregular and disorderly.[6] Although Calvin concedes that there may be some good monks left in the various houses, they form a scattered and hidden band, a *vestigium purioris ecclesiae* in an institution which is otherwise hopelessly corrupt.[7]

Nevertheless, in spite of Calvin's energetic criticism of monastic abuses (a criticism which does not in the main distinguish between communities of monks and friars), his principal energies are concentrated in an assault on the institution itself, especially on its intellectual foundations. In order to understand the force of Calvin's critique of monasticism, it may be useful to place his criticism in the context of medieval debates over the status of the religious life.

I

The thirteenth-century theologian, Thomas Aquinas (d. 1274), argued vigorously for the monastic life as a state of perfection. Thomas did not mean to assert that all monks are in fact perfect or that it is impossible for secular priests or laity to attain perfection. Monks are in a state of perfection only because they have put themselves under obligation by their vows to strive for perfection in love.[8] It is the vow and the obligation which it entails that marks the crucial difference between the status of a monk and the status of a secular priest or layperson.[9]

Monks do not tread the only path to perfection, but they do walk a better way. Fundamental to this belief is Thomas's understanding of the distinction between commands and counsels.[10] The old law, the law of Moses, which the Church now recognizes after the advent of Christ to be a law of bondage, contained only commands, such as the prohibition of theft or murder. The new law, however, the law of liberty, contains both commands and counsels, including the counsels to embrace celibacy and voluntary poverty. While all Christians are summoned to obey the commands, the religious have obligated themselves by a vow to follow the evangelical counsels as well. The counsels make it easier to attain perfection; therefore mendicant friars (like the Dominicans in Thomas's own order) find themselves in a more advantageous position in the quest for holiness.

There is, of course, another sense in which one may be in a state of perfection. Bishops are in a state of perfection as well as monks, not because they are obligated by their vows to the quest for sanctity, but because they are obligated by their ordination to a perpetual cure of souls.[11] Bishops are in a state of perfection by virtue of their *cura animarum perpetua*. Their task is to lead others to perfection.[12] Ordinary priests, who for Thomas are only bailiffs of the bishop, are not obligated to a perpetual cure of souls and are therefore not in a state of perfection.[13] The very fact that they may be released from the cure of souls without the permission of their bishop to become monks—as a bishop may not without the permission of the pope—is proof for Thomas that the state of perfection is only a status for monks and bishops.[14]

Theoretically Thomas gives preeminence to bishops when he concludes that "the state of perfection is more potent and perfect in prelates and bishops than in the religious."[15] Against this theoretical preeminence of bishops must be set such practical monastic advantages as the greater meritoriousness of their good works. Thomas affirms, and that affirmation is hotly contested by John Pupper of Goch, that good works performed because of a vow are higher and more meritorious than other works.[16] He holds this view because he believes that a vow is an *actus latriae*, the highest of the moral virtues and can therefore confer an additional dignity on good works that result from it.[17]

Furthermore, monks who profess vows undergo a second baptism.[18] Thomas does not go as far as some later theorists who press the analogy of baptism and monastic vows to the extent of believing that the monk has been forgiven both the guilt and penalty of his postbaptismal sin. Vows only alleviate the penalty of sin through the obligation of a perpetual satisfaction. But profession of a monastic vow places monks in a higher spiritual state than priests and laity. All Christians have died to sin through baptism. Monks have died through the second baptism of their vows, not only to sin, but also to the world. Since only a few secular priests become bishops whereas all monks by reason of their vows are in a state of perfection, the overall impact of Thomas's argument is to stress the advantages enjoyed by the mendicant orders in comparison with the secular priesthood.

II

While the fifteenth-century theologian, Jean Gerson (d. 1429), draws the same distinction between commands and counsels as does Thomas Aquinas, he is led to a quite different set of conclusions.[19] The essence of the commands may be summarized for Gerson in the dual commandment of love of God and neighbor. Perfection is found, therefore, in the commands, in perfect charity, and not in the counsels which are added to the commands.[20] Counsels contribute instrumentally and accidentally to perfection, but not essentially.[21]

Vows, which have a central importance for Thomas, are downgraded by Gerson. The monastic vow only has an instrumental character.[22] Perfection can be reached without it, and *perfecti* can be found among the faithful in every *status*, *gradus*, and *sexus*. Gerson agrees with Thomas that a vow increases merit, since the offering of the fruit and the tree is worth more than the offering of the fruit alone.[23] Still he does not press the point and even observes that "many works completed without a vow are more perfect and better than some others that take their origin from a vow."[24]

The real attack on Thomas's thought is concentrated in Gerson's view that the state of the secular clergy is more perfect than the state of the religious. While the monk is obligated by his vow to acquire perfection, the bishop is obligated to exercise it in the church.[25] The task of the secular clergy is higher because it is directed toward the common good, whereas the monk's quest for sanctity is directed to his own private good.[26] Gerson can thus conclude that the status of a priest is higher than the status of the religious because of the greater proximity of the office of a priest to the office of a bishop.[27]

Gerson buttresses his argument by affirming that the priesthood was founded by Christ and therefore has its own independent dignity.[28] The priest is not the bailiff of the bishop but a minister in his own right. Indeed, the sanctity of ordination to priesthood is higher than the sanctity of monastic vows. Whereas a monk may be released from his religious vows, no power on earth can dissolve ordination to priesthood.

The locus of the state of perfection is found for Gerson above all in the office of a bishop and secondarily in the office of a priest.[29] The churchly dimension, which is also stressed in Thomas, receives greater attention at the hands of Jean Gerson. At the same time, Gerson is less interested in a spiritual elite than Thomas. He wishes to take mystical theology out of the hands of a favored few and make it the concern of the whole people of God. Perfection is found essentially in the commands, in the call to perfect love of God and neighbor that summarizes the whole law and prophets.

III

Very little is known for certain about John Pupper of Goch (d. 1475), one of the severest critics of Thomas's understanding of the religious life before the Reformation. He appears to have been a priest of the archdiocese of Utrecht, who founded a house of Augustinian canonesses in Malines in 1459 and who had previously been a rector in Sluis. He may have studied in Cologne, though that is subject to some doubt, or even in Paris, though that remains to be proven. His historical importance rests on four theological treatises he composed that attacked scholastic theology and monastic theory in the name of Christian liberty.[30]

Perfection consists for Goch in the perfect conformity of the will of the Christian to the will of God.[31] Goch resists both the Thomistic tendency to locate perfection in the intellect and the Franciscan propensity to equate it with poverty.[32] He finds no bar to perfection in the legal ownership of material goods, provided that the heart is not attached to its possessions.[33] To the degree that the will is conformed to the will of God, to that degree the believing man or woman is perfect.

Goch rejects the Thomistic understanding of the distinction between commands and counsels, though he does not reject the distinction as such or affirm with Gerson that one should seek perfection in the commands.[34] He argues, rather, that both commands and counsels belong to the one perfection of evangelical law and that both contribute to perfection in charity.[35] What Goch rejects is the notion that commands are for ordinary Christians while counsels are for the religious, who have bound themselves by a vow to seek perfection in love. All Christians stand under the claim of the whole law of God, which embraces both commands and counsels. If one objects that married couples are barred by that understanding from the higher degree of perfection that virginity confers, one may respond that most monks are similarly barred from the higher perfection granted to martyrs.[36] All the faithful are called to conform their wills to the will of God so far as the special circumstances of their own vocation and situation allow. All the faithful can merit beatitude, but not all can attain the same degree of perfection *in via*.[37] Some of the faithful embody the apostolic life more perfectly than others.

Goch does not, in other words, deny that there is a state of perfection. What he does find unacceptable is Thomas's contention that mendicant friars are in it. Goch's attack on the Thomistic understanding of the state of perfection concentrates on three points: (1) the meaning and importance of the religious vow; (2) the notion that the vow is a second baptism; and (3) the concept of ministry and ordination implicit in monastic theology.

Goch denies that the profession of vows has any warrant in the New Testament.[38] The exegetical evidence traditionally cited by monks and friars to buttress their claims is weighed briefly by Goch and found wanting.[39] Indeed, vows are incompatible with Christian freedom since they introduce an element of compulsion and constraint that is foreign to it.[40] The gospel is the message of the restoration of freedom to sinners to perform the will of God through charity. Whoever has been liberated by the Spirit to do God's will does not need the compulsion and constraint of vows and rules to elicit a grudging consent.

Goch dismisses with undisguised contempt Thomas's idea that a vow increases merit.[41] On the contrary, since vows are incompatible with Christian freedom, they tend to undercut merit.[42] Does that mean that a vow can never be meritorious? Goch is unwilling to go that far. A vow can be meritorious if it springs spontaneously from the activity of the indwelling Spirit and is accepted by God.[43] It is meritorious, not because it is a vow, but because God has accepted it.[44] The dignity of a vow is distinguished in no special way from the dignity of any good act of whatever sort.

If a vow is not automatically meritorious and even tends to undercut the merit of other acts performed because of it, of what use is a vow? Goch holds that monasticism and monastic vows are a positive constitution of the church.[45] Monasticism is not grounded in natural law nor in an explicit teaching of revelation, but in a tactical decision of the church to establish certain structures to gain certain ends. Monasticism was founded, not as the most exemplary form of the state of perfection, but as a hospital where the spiritually weak can be supervised and assisted to make at least some small progress in their spiritual life.[46] The mendicant orders are the home of the spiritually infirm rather than an encampment of the spiritually elite.

Goch does not appear to dispute the contention that monasticism is a state of penance.[47] The idea that the monk is one who performs perpetual satisfaction for his sins is not in itself an objectionable idea. Goch does not, however, accept the view of Thomas that monasticism is a second baptism in which monks who had previously died to sin now die to the world. Such a viewpoint tends to exalt the status of monks over the status of priests and laity. Goch rejects it by denying that it is in any sense possible to draw an analogy with baptism. It is not a vow but an intention that is required of the candidate for baptism.[48] Nor is baptism, which is necessary for salvation, in any sense comparable with religious vows, which are not.[49]

If Christian perfection is possible without a vow, does Goch reject altogether the notion of a spiritual elite? The answer, clearly, is no. The highest status in the church is the status of a priest, whose dignity derives from his ordination to celebrate the sacraments, above all, the sacrament of the eucharist.[50] The bishop does not differ from the priest in order but solely in jurisdiction.[51] Just as ordination to the priesthood is the highest order in the church militant, so, too, the state of a priest is the state of highest perfection.[52] Bishop and presbyter share the same order because each has an equal right to confect a valid eucharist. The priesthood as such is the state of perfection. With respect to jurisdiction, the bishop is a unique successor of the apostles; with respect to order, the bishop is only a priest among priests.[53]

While Goch rejects the notion that monasticism is a state of perfection and only admits in a very limited sense that it is a state of penance, he does not reject altogether the ideal of a common life. The best expression of the apostolic life is a community of Augustinian canons—that is, a community of secular priests—who live a common life with their bishop in obedience to both commands and counsels.[54] The pattern of life established by St. Augustine with his cathedral clergy and maintained by the Augustinian canons perpetuates the pattern of life taught by the apostles and given its highest expression in the relationship of Jesus to his disciples. While the mendicant orders have a foundation in the positive law of the church, the Augustinian canons can claim legitimation for their societies in revelation itself. The priesthood, Goch concludes, is the *status perfectionis* and the communal societies of priests the best embodiment of the apostolic life. On the whole, it is not surprising that the founder of a house of Augustinian canonesses should find in the Augustinian norm a corrective for the less authentic life of the mendicants.

IV

Calvin shares with Goch a respect for the moderate monasticism practiced by Augustine and uses Augustine's description of early monastic practice as a norm by which to judge the defects of contemporary monasticism.[55] It is clear, for example, that early monks thought of themselves as a community in aid of piety, whose rule was tempered by the goal of brotherly love.[56] Monks who could not live a celibate life were released from the community and allowed to marry.[57] Unlike modern monks who are constrained by rigid rules, ancient monks followed a flexible discipline moderated by the practical rule of charity.

Furthermore, ancient monks were more fully integrated into the life of ordinary Christian congregations.[58] They had no separate chapels of their own and worshiped in the parish church. While some monks were chosen to be clergy or bishops, most monks were not.[59] As monks they were not regarded by early Church Fathers as a separate order, but were ruled by priests. Jerome lists five church orders: bishops, presbyters, deacons, believers, and catechumens: "He gives no special place to the remaining clergy and monks."[60]

Indeed, Calvin wonders whether on Catholic principles priesthood and monasticism are not mutually exclusive.[61] A priest is ordained to a service of Word and sacrament in the world; a monk is called to a life of prayer and contemplation withdrawn from it. Gregory the Great had ordered abbots to withdraw from the clergy "on the ground that no one can properly be both a monk and a cleric."[62] To be sure, Calvin concedes, "some of the mendicants preach"; but "all the rest . . . either chant or mutter masses in their dens."[63]

Of course, monastic theologians may appeal to the decrees of Innocent and Boniface, which support the ordination of cloistered monks. But Calvin is unimpressed by innovations introduced into church life by medieval popes. "What sort of reason is this," he demands, "that every ignorant ass, as soon as he has occupied the see of Rome, may overthrow all antiquity with one little word?"[64] Calvin is far more impressed by the example of the early church that considered it "a great absurdity for a monk to function in the priesthood. . . . For when they are ordained they are expressly forbidden to do those things that God has enjoined on all the presbyters."[65]

The appeal of Catholic defenders of monastic life to antiquity is regarded by Calvin as a formal appeal devoid of content. The role of monks in early Christianity is strikingly different from their role in sixteenth-century society. "By this comparison of ancient and present-day monasticism," concludes Calvin, "I trust I have accomplished my purpose: to show that our hooded friends falsely claim the example of the first church in defense of their profession—since they differ from them as much as apes from men."[66]

Although Calvin prefers ancient monasticism to modern, he does not regard ancient monasticism as beyond criticism. Even ancient monks were not exempt from "immoderate affectation and perverse zeal" in the exercise of outward discipline.[67] While it is a beautiful act to abandon one's possessions for the sake of Christ, it is an even more beautiful act to rule one's household in the love and fear of God. Calvin rejects the ancient vision of voluntary poverty: *nudus nudum Christum sequens*.[68] Poverty is worthless if love is lacking. The story of the rich young ruler must be read in the context of 1 Corinthians 13. God calls us to perform the duties he has commanded. Withdrawal from the world to a contemplative life is finally for Calvin a lesser calling than an active life of obedient love in society.

Among the principal criticisms Calvin levels against modern monasticism is the charge that it is schismatic.[69] "All those who enter into the monastic life break with the Church" and every cloister and monastic house is a "conventicle of schismatics."[70] The schismatic character of monasticism is evident in the monastic understanding of the vow as a second baptism. A second baptism lacks biblical support and establishes "a double Christianity" that separates monks from the whole body of the church.[71]

The advocates of such a double Christianity claim to follow the counsels as well as the commands, but Christ's rule of life embraces both commands and counsels and is intended for all Christians.[72] All Christians, not merely the religious, are enjoined to love their enemies; all Christians, not merely monks and nuns, are forbidden to seek revenge. The Sermon on the Mount is not restricted to a monastic elite within the church. Indeed, the distinction between commands and counsels "never entered the minds of the ancients" at all. Every early Christian writer declares "with one voice that men must of necessity obey every little word uttered by Christ."[73]

Monks have set themselves further apart from ordinary Christians by claiming to be in a state of perfection. Calvin is well aware that to claim to be in a state of perfection is not to be confused with the claim that one is already perfect. "I am not ignorant," he observes, "of their sophistical solution: that monasticism is not to be called perfect because it contains perfection within itself, but because it is the best way of all to attain perfection."[74] This "intolerable mockery" deceives "untutored and ignorant youths." Moreover, it gives great honor to an institution nowhere approved by God and makes all other callings seem "unworthy by comparison." "How great an injury, I beg of you, is done to God when some such forgery is preferred to all the kinds of life ordained by him and praised by his own testimony?"[75]

Of the vows taken by religious orders the vow on which Calvin comments most extensively is the promise of perpetual virginity. Calvin shares the widely held Protestant viewpoint that celibacy is a gift and cannot be made a law for every person.[76] When Catholic defenders of celibacy point to the ancient order of widows as an example of a celibate community in the early church, Calvin replies that these widows were celibate, not as something religious in itself, but "because they could not carry on their function without being their own masters and free of the marriage yoke."[77] In order to avoid as much as possible a conflict between the calling of a widow and the normal desire for sexual fulfillment, Paul set an age commonly beyond danger for entrance into this group.[78]

At any rate, widows were never nuns.[79] Nuns offer their celibacy to God as some kind of service. Unlike widows who gave up family life in order to devote themselves to a life of strenuous activity for sake of the gospel, modern nuns are all too frequently idlers, who attempt to appease God with their songs and mumblings. Many take their vows too young and find themselves in difficulty, when they are no longer able to reconcile their vow of celibacy with their sexual longings.

The good news, however, is that monastic vows are not indissoluble.[80] Men and women who feel that they must keep on as celibate monks and nuns simply because at an early age they made a solemn promise to God should know that unlawful vows are not binding.[81] Otherwise Christians would be bound to what God does not require.

V

In the movement from Thomas Aquinas to John Calvin, the argument over the status of monks has come full circle. Thomas regarded both bishops and monks as participants in the state of perfection on earth, bishops by virtue of their perpetual cure of souls and monks by virtue of their vows. Secular priests and laity, who had no such perpetual cure, were excluded from the state of perfection. What separated monks from other Christians was the obligation they had incurred to keep the counsels as well as the commands.

Gerson agreed with Thomas that both monks and bishops were in a state of perfection, but emphasized that perfection was to be found in the commands rather than the counsels. Counsels play an instrumental rather than an essential role in the quest for perfection. Moreover, bishops were not only in a higher state of perfection than monks (a point admitted by Thomas), but even shared their dignity with secular priests (a point that Thomas explicitly denied).

Goch pushed the argument still further by stressing the sacramental equality of priests and bishops, who differ only in jurisdiction. The *status perfectionis* is the state of the priesthood as such, in which bishops share by virtue of their ordination to celebrate the eucharist. Goch rejected the Thomistic theology of the vow as a second baptism that added an additional dignity to good works and excluded monks from the state of perfection. Monasteries are institutions the church has created to assist the spiritually infirm.

Calvin took the argument to yet another stage when he suggested that the state of perfection is the state of every Christian, clerical and lay, who is discharging a lawful vocation. All Christians are bound to follow the rule of Christ whose final end is the perfection of the elect. The notion of a *status perfectionis* is, in a certain sense, broadened to include all the faithful, with the exception of monks and nuns, who are pursuing a vocation not authorized by Scripture. They, too, may be included in the state of perfection, rightly understood, if they will renounce their dissoluble vows, abandon their schismatic conventicles, and reintegrate themselves into the community of the faithful. The distinction between commands and counsels dissolves into a general obligation for Christians to keep every word of Christ and to reaffirm marriage as the normal state of the Christian man and woman.

If there is a distinctive note in Calvin's criticism of monasticism, it may lay in his emphasis on Christian unity. Calvin found no place for the monastic ideal, which he regarded as unavoidably schismatic, in a church that is one, holy, catholic, and apostolic. To tolerate monasticism is to admit a double Christianity, a second baptism, a dual path to the heavenly Jerusalem, and a spiritual elite. Whatever other faults monasticism might have had in Calvin's eyes, this fault alone was sufficient to condemn it.

NOTES

1. *Inst*. IV.xiii.15.
2. *Inst*. IV.xiii.15.
3. *Inst*. IV.xiii.15.
4. Comm. on Acts 15:5 (CO 48.342); II Cor. 10:12 (CO 50.120).
5. Comm. on Jer. 5:30–31.
6. *Inst*. IV.xiii.10; Comm. on II Thess. 3:11.
7. *Inst*. IV.xiii.15.
8. Thomas Aquinas, *Summa Theologiae* II–IIae q.186 a.1 ad 3. Cf. q.184 a.5 ad 2; q. 184 a.4 concl.
9. Thomas Aquinas, *Summa Theologiae* II–IIae q.184 a.4.
10. Thomas Aquinas, *Summa Theologiae* I–IIae q.108 a.4.
11. Thomas Aquinas, *Summa Theologiae* II–IIae q.184 a.5.
12. Thomas Aquinas, *Summa Theologiae* II–IIae q.184 a.7.
13. Thomas Aquinas, *Summa Theologiae* II–IIae q.184 a.6 ad 2.
14. Thomas Aquinas, *Summa Theologiae* II–IIae q.184 a.6 concl.

15. Thomas Aquinas, *Summa Theologiae* II–IIae q.184 a.7 concl.

16. Thomas Aquinas, *Summa Theologiae* II–IIae q.189 a.2.

17. Thomas Aquinas, *Summa Theologiae* II–IIae q.88 a.6.

18. Thomas Aquinas, *Summa Theologiae* II–IIae q.189 a.3 ad 3.

19. For a discussion of Gerson's criticism of Thomas, see D. Catherine Brown, *Pastor and Laity in the Theology of Jean Gerson* (Cambridge: Cambridge University Press, 1987), pp. 73–78.

20. Jean Gerson, "De consiliis evangelicis et statu perfectionis," in *Oeuvres Complétes*, III: *L'Oeuvres Magistrale*, ed. P. Glorieux (Paris, 1962), pp. 10–11. The treatise covers pages 10–26.

21. Gerson, *O'euvres Complètes*, p. 14.

22. Ibid., pp. 20–21.

23. Ibid., pp. 20–21.

24. Ibid., p. 21.

25. Ibid., p. 22.

26. Ibid., p. 25.

27. Ibid., pp. 23–24.

28. Ibid., p. 25.

29. Ibid., p. 22.

30. Goch's works include the following: *De quatuor erroribus circa legem evangelicam exortis et de votis et religionibus factitiis dialogus* (abbreviated as *Dial.*), ed. C. G. F. Walch, *Monimenta medii aevi*, Vol. I.4 (Göttingen, 1760), pp. 74–239; *De scholasticorum scriptis et religiosorum votis epistola apologetica* (abbreviated as *Epist. Apol.*), ed. C. G. F. Walch, *Monimenta medii aevi*, Vol. II.1 (Göttingen, 1761), pp. 1–24; *De libertate christiana* (abbreviated as *De lib. chr.*), ed. F. Pijper, *Bibliotheca Reformatoria Neerlandica*, Vol. VI (Hague, 1910), pp. 1–263; *Fragmenta* (abbreviated as *Frag.*), ed. F. Pijper, *Bibliotheca Reformatoria Neerlandica*, Vol. VI (Hague, 1910), pp. 267–347.

31. *Dial.* X.132, 138; XII.158; XVIII.186; XIX.196.

32. *Dial.* X.132, 135; XIX.191–92.

33. *Dial.* XXII.234–35.

34. *De lib. chr.* IV.10.247.

35. *De lib. chr.* IV.11.251.

36. *Dial.* XIX.194–95. Thomas Aquinas regards martyrdom as the *actus maximae perfectionis* (*Summa Theologiae* II–IIae q.124 a.3 and q.184 a.5 ad 3).

37. *Dial.* XIX.192.

38. *De lib. chr.* IV.1.226.

39. *De lib. chr.* I.6.53; *Epist. Apol.* 15.

40. *De lib. chr.* I.7.55.

41. *Dial.* XVII.181; *De lib. chr.* III.4.190–91, 5.193.

42. *Epist. Apol.* 19; *Dial.* XVII.181, XVIII.183; *De lib. chr.* IV.3.229, 4.231–32, 6.238.

43. *Dial.* XVIII.184.

44. *Frag.* 309. Cf. *Frag.* 307; *De lib. chr.* I.22.83, 23.85, 24.89, 24.90; II.23.128; III.4.191, 5.195.

45. *Dial.* XVII.178; XVIII.183.
46. *Dial.* XII.159; XIV.164–65; XV.167.
47. *Dial.* XXII.211.
48. *De lib. chris.* IV.1.228.
49. *Dial.* XII.153.
50. *Dial.* XX.199, 201, 205, 206.
51. *Dial.* XX.209–10.
52. *Dial.* XX.199, 201, 205, 206.
53. *Dial.* XX.209–10.
54. *Dial.* XX.212.
55. *Inst.* IV.xiii.9.
56. *Inst.* IV.xiii.10.
57. *Inst.* IV.xiii.17.
58. *Inst.* IV.xiii.14.
59. *Inst.* IV.xiii.8.
60. *Inst.* IV.iv.1.
61. *Inst.* IV.v.8.
62. *Inst.* IV.v.8.
63. *Inst.* IV.v.8.
64. *Inst.* IV.v.8.
65. *Inst.* IV.v.8.
66. *Inst.* IV.xiii.16.
67. *Inst.* IV.xiii.16.
68. *Inst.* IV.xiii.13.
69. *Inst.* IV.xiii.10.
70. *Inst.* IV.xiii.14.
71. *Inst.* IV.xiii.14.
72. *Inst.* IV.xiii.12.
73. *Inst.* IV.xiii.12.
74. *Inst.* IV.xiii.11.
75. *Inst.* IV.xiii.11.
76. *Inst.* IV.xiii.17.
77. *Inst.* IV.xiii.18.
78. *Inst.* IV.xiii.18.
79. *Inst.* IV.xiii.19.
80. *Inst.* IV.xiii.21.
81. *Inst.* IV.xiii.20.

14

Calvin and the Civil Magistrate

Philip Melanchthon has given us a great deal of light by reason of the outstanding character of both his learning, industry, and the skill in all kinds of knowledge in which he excels, in comparison with those who have published commentaries before him. His only object, however, seems to have been to discuss the points which were especially worth noting. He therefore dwells at length on these, and deliberately passes over many matters which can cause great trouble to those of average understanding.[1]

Melanchthon is the only commentator from Wittenberg that Calvin cites by name in the preface to his Commentary on Romans, though Melanchthon was not the first theologian on the Wittenberg faculty to lecture on Romans. Martin Luther[2] and Johannes Lang[3] had lectured on Romans before him. Their unpublished lectures are interesting as a chapter in the evolution of the new Reformation theology. But it was Melanchthon who served as the principal commentator on Romans at Wittenberg in the formative period of early Lutheranism, even when his reading of Paul differed from Luther's.

Calvin does not tell us which commentary by Melanchthon on Romans he is using. The question is not frivolous. Melanchthon's first commentary was an unauthorized edition, drawn from student notes and published in Nuremberg in 1522 by Luther without Melanchthon's approval under the title, the *Annotationes Phil. Melanchthonis in Epistolas Pauli ad Romanos et ad Corinthios.*[4] Melanchthon's second commentary, his *Dispositio orationis in Epistola Pauli ad Romanos*, was published in 1529 in Hagenau. The *Dispositio* emphasized the rhetorical rules which Paul used in the development of his themes.

In 1532 Melanchthon lectured once again on Romans. In these lectures from the period following the composition of the Augsburg Confession, Melanchthon attempted to clarify differences between Paul and Augustine (a tension which Luther was always reluctant to mention) and to define more precisely, with the help of Aristotle, the meaning of "righteousness." The 1532 lectures were published in the fall at Wittenberg as the *Commentarii in Epistolam Pauli ad Romanos*. A later edition of this work with a new dedication and various other changes was published in 1540. After the death of Luther and eight years before his own death, Melanchthon returned one final time to Romans, publishing his last commentary on this book, the *Enarratio Epistolae Pauli ad Romanos*, in 1556.

It seems unlikely that Calvin made use of Melanchthon's last commentary on Romans. Although both Melanchthon's last commentary and Calvin's final revision appeared in 1556, Calvin completed his revision no later than January 24, 1556 and thus so early in the year that it seems impossible for him to have made use of Melanchthon's *Enarratio*.[5] In all probability Calvin consulted the 1532 commentary by Melanchthon in one of its many printings. It seems likely that Calvin was influenced, if at all, by the mature rather than the young or aging Melanchthon.

I

I want to use Romans 13:1–7 as a focal point for a comparative study of the exegesis of these two seminal commentators on Paul.[6] Do Melanchthon and Calvin read this text in a similar way? How seriously should we regard Calvin's praise of Melanchthon's skill as an interpreter? Does Calvin read this text with spectacles provided by Melanchthon? Or does Calvin's criticism of Melanchthon's method imply a criticism of his substantive comments as well? To what extent can Melanchthon be numbered among Calvin's teachers in the art of biblical interpretation?

Melanchthon cites a wealth of authorities in his exposition of Paul, beginning with the Bible itself: Gen. 9:6, 14, 25, 41:40ff., Deut. 32:35, 2 Chron. 19:6, Ps. 82:6, Prov. 8:15, 16:11, Eccl. 8:8, Isa. 11:9, Jer. 29:7, Dan. 2:48, Micah 4:3, Matt. 5:39, 8:10, Luke 3:14, 22:25, Acts 5:29, 10:1ff., 15:10, 28, Rom. 12:19, 1 Cor. 6:7, 13:4–7, Col. 3:14, 1 Tim. 1:9, 2:1ff., and 1 Peter 2:13–18. Among the ancient authors he cites Aristotle, Plato, Xenophon, and Herodotus, and alludes to such other classical and historical figures as Alexander the Great and Julian the Apostate. More surprising are his allusions to Roman and canon law. He cites legal texts, ancient and modern, from Canon 12 of Nicaea to the Code of Justinian and from the Decretum of Gratian to the pronouncements of Innocent IV and John XXII. He even refers to such teachers of law as Baldus Ubaldus from the fourteenth century and C. Cassius Longinus from the first. While he does not mention any scholastic theologians, except Gerson by name, he does report in a general way on a question disputed by scholastic theology. Apparently, Melanchthon feels it is appropriate to enlist the full range of one's learning in the task of biblical interpretation and to exhibit that learning in the exegesis itself.

Calvin, astonishingly enough, makes few biblical allusions. He seems more interested in uncovering the *Sitz im Leben* of the text than in tracing parallel passages, however appropriate and suggestive. He believes that Paul wrote Romans 13 in order to restrain the "restless spirits" who thought that Christian liberty means the abolition of all earthly powers. Since the Roman Empire was involved in the persecution of early Christian communities, it seemed doubly absurd to many Christians to render obedience to authorities who were "contriving to snatch the kingdom from Christ." In Calvin's view it was, therefore, particularly important for Paul to lay great stress on the authority of magistrates. Calvin draws an analogy between the restless spirits of the first century and the malcontents of his own century, though the reference is veiled and no group is singled out by name.

Calvin's philological interests in this passage are fairly minor. He appeals to the causative *gar* in Greek (13:3a), mentions the Hebrew usage of the word, *praise* (13:3b), and alludes generally and vaguely to the political teaching of "the philosophers" (13:3b). He does not, however, cite a single authority by name, biblical, philosophical, literary, legal, or theological. Such citations appear to interfere with the "lucid brevity" for which Calvin is striving.

II

Several questions trouble both commentators. Who, for example, are the higher powers to whom Christians should be subject? Does Paul have in mind both secular magistrates and ecclesiastical superiors? Do Christians owe such powers unqualified obedience? On what grounds is obedience owed to any human power? May Christians discharge the role of a magistrate with a tranquil conscience? Or does obedience to God inevitably set Christians at odds with the state?

Identity of the Powers

There is a medieval exegetical tradition that identifies the higher powers to which Christians owe obedience as both secular and spiritual. According to this tradition, when Paul says that the ruler does not bear the sword in vain, he means both the physical sword of temporal magistrates and the spiritual sword of ecclesiastical prelates. Christians owe obedience to both, princes and bishops, and Paul is articulating a principle of universal applicability.

Sixteenth-century interpreters of Paul divide on this question and not necessarily along confessional lines. Thomas de Vio Cardinal Cajetan[7] and Girolamo Cardinal Seripando[8] think that Paul is referring solely to secular magistrates. Martin Luther[9] and Jacopo Cardinal Sadoleto[10] do not agree. In his 1515–1516 lectures on Romans, Luther argues that Paul had in mind both secular and spiritual authorities. Having made this point, Luther shows very little curiosity about secular rulers, who seem to him to be doing a capable enough job—certainly better than the spiritual authorities, whose stewardship of the church has left it in rags and tatters.

Sadoleto, on the other hand, agrees with Luther's reading of Paul's intention, but not with Luther's criticism of the church. For Sadoleto, the papacy is unarguably the highest of the higher powers. He therefore heaps scorn on the Protestants who grovel before petty German princes (whose title to power is often, to say the least, ambiguous) while rebelling against the spiritual sword held by the church, given directly to Peter by Christ.

In this dispute Melanchthon and Calvin side with Cajetan and Seripando against Luther and Sadoleto. Paul has in mind only secular magistrates. Whatever needs to be said about offices and order in the institutional church (and Melanchthon and Calvin agree that a good deal needs to be said) is simply not the subject of this passage. Calvin sums up the views of Melanchthon as well as his own when he writes:

> The whole of this discussion concerns civil government (*de civilibus praefecturis*). Those, therefore, who bear rule over men's consciences attempt to establish their blasphemous tyranny from this passage in vain.[11]

Grounds for Obedience

Melanchthon offers two grounds for the Christian's obedience to the magistrate. The first ground is reason and natural law. The gospel, after all, does not teach political science or offer a divinely sanctioned pattern for the state. The positive laws of the state are derived from the principles of natural law that are prehensible to human reason. Not every society views the fundamental principles of law in exactly the same way and there are legitimate differences between the polity of the Saxons and the French. When Paul urges every Christian to be subject to the higher powers, he does not expect Saxon citizens to obey the laws of France or the French to obey the laws of England. Nor does Paul expect all Christians to model their polity on the law codes of Moses. Indeed, in matters of polity the law codes of Moses are binding on Christians only to the extent that they conform to the principles of natural law.

On the other hand, reason has its limitations. It does not see that there is a second ground for Christian obedience in God's own ordination of the state and the rule of law. The state and the political order are ordained by God, not as an unavoidable evil that must be tolerated, but as a good that should be revered and celebrated. The state protects the bodily life of its citizens and promotes the welfare of the human race. The magistrate must be obeyed, not only because the rule of law is better for human life than anarchy, but because God has made such obedience mandatory. To disobey the state in those matters in which the state licitly commands is to commit mortal sin and put oneself in danger of eternal damnation.

There are, of course, objections that can be raised against this view. While Melanchthon only lists monks as critics who have misunderstood the intention of Paul in this matter, it is clear from the way in which he echoes the common objections of the Anabaptists to civil power that he has them in mind also. There are three objections which these critics lodge: (1) that the gospel commends nonresistance to evil; (2) that Christians are called to a higher moral standard than the law codes of the Roman Empire; and (3) that Christians cannot serve as magistrates.

The first objection is the one that seems to concern him most. Melanchthon repeats themes from Luther's social ethic when he distinguishes between public vindication of the law and private vengeance and between what one may do as a public officer of the state and as a private individual.[12] The gospel clearly forbids vengeance by private individuals. There is no divine sanction for blood feuds or mob justice. The right to reward the good and punish the wicked has been given by God to public officials who may wield the sword and shed human blood in the discharge of their public office. Kings have no more right to murder private enemies than do peasants. But unlike peasants they can execute criminals who have broken the laws and violated the just order of the state.

The second objection, that Christians are called to a higher moral standard than the minimal righteousness enforced by the law, is conceded. What Melanchthon denies is that commitment to a higher righteousness necessarily puts Christians in conflict with the requirements of the state. Melanchthon seems to see the higher justice of the Christian community as a completion or perfection of the lower justice of the state rather than as a dissent from it. Grace perfects nature; it does not abolish it.

The third objection, that Christians cannot be magistrates, is met by a flat denial. God has ordained this work, reason demonstrates its utility, and therefore Christians ought not to shrink from its demands. The service of the state is Christian service and the magistrate, the living law, is the highest embodiment of the political order. Even though Melanchthon does not call princes *Wunderleute* or disparage lawyers and law books in favor of the political intuitions of princes, as Luther sometimes does, he clearly regards the magistrate as more than a bureaucrat who applies society's rules to society's ills in a mechanical and unimaginative way. The magistrate is not a law clerk. The magistrate directs public affairs, inspires other public officials in the discharge of their duties, and even leads armies into battle. The task is as complex as the tangled affairs of human life to which it responds. Christians ought to be grateful for the state with its magistrates, laws, and judgments, and to give the state the reverence, honor, and support that is its due.

At this point Melanchthon launches a fairly long discussion of several matters, not all of which have been brought up by Paul, but all of which are implicit for Melanchthon in the Christian acceptance of a stable political order—namely, taxes, private property, enforceable contracts, and litigation. What Melanchthon wants to show, against Anabaptist criticisms of the political order, is that all of these matters are licit for the Christian. If the Anabaptists reject private property in favor of communal, if they refuse to pay war taxes, if they suggest that Christians may not sue Christians in court, they are in fact rejecting the higher powers to whom Paul commands all Christians to render obedience.

Calvin takes a somewhat different attitude about the state and its polity, though he agrees with Melanchthon about a number of issues. He agrees, for example, that the state has been ordained by God for the well-being of the human race and not as a punishment to afflict it. He agrees that the magistrate has a legitimate right to collect taxes, though he adds the caveat, missing from Melanchthon, that taxes are public property to be used in the promotion of the public good rather than private funds to be squandered by rulers in the gratification of their own lusts. He even agrees with Melanchthon that the magistrate has been given by God the right to shed human blood in the public interest.

But the tone of Calvin's exposition is quite different. There is less of a polemical edge, less inclination to bring up matters not explicitly brought up by Paul. Furthermore, whereas Melanchthon, breathing out counter-revolutionary sentiments, stresses the dark side of state power (such as its right to punish criminals and wage war), Calvin emphasizes the positive side of political order (such as the promotion of domestic peace and the prevention of armed conflict).

They even differ in their starting-points. While Melanchthon grounds the state in both human reason and divine ordination, Calvin stresses divine ordination alone. It is vain curiosity to ask by what right rulers rule. For Calvin, it is enough that they rule by divine ordination. To despise human government is to despise the providence which set that government in place. Rulers must be obeyed, not on the grounds of human necessity, but on the grounds of obedience to God.

Having taken this position, however, does not prevent Calvin from discussing the utility of the magistracy as an instrument for the promotion of the public good and the restraint of human wickedness. Sin is such a dangerous reality that anyone who opposes the legitimate functioning of the state marks himself as an enemy of the human race. Wicked rulers are to obeyed and even rulers who have no power to enforce their will on their subjects. Both Melanchthon and Calvin agree that there is no tyranny so vile that it lacks all semblance of justice. The duty to obey does not rest on the goodness of princes or on their power but on the commandment of God. Indeed, Calvin even ventures the uncomfortable suggestion that God may from time to time send malicious and tyrannical rulers to Christians as a just punishment for their sins.

Limits of Obedience

Since Melanchthon and Calvin have taken such a strong stand on the duty of Christians to obey magistrates, it will come as no surprise that they have very little to say about legitimate restrictions on that obedience. Melanchthon approaches the question from the perspective of the subject. Since Christians ought not to value their own judgments more than the judgments of their magistrates (and thus give those magistrates the benefit of any doubt), they cannot and should not obey princes or governors who command them to act against God or the laws of God. What Melanchthon seems to have in mind is civil disobedience rather than any form of armed rebellion. Still he does allow for passive disobedience.

Calvin, on the other hand, focuses on magistrates and the inherent limitations of their power. Magistrates are servants rather than lords. Their power is restrained and limited by what promotes the common welfare of their people. They are ministers and stewards of God and therefore answerable to God for abuses of their power. Calvin even suggests that dictatorships are not ordained governments, though he does not amplify what he means by that remark. We know from other contexts that Calvin does allow lesser magistrates the right to act in concert against the abuse of power by a despotic ruler. But since there is nothing in Paul's text on the subject of civil disobedience, Calvin does not bring the matter up.

Calvin may also ameliorate the absolute and unqualified nature of Paul's injunction to obey magistrates by his comments on the original setting of the text. Paul spoke so absolutely because he had to put an end to the fanaticism that believed redemption in Christ placed one outside the civil

order. Even un-Christian governments have their legitimate rights and are
owed honor, obedience, and taxes from their Christian subjects. Nevertheless, it is clear from what they say that both Calvin and Melanchthon are
uneasy with Paul's unqualified endorsement of the rights of the magistrate
and wish to soften it with themes drawn from elsewhere in the Bible.

It is also worth noting that Melanchthon's most enthusiastic endorsement of state power comes in the period immediately following the Peasants' Revolt and the Diet at Augsburg. The reformers at Wittenberg had
good reason to be grateful to Protestant princes for their protection and
optimistic about the benign influence of state power in furthering the cause
of the Reformation. By 1556 Melanchthon's early optimism has waned. In
his final commentary on Romans he presses the point that pastors have the
right to rebuke princes and to be obeyed in those matters that touch on the
ministry of the gospel. Whoever disobeys the divine commandments that
sound from the pulpit commits mortal sin. As an example of what he has
in mind, Melanchthon cites the excommunication of the emperors Theo-
dosius and Valens by Ambrose and Basil. For old Melanchthon, the church
has once again become a buffer against the unbridled power of the state.

III

It would be a mistake to draw large conclusions from such a relatively small
sample of the biblical exegesis of Calvin and Melanchthon. Nevertheless,
there are some observations that we can make.

1. At first glance Calvin and Melanchthon seem to form a common front
on the question of the power and legitimate functions of the state. However, when we look more closely at them we find there are in fact a great
many differences between their views, not all of which are attributable to
differences in method. It may, of course, be a difference in method that
prevents Calvin from talking about many of the questions concerning property, contracts, and litigation that seem to trouble Melanchthon. Calvin
usually reserves lengthy discussions of related issues to the pages of the
Institutes, where they do not interrupt the flow of biblical exegesis.

Less easy to categorize as a difference of method is Calvin's dismissal of
Melanchthon's view of the role of reason and natural law in providing a
foundation for the political order. Calvin does not, of course, contradict
Melanchthon's arguments or mention him by name. But he does relegate
Melanchthon's carefully articulated position to the realm of vain curiosity.
Vainly curious questions are questions that are neither necessary nor useful
to ask. They are, generally speaking, the kinds of questions scholastic theologians are inordinately fond of asking. Calvin, however, wants to follow
in his exegesis the simpler structure of Paul's argument. It is enough for

him to know that the political order in Strasbourg (and later in Geneva) is an order ordained by the providence of God.

2. Calvin and Melanchthon are both uneasy about the absolute endorsement of state power that Paul seems to offer. Each tries, in characteristically different ways, to soften that endorsement. Melanchthon appeals to the right of passive disobedience by ordinary Christians and the duty of pastors to confront the established powers in the name of the gospel. Calvin calls attention to the original setting of this passage and reminds rulers that the only legitimate state power is power directed toward the welfare of their subjects.

Still it does not appear that Calvin and Melanchthon have altogether escaped a reading of Paul that provides an ideological justification in religion for the power and privileges of the ruling classes. Melanchthon in particular lays such heavy emphasis on the rights and privileges of magistrates that Christian subjects are given almost no leverage against wicked and unjust rulers. Even the right of pastors to rebuke the powerful and defend the defenseless does not have the same force or reliability as a constitutional restraint. Will pastors protest in time? Will princes listen? Are ordinary Christians willing to suffer the grisly penalties of civil disobedience?

On the other hand, if Calvin and Melanchthon offer little in the way of restraint on the powerful, Paul offers even less. His statement is absolute; theirs at least is qualified. Both commentators have softened the seemingly harsh character of Paul's dictum by introducing qualifications not found in the text. Perhaps Calvin is right when he argues that Paul is combating a tendency toward an illegitimate freedom in the Roman Christian community. This is certainly the interpretation that Cajetan also embraces. Perhaps (as Calvin does not suggest) Paul is only articulating an interim ethic to describe Christian conduct in the brief period before the Lord's return. Whatever is the case, Paul provides the text that Melanchthon and Calvin must interpret and from which they cannot escape.

3. Confronted as we are by worldwide abuses of civil power, it is very difficult for us to see with Melanchthon and Calvin the state and the magistracy as good gifts of God. Understandably, our generation has been more interested in rediscovering the biblical underpinning for political dissent than in reevaluating the biblical basis for civil obedience. It may therefore be appropriate for us to engage in an experiment in thought, to look at government and political power with the eyes provided by these sixteenth-century commentators on Paul, to see the tolerably just state once again as a gift of God for the benefit of the human race. Anarchy does not provide the conditions necessary for the orderly development of human life and even revolutionary governments must build roads and bridges, regulate medications, grade meat, pay pensions, put out fires, arrest criminals, educate

children, provide water and sewers, certify drivers, collect customs duties and taxes, provide health care for the indigent and elderly, combat acid rain, protect endangered species, rescue flood victims, provide temporary shelter for the homeless, and defend the safety of its citizens.

Of course, we cannot and should not substitute the exegesis of Melanchthon and Calvin for our own. We stand in different circumstances and must discharge our theological task in light of the church's knowledge at the present time. We can, however, learn from Melanchthon and Calvin what we can no longer learn from each other—that a tolerably just political order enhances human life and that Christians have legitimate reason to be grateful for it.

NOTES

1. T. H. L Parker, ed., *Iohannis Calvini Commentarius in Epistolam Pauli ad Romanos* (Leiden: E.J. Brill, 1981), p. 2, abbreviated as Calvin, *Commentarius*. The Latin text of Melanchthon's 1532 commentary is found in *Römerbrief-Kommentar 1532*, ed. Rolf Schäfer, in *Melanchthons Werke in Auswahl* 5 (Gütersloh: Gerd Mohn, 1965). Melanchthon's 1556 commentary is published in the Corpus Reformatorum 15.

2. WA 56.

3. Reinhold Weijenborg, O.F.M., "Die Wittenberger Römerbriefvorlesung des Erfurters Augustiners Johannes Lang. Erstausgabe nach dem *Vat. Pal. Lat. 132* mit Einleitung und Kommentar," *Antonianum* 52 (1976): 394–494.

4. For a history of Melanchthon's commentaries, see the introduction by Rolf Schäfer, *Römerbrief-Kommentar*, pp. 15–24.

5. For the history of Calvin's commentary on Romans, see T. H. L. Parker, *Calvin's New Testament Commentaries* (Grand Rapids, Mich.: Wm B. Eerdmans, 1971) and Calvin, *Commentarius*, pp. ix–xvii.

6. Calvin, *Commentarius*, pp. 281–85; Melanchthon, *Römerbrief-Kommentar*, pp. 302–25. Cf. CR 15.1009–17.

7. Thomas de Vio (Cajetan), *Epistolae Pauli et aliorum Apostolorum* (Paris: Carola Guillard et Jean de Roigny, 1540), pp. 83–85.

8. Girolamo Seripando, *In D. Pauli Epistolas ad Romanos et Galatas Commentaria* (Naples, 1601), pp. 220–24.

9. WA 57.476–82.

10. Jacopo Sadoleto, *In Pauli Epistolam ad Romanos Commentariorum*, Opera Omnia 4 (Verona: Joannes Albertus Tumermanus), pp. 307–12.

11. Calvin, *Commentarius*, p. 285.

12. On this question see my essay, "Luther and the Two Kingdoms," in David C. Steinmetz, *Luther in Context* (Bloomington: Indiana University Press, 1986), pp. 112–25.

15

Concluding Observations

What holds this book together, aside from the fact that it deals in every chapter with the theology of John Calvin, is its methodology. The principal thesis of the book is, after all, methodological; namely, that the best and most productive way to study Calvin is to place him in the context of the theological and exegetical traditions that formed him and in the lively company of the friends and enemies from whom he learned and with whom he quarreled. In each chapter I have attempted to examine him in a some-what different context, comparing what he wrote with what had been written by a wide range of Christian theologians from Chrysostom and Ambrosiaster in the remote past to Tilemann Hesshusen and Ambrosius Catherinus Politus in his own time. The purpose of this exercise has not merely been to broaden our knowledge of the context within which he lived and thought, but to sharpen our image of Calvin by clarifying the actual range of intellectual options open to him.

If there is a subthesis, it is that, while every genre of Calvin's writings is important and none should be omitted, Calvin's biblical commentaries offer an opportunity for comparative study not easily duplicated in his other writings. By comparing his exegesis of Genesis 38 or Romans 7 with the exegesis of his contemporaries and the traditional authorities they routinely consulted, we can quickly gain a sense of the boundaries of the intellectual world he inhabited and identify what was original in his thought.

Of course, the test of any method is whether in fact it illuminates its subject. In that respect, the results of this inquiry have been, on the whole, gratifying. For example, the study of Calvin's interpretation of Romans 4 disclosed the unexpected depth of his dependence on antecedent exegetical tradition, not only for important theological insights (that, of course, was to be expected) but also for more trivial exegetical details. Similarly, a comparison of Calvin's exegesis of Romans 1 with the exegesis of a representative group of his friends and rivals clarified what one could never have learned from reading the *Institutes* in isolation; namely, that Calvin seems to have been alone or, at the very least, belonged to a tiny minority of his contemporaries, when he insisted on noetic impairment as a consequence of sin. These results are duplicated in other chapters, where we see Calvin embracing, modifying, or rejecting the options presented to him.

The picture of Calvin that emerges from this book is of a theologian who extols the ancient Christian Fathers and is clearly influenced by them, but who also maintains a fierce independence of their authority. He uses scholastic distinctions, but not always correctly, and even puzzles his own followers by his rejection of the distinction between the absolute and ordained power of God. He accepts the majority opinion that prefers the older Augustine's interpretation of Romans 7, but stands alone (or nearly so) in his emphasis on the noetic effects of sin in Romans 1. He is closer to Zwingli than to Luther in his opposition to the use of images but closer to Luther than to Zwingli in his doctrine of the eucharist (a point not conceded by Hesshusen). Like Luther, though with a somewhat different focus, he offers a christological interpretation of the story of Judah and Tamar; unlike Luther, he lapses into moralizing aphorisms. Although he is close to Thomas Aquinas and the ex-Dominican Bucer in his view of predestination (though without Thomas's inclination to engage in apologetics), he rejects the medieval tendency to draw a sharp line between the Old and New Testaments, especially with respect to the sacrament of baptism. He is heavily dependent in his biblical interpretation on antecedent theological and exegetical traditions, including what I have called, for want of a better term, *exegetical lore*. The weight of such exegetical tradition sometimes inhibits him from indulging opinions that he feels freer to express in his polemical or dogmatic writings. He repeats traditional criticisms of monasticism, some quite ancient, others developed in the high and later Middle Ages, though his principal objection is leveled against what he regards as its inherently schismatic character. While he offers an essentially positive account of the state and the role of the magistrate, he is, like Melanchthon, not satisfied to leave state power unqualified.

At the same time the results of this study cannot easily be reduced to a list of positions Calvin embraced, modified, or rejected. It is, of course, important to know that Calvin agreed with the older Augustine when he concluded that the divided self of Romans 7 referred to the life of believers under grace rather than to pre-Christian existence under the law. But such knowledge takes on a different weight and texture when we discover that a representative group of Calvin's contemporaries—Catholic, Reformed, and Lutheran—also agreed with this reading. From the perspective of the sixteenth century, it was therefore not astonishing that Calvin pitted the older Augustine against the younger; it would have been far more astonishing to his friends and enemies alike had he not.

Traditional Calvin scholarship has frequently been satisfied to study Calvin in greater or lesser isolation from his historical context and to reconstruct his theology with little or no reference to his contemporaries. For the most part these studies have focused on the internal logic and development of Calvin's thought and on the relationship of the parts to the whole. Often such studies were motivated more by systematic-theological interests than by historical. What seemed to interest their authors was a usable Calvin whose historical limitations could be transcended and whose theology could be invoked to reinvigorate the theological discourse of their own time; a Calvin who could address them, not as an alien figure from the past, but as a familiar contemporary.

Although this approach to Calvin has produced important studies of his thought, it has, by unnecessarily limiting the questions historians could ask and answer, left itself open to anachronistic misunderstandings. After all, Calvin is a citizen of his own age rather than ours, an inhabitant of early modern Europe who shared its unique glories and its sometimes brutal limitations. There is no way to modernize him without, to some degree, distorting his thought. As a theologian nurtured in the late medieval Catholic church, Calvin is uncomfortable in the world of traditional Protestants like Hodge and Barth. Whatever relevance Calvin may have for theology in the present is a relevance that acknowledges, even perhaps celebrates, the particularities of his location in space and time.

This book is an essay in historical theology. It has attempted to place Calvin squarely in his own age and evaluate him according to the standards by which he and his contemporaries judged themselves. The goal of this study has been to uncover the structures of Calvin's thought by clarifying the structures of thought of his immediate contemporaries. To achieve this goal, I focused on Calvin in the public act of interpretation and tried to explain what he was doing by explaining what other Christian theologians, past and present, have done when faced with the same texts. By doing so, this book has, I hope, furthered our understanding of the historical Calvin.

SELECTED BIBLIOGRAPHY

JOHN CALVIN

Iohannis Calvini Commentarius in Epistolam Pauli ad Romanos, ed. T. H. L. Parker. Studies in the History of Christian Thought 22. Leiden, 1981.

Ioannis Calvini Opera Quae Supersunt Omnia, 59 vols., ed. Wilhelm Baum, Eduard Cunitz, and Eduard Reuss. *Corpus Reformatorum* 29–87. Brunswick and Berlin, 1863–1900. Abbreviated as CO.

Ioannis Calvini Opera Selecta, 5 vols., ed. Peter Barth and Wilhelm Niesel. Munich, 1926–1952. Abbreviated as OS.

Opera Calvini denuo recognita. Geneva, 1992– .

Registres de la compagnie des pasteurs de Genève au temps de Calvin, 3 vols., ed. R. M. Kingdon and J. F. Bergier. Geneva, 1962–69.

Supplementa Calviniana, sermons inédits. Neukirchen, 1936– .

COMMENTARIES ON GENESIS

Alcuin of York. *In Genesim Quaestiones, a Menrado Moltero restitutae*. Hagenau, 1529.

Alsted, Heinrich. *Pentateucha Mosaica*. Herbord, 1631.

Babington, Gervase. *Certain Plaine, Brief, and Comfortable Notes, upon Every Chapter of Genesis*. London, 1592.

Becker [Artopoeus], Peter. *De prima rerum origine, et vita . . . patrum, ex libro Geneseos*. Basel, 1546.

Borrhaus [Cellarius], Martin. *In Mosem, divinum legislatorem, paedagogum ad Messiam servatorem mundi*. Basel, 1555.

Brocardus, Jacobus. *Mystica et prophetica libri Geneseos interpretatio*. Leiden, 1580.

Brucioli, Antonio. *Commento in tutti i sacrosanti libri del Vecchio et Nuovo Testamento, tomo primo*. Venice, 1544.

Calvin, John. *Mosis libri v cum Iohannis Calvini commentarii*. Geneva, 1563.

Capito, Wolfgang. *Hexaemeron Dei opus explicatum*. Strasbourg, 1539.

Chytraeus, David. *In Genesin enarratio*. Wittenberg, 1557.

Del Rio, Martin. *Pharus sacrae sapientiae*. Lyon, 1608.

Denis the Carthusian [Rickel]. *Enarrationes piae et eruditae in quique Mosaicae legis libros*. Cologne, 1534.

Drusius [Dreisschus], Johannes. *Ad loca difficiliora Pentateuchi, id est quinque librorum Moysis commentarius*. Arnhem, 1616.

Eitzen, Paul von. *Commentariorum in Genesim, liber primus*. Frankfurt, 1560.

Eugubinus, Augustinus Steuchus. *Cosmopoeia, vel de mundo opificio, expositio trium capitum Genesis, in quibus de creatione tractat Mosis*. Venice, 1591.

————. *Recognitio Veteris Testamenti ad Hebraicam Veritatem*. Venice, 1591.

Faber, Martin. *Glossa über die fünf Bücher Mose*. Jena, 1576.

Fabricius, George. *Commentarius in Genesin brevis, eruditus et valde utilis*. Leipzig, 1584.

Fagius [Büchlein], Paul. *Exegesis sive expositio dictionum Hrbraicorum literalis et simplex, in quatuor capita Geneseos*. Isen, 1542.

Fernandez, Benedict. *Commentariorum atque observationum moralium in Genesim*. Lyon, 1618–1627.

Gerhard, Johannes. *Commentarius super Genesin*. Jena, 1653.

Gesner, Salomon. *Genesis sive primus liber Mosis disputationibus xxxviii breviter comprehensus*. Wittenberg, 1603.

Gibbens, Nicholas. *Disputation concerning the Holy Scripture . . . the First Part of the First Tome*. London, 1601.

Honcala, Antonius. *Commentaria in Genesim*. Alcala, 1555.

Hugh of St. Cher. *Repertorium apostillarum utriusque Testamenti*. Basel, 1503.

Hyperius [Gerhard], Andreas. *De formandis concionibus sacris, seu de interpretatione scripturarum populari*. Marburg, 1553.

Lapide, Cornelius a. *Commentaria in Pentateuchum Moysis*. Antwerp, 1616.

Linck, Wenzeslaus. *Annotation in die fünf Bücher Mosi*. Wittenberg (?), 1543.

Lipomanus, Luigi. *Catena in Genesim*. Paris, 1546.

Luther, Martin. WA 42–44.

Lyra, Nicholas of. *Postilla super Genesim*. Nuremberg, 1498.

Maldonado, Juan. *Commentarii in praecipuos sacrae scripturae libros Veteris Testamenti*. Paris, 1643.

Marius, Leonard. *Commentariorum in universam s. scripturam tomus primus*. Cologne, 1621.

Marlorat, Augustin. *Genesis cum catholica expositione ecclesiastica*. Morsée, 1585.

Martinius, Matthias. *Commentariolus de creatione mundi*. Bremen, 1613.

Melanchthon, Philip. *In obscuriora aliquot capita Geneseos annotationes*. Hagenau, 1523.

Mercier, Jean. *In Genesin, primum Mosis librum sic a Graecis appelatum, commentarius*. Geneva, 1598.

Mersenne, Marin. *Quaestiones celeberrimae in Genesim*. Paris, 1623.

Musaeus, Simon. *Richtigg und reine Auslegung des ersten Buchs Mosy*. Magdeburg, 1576.

Musculus, Wolfgang. *In Mosis Genesim plenissimi commentarii*. Basel, 1565.

Oecolampadius, Johannes. *In Genesim enarratio*. Basel, 1536.

Oleaster, Jerome. *Commentaria in Mosi Pentateuchum*. Lisbon, 1556.

Palladius, Peder. *Librorum Moisi, qui sunt fons doctrinae ecclesiae, explicatio brevis et ad usum piorum accommodata*. Wittenberg, 1559.

Pareus, David. *In Genesin Mosis commentarius*. Frankfurt, 1609.

Pelargus [Storch], Christophor. *Commentarius in Genesin*. Wittenberg, 1598.

Pellikan, Conrad. *Commentaria Bibliorum, tomus primus.* Zurich, 1536.

Pepin, Guillaume. *Expositio in Genesin.* Paris, 1528.

Pererius, Benedict. *Commentarius in Genesin.* Cologne, 1606.

Pezel, Christophor. *In primum librum Mosis, qui inscribitur Genesis commentarius.* Neustadt, 1599.

Piscator, Johannes. *Commentarius in Genesin.* Herborn, 1601.

Pitigianis, Franciscus de Arreti. *Commentaria scholastica in Genesim.* Venice, 1615.

Politus, Ambrosius Catherinus. *Commentarius in Genesin.* Venice, 1551.

Rivet, Andreas. *Theologicae et scholasticae exercitationes centum nonaginta in Genesin.* Leiden, 1633.

Ross, Alexander. *An Exposition of the Fourteene First Chapters of Genesis by way of Question and Answer.* London, 1626.

Selnecker, Nicholas. *In Genesin, primum librum Moysi, commentarius.* Leipzig, 1569.

Spangenberg, Cyriakus. *In sacri Mosis Pentateuchum tabulae ccvi.* Basel, 1567.

Stephanus, Henri. *Commentarius in Genesin.* Augsburg, 1562.

Strigel, Victorinus. *Primus liber Moysi, qui inscribitur Genesis.* Leipzig, 1566.

Vermigli, Peter Martyr. *In primum librum Mosis, qui vulgo Genesis dicitur, commentarii.* Zurich, 1569.

Vio [Cajetan], Thomas de. *Opera omnia,* Vol. 14. Lyon, 1639.

Wild [Ferus], Johannes. *In totam Genesim enarrationes.* Cologne, 1572.

Willet, Andrew. *Hexapla in Genesin.* Cambridge, 1605.

Ystella, Luis Valentino. *Commentaria in Genesim et Exodum.* Rome, 1601.

Zanchi, Jerome. *De operibus Dei intra spacium sex dierum creatis opus.* Neustadt, 1591.

Ziegler, Jacob. *Conceptionum in Genesim mundi, et Exodum, Commentarii.* Basel, 1560.

Zwingli, Huldrych. *Farrago annotationum in Genesim.* Zurich, 1527.

COMMENTARIES ON JOHN

Alesius, Alexander. *Commentaria in Evangelium Ioannis.* Basel, 1553.

Arboreus, Johannes. *Doctissimi et uberimi commentarii in quatuor Domini evangelistas.* Paris, 1551.

Aretius, Benedict. *Commentarii in quatuor evangelistas.* Lausanne, 1581.

Arias Montanus, Benedict. *Elucidationes in quatuor evangelia Matthaei, Marci, Lucae et Johannis.* Antwerp, 1575.

Beda, Noel. *Annotationum Natalis Bedae Theologi Parisiensis in Iacobum Fabrum Stapulensem, libri duo, et in Desiderium Erasmum Roterodamum liber unus, qui ordine tertius est.* Paris, 1526.

Beza, Theodore. *Annotationes majores in Novum Dn. nostri Iesu Christi Testamentum.* Geneva (?), 1594.

Brenz, Johannes. *In D. Johannis Evangelion Exegesis.* Hagenau, 1528.

Brucioli, Antonio. *Nuovo commento ne divini et celesti libri evangelici secondo Mattheo, Marco, Luca et Giovanni, tomo quarto.* Venice, 1542.

Brunfels, Otto. *Annotationes in quatuor Evangelia et Acta Apostolorum.* Strasbourg, 1535.

Bucer, Martin. *Enarratio in Evangelion Johannis.* Strasbourg, 1528.

Bullinger, Heinrich. *In divinum Iesu Christi Domini nostri Evangelium secundum Ioannem commentariorum libri x.*

Calvin, John. *In Evangelium secundum Iohannem commentarius.* Geneva, 1553.

Chrysostom, John. *In sanctum Iesu Christi Evangelium secundum Ioannem commentarii.* Antwerp, 1542.

Chytraeus, David. *In Evangelion Ioannis scholia.* Frankfurt, 1588.

Cruciger, Caspar. *In Evangelium Iohannis apostoli enarratio.* Strasbourg, 1546.

Cyril of Alexandria. *In Evangelium Ioannis commentarii.* Basel, 1524.

Denis the Carthusian [Rickel]. *In quatuor evangelistas enarrationes.* Cologne, 1532.

Dietrich, Veit. *Annotationes compendiariae in Novum Testamentum.* Frankfurt, 1545.

Erasmus, Desiderius. *Paraphrasis in Evangelium secundum Ioannem.* Basel, 1523.

———. *In Novum Testamentum annotationes.* Basel, 1535.

Gagney, Jean de. *In iv sacrosancta Evangelia, necnon Actus Apost. facillima clarissimaque scholia.* Paris, 1631.

Gorran, Nicholas de. *Commentaria in quatuor Evangelia.* Cologne, 1537.

Guilliaud, Claude. *In sacrosanctum Evangelium secundum Ioannem.* Paris, 1548.

Gwalther, Rudolf. *In Evangelium Iesu Christi secundum Ioannem homiliae clxxx.* Zurich, 1568.

Hegendorf, Christoph. *Annotationes in Evangelium Marci, in Epistolam Pauli ad Hebraeos, in Epistolam Petri priorem, in passionem Matthaei, et Joannis.* Nuremberg, 1525.

Hemmingsen, Niels. *Commentariorum in sacrosanctum Domini nostri Iesu Christi Evangelium secundum Iohannem.* Basel, 1590.

Hunnius, Aegidius. *Commentarius in Evangelium de Iesu Christo secundum Ioannem, editio tertia.* Frankfurt, 1595.

Lee, Edward. *Annotationes Edovardi Leei in Annotationes Novi Testamenti Desiderii Erasmi.* Basel, 1520.

Lefèvre d'Etaples, Jacques. *Commentarii initiatorii in quatuor Evangelia.* Cologne, 1521.

Lossius, Lukas. *Annotationes scholasticae in Evangelia, quae leguntur in praecipuis festis sanctorum Iesu Christi.* Wittenberg, 1554.

Luther, Martin. WA 33, 45–47.

Lyra, Nicholas of. *Glossae in universa Biblia. Postilla.* Nuremberg, 1481.

Maldonado, Juan. *Commentarii in quatuor evangelistas.* Lyon, 1682.

Marlorat, Augustin. *Novi Testamenti catholica expositio ecclesiastica.* Geneva, 1593.

Melanchthon, Philip. *In Evangelium Ioannis annotationes.* N.p., 1523.

Musculus, Wolfgang. *Commentariorum in evangelistam Ioannem.* Basel, 1545.

Oecolampadius, Johannes. *Annotationes piae et doctae in Evangelium Ioannis.* Basel, 1533.

Pellikan, Conrad. *In sacrosancta quatuor Evangelia et Apostolorum Acta.* Zurich, 1546.

Piscator, Johannes. *Commentarii in omnes libros Novi Testamenti.* Herborn, 1658.

Rollock, Robert. *In Evangelium Domini nostri Iesu Christi secundum S. Iohannem.* Geneva, 1599.

Rupert of Deutz. *Commentariorum in Evangelium Ioannis libri xiii.* Nuremberg, 1526.

Salmeron, Alfonso. *Commentarii in evangelicam historiam et in Acta Apostolorum.* Cologne, 1602.

Sarcerius, Erasmus. *In Ioannem evangelistam iusta scholia.* Basel, 1540.

Sozzini, Fausto. *Explicatio primae partis primi capitis Iohannis.* Rakow, 1618.

Strigel, Victorinus. *Hypomnemata in omnes libros Novi Testamenti.* Leipzig, 1565.

Toledo, Francisco de. *In sacrosanctum Ioannis Evangelium commentarii.* Cologne, 1584.

Valla, Lorenzo. *In Novum Testamentum annotationes.* Basel, 1526.

Vio [Cajetan], Thomas de. *In iiii Evangelia, ad Graecorum codicum fidem emendata, commentarii luculentissimi, ad sensum literalem quam maxime accommodati.* Lyon, 1556.

Wigand, Johannes. *In Evangelium S. Johannis explicationes.* Königsberg, 1575.

Wild [Feri], Johannes. *In sacrosanctum Iesu Christi Evangelium secundum Ioannem enarrationes.* Mainz, 1550.

Zwingli, Huldrych. *In evangelicam historiam de Domino nostro Iesu Christo, per Matthaeum, Marcum, Lucam et Ioannem conscriptam.* Zurich, 1539.

COMMENTARIES ON ROMANS

Alesius, Alexander. *Omnes disputationes de tota Epistola ad Romanos diversis temporibus ab ipso in celebria Academia Lipsensi.* Leipzig, 1553.

Ambrosiastri qui dicitur Commentarius in Epistulas Paulinas; pars prima, In Epistulam ad Romanos, CSEL 81, ed. H. J. Vogels. Vienna, 1966.

Aquinas, Thomas. *Opera Omnia* 13. Parma, 1872.

Arboreus, Jean. *Doctissimi et lepidissimi commentarii in omnes divi Pauli Epistolas.* Paris, 1553.

Aretius, Benedict. *Commentarii in Epistolam d. Pauli ad Romanos.* Lausanne, 1579.

Arias Montanus, Benedict. *Elucidationes in omnia sanctorum apostolorum scripta.* Antwerp, 1588.

Beda, Noel. *Annotationum Natalis Bedae theologi Parisiensis in Iacobum Fabrum Stapulensem libri duo: et in Desiderium Erasmum Roterodamum liber unus, qui ordine tertius est.* Paris, 1526.

Beza, Theodore. *Annotationes maiores in Novum Dn. nostri Iesu Christi Testamentum.* Geneva, 1594.

Brenz, Johannes. *In Epistolam, quam Apostolus Paulus ad Romanos scripsit. commentariorum libri tres.* Basel, 1565.

Brucioli, Antonio. *Nuovo commento in tutti le celesti et divine epistole di San Paolo, tomo sesto.* Venice, 1544.

Bucer, Martin. *Metaphrases et enarrationes perpetuae epistolarum d. Pauli Apostoli. Tomus primus continens metaphrasim et enarrationem in Epistolam ad Romanos.* Strasbourg, 1536.

Bugenhagen, Johannes. *In Epistolam ad Romanos interpretatio.* Wittenberg, 1527.

Bullinger, Heinrich. *In sanctissimam Pauli ad Romanos Epistolam commentarius.* Zurich, 1533.

Calvin, John. *Commentarii in Epistolam Pauli ad Romanos.* Strasbourg, 1540.

Chrysostom, John. *In omnes d. Pauli epistolas commentarii.* Antwerp, 1544.

Colet, John. *Opera.* Reprint of 1867–76 edition. London, 1955.

Contarini, Gasparo. *Scholia in epistolas divi Pauli.* Paris, 1571.

Cornerus [Körner], Christoph. *In Epistolam d. Pauli ad Romanos scriptam commentarius.* Heidelberg, 1583.

Corro, Antonio del. *Dialogus in Epistolam d. Pauli ad Romanos.* Frankfurt, 1587.

Crellius, Johannes. *Commentarii in Evangelium Matthaei et Epistolam Pauli ad Romanos.* Rakow, 1636.

Cruciger, Caspar. *In Epistolam Pauli ad Romanos scriptam commentarius.* Wittenberg, 1567.

Denis the Carthusian [Rickel]. *In omnes beati Pauli epistolas commentaria.* Cologne, 1545.

Dietrich, Veit. *Annotationes compendiariae in Novum Testamentum.* Frankfurt, 1545.

Erasmus, Desiderius. *Paraphrases in omnes epistolas Pauli.* Basel, 1523.

————. *In Novum Testamentum annotationes.* Basel, 1535.

Gagney, Jean de. *Brevissima et facillima in omnes d. Pauli epistolas scholia.* Paris, 1529.

————. *Epithome paraphrastica enarrationum in Epistolam divi Pauli Apostoli ad Romanos.* Paris, 1533.

Grandis [le Grand], Nicholas. *In Epistolam ad Romanos aeditio.* Paris, 1546.

Grimani, Marino. *In Epistolas Pauli ad Romanos, et ad Galatas commentarii.* Venice, 1542.

Grynaeus, Johann Jacob. *Exegesis beati Pauli Apostoli ad Romanos.* Basel, 1591.

Guilliaud, Claude. *In omnes divi Pauli Apostoli epistolas, collatio.* Paris, 1548.

Gwalther, Rudolf. *In d. Pauli Epistolam ad Romanos homiliae.* Zurich, 1572.

Haymo of Auxerre. *In d. Pauli epistolas omnes interpretatio.* Cologne, 1539.

Haresche, Philibert. *Expositio Epistolae divi Pauli ad Romanos.* Paris, 1536.

Hemmingsen, Niels. *Commentarius in Epistolam Pauli ad Romanos.* Leipzig, 1562.

Hesshusen, Tilemann. *Explicatio Epistolae Pauli ad Romanos.* Jena, 1572.

Hugh of St. Cher. *In epistolas d. Pauli, Actus Apostolorum,* Epist. *septem canonicas, Apocalypsim b. Joannis, tomus septimus.* Venice, 1732.

Hunnius, Aegidius. *Epistolae divi Pauli Apostoli ad Romanos expositio plena et perspicua.* Frankfurt, 1590.

Hyperius, Andreas. *Commentarii in omnes d. Pauli Apostoli epistolas.* Zurich, 1584.

Knöpken, Andreas. *In Epistolam ad Romanos interpretatio.* Nuremberg, 1524.

Lang, Johannes. "Die Wittenberger Römerbriefvorlesung des Erfurter Augustiners Johannes Lang. Erstausgabe nach dem Vat. Pal. 132 mit Einleitung und Kommentar," *Antonianum* 52 (1976): 394–494.

Lefèvre d'Etaples, Jacques. *Epistole divi Pauli: cum commentariis praeclarissimi viri Jacobi Fabri Stapulen.* Paris, 1517.

Lonicer, Ioannis. *Veteris cuiuspiam theologi Graeci succincta in d. Pauli ad Romanos Epistolam exegesis.* Basel, 1537.

Lossius, Lukas. *Annotationes scholasticae in epistolas dominicales, et eas quae in festis Iesu Christi, et sanctorum ipsius praecipuis leguntur in ecclesia per totum annum.* Frankfurt, 1554.

Luther, Martin. *Der Brief an die Römer*, WA 56. Weimar, 1938.

Lyra, Nicholas of. *Glossae in universa Biblia. Postilla.* Nuremberg, 1481.

Major, George. *Series et dispositio orationis in Epistola Pauli ad Romanos.* Wittenberg, 1556.

———. *Enchiridion Epistolae S. Pauli ad Romanos.* Wittenberg, 1557.

Marlorat, Augustin. *In Pauli epistolas catholica expositio ecclesiastica.* Geneva, 1593.

Melanchthon, Philip. *Annotationes in Epistolas Pauli ad Romanos et ad Corinthios.* Nuremberg, 1522.

———. *Commentarii in Epistolam Pauli ad Romanos.* Wittenberg, 1532.

Musculus, Wolfgang. *In Epistolam Pauli ad Romanos commentarii.* Basel, 1555.

Mylius, Georg. *In Epistolam d. Pauli ad Romanos explicatio orthodoxa atque methodica.* Jena, 1595.

Ochino, Bernardino. *Expositio divi Pauli ad Romanos.* Augsburg, 1545.

Oecolampadius, Johannes. *In Epistolam b. Pauli Apostoli ad Rhomanos adnotationes.* Basel, 1525.

Oecumenius [Pseudo-]. *Commentaria luculentissima vetutissimorum Graecorum theologorum in omnes d. Pauli epistolas ab Oecumenio exacte et magna cura ad compendium collecta.* Paris, 1547.

Osiander, Lukas. *Epistolae S. Pauli Apostoli omnes.* Tübingen, 1583.

Pareus, David. *In divinam ad Romanos S. Pauli Apostoli Epistolam commentarius, editio tertia.* Heidelberg, 1620.

Pellikan, Conrad. *In omnes apostolicas epistolas, Pauli, Petri, Iacobi, Ioannis et Iudae commentarii.* Zurich, 1539.

Piscator, Johannes. *Commentarii in omnes libros Novi Testamenti.* Herborm, 1658.

Politus, Ambrosius Catherinus. *Commentaria in omnes divi Pauli et alias septem canonicas epistolas.* Venice, 1551.

Rollock, Robert. *Analysis dialectica in Pauli Apostoli epistolam ad Romanos.* Edinburgh, 1594.

Sadoleto, Jacopo. *In Pauli Epistolam ad Romanos commentariorum libri tres.* Venice, 1536.

Salmeron, Alfonso. *Commentarii in omnes epistolas b. Pauli et canonicas.* Cologne, 1604.

Sarcerius, Erasmus. *In Epistolam ad Romanos pia et erudita scholia.* Frankfurt, 1541.

Selnecker, Nicholas. *In omnes epistolas d. Pauli Apostoli commentarius plenissimus.* Leipzig, 1595.

Seripando, Girolamo. *In d. Pauli Epistolas ad Romanos et Galatas commentaria.* Naples, 1601.

Soto, Domingo de. *In Epistolam divi Pauli ad Romanos commentarii.* Antwerp, 1550.

Sozzini, Fausto. *De loco Pauli Apostoli in Epistola ad Rom. cap. septimo.* Rakow, 1612.

———. *Defensio disputationis suae de loco septimi capitis Epistolae ad Romanos.* Rakow, 1618.

———. *Explicatio primae partis primi capitis Iohannis. Adjectae sunt cap:9 Epist. ad Rom: et aliorum quorundam S. Scripturae locorum, eiusdem auctoris explanationes.* Rakow, 1618.

Spangenberg, Cyriakus. *Auslegung der ersten acht Capitel der Episteln Pauli an die Römer.* Strasbourg, 1566.

―――――. *Auslegung der letsten acht Capitel der Episteln Pauli an die Römer.* Strasbourg, 1569.

Strigel, Victorinus. *Hypomnemata in omnes epistolas Pauli et aliorum Apostolorum et in Apocalypsin.* Leipzig, 1565.

Theodoret of Cyr. *In quatuordecim Sancti Pauli Epistolas commentarius.* Florence, 1552.

Titelmans, Franciscus. *Elucidatio in omnes epistolas apostolicas, quatuordecim Paulinas, et canonicas septem.* Antwerp, 1529.

Toledo, Francisco de. *Commentarii et annotationes in Epistolam beati Pauli Apostoli ad Romanos.* Lyon, 1603.

Valdès, Juan de. *Commentario o declaracion breve y compediosa sobre la epistola de S. Paulo Apostol a los Romanos.* Venice, 1556.

Valla, Lorenzo. *In Novum Testamentum annotationes.* Basel, 1526.

Vermigli, Peter Martyr. *In Epistolam Pauli ad Romanos.* Basel, 1559.

Vio [Cajetan], Thomas de. *Epistolae Pauli et aliorum apostolorum ad Graecam veritatem castigatae, et iuxta sensum literalem enarratae.* Paris, 1540.

Weinrich, Georg. *Commentarii super auream et insignem d. Pauli gentium Apostoli epistolam Romanis inscriptam et nuncupatam.* Leipzig, 1608.

Wigand, Johannes. *In Epistolam S. Pauli ad Romanos annotationes.* Frankfurt, 1580.

Zwingli, Huldrych. *In evangelicam historiam de Domino nostro Iesu Christo, per Matthaeum, Marcum, Lucam et Ioannem conscriptam; epistolas aliquot Pauli annotationes.* Zurich, 1539.

THEOLOGICAL TREATISES

Beza, Theodore, *Abstersio calumniarum, quibus aspersus est Ioannes Calvinus a Tilemanno Heshusio.* Geneva, 1561.

―――――. *Kreophatia sive cyclops. Onos syllogizomenos sive sophista. Dialogi duo de vera communicatione corporis et sanguinis Domini adversus Tilemanni Heshusii somnia.* Geneva, 1561.

Biel, Gabriel. *Collectorium circa quattuor libros Sententiarum* IV/1, ed. W. Werbeck and U. Hoffmann. Tübingen, 1975.

Calvin, John. *Dilucida explicatio sanae doctrinae de vera participatione carnis et sanguinis Christi in sacra coena, ad discutiendas Heshusii nebulae.* Geneva, 1561.

Carlstadt, Andreas Bodenstein von. *Andreas Karlstadt, Von Abtuhung der Bilder*, ed. Hans Lietzmann, Kleine Texte 74. Bonn, 1911.

―――――. *Karlstadts Schriften aus den Jahren 1523–25*, ed. E. Hertsch. Halle, 1956.

Eck, John. *Enchiridion locorum communium adversus Lutherum et alios hostes ecclesiae (1525–1543)*, ed. Pierre Fraenkel, Corpus Catholicorum 34. Münster, 1979.

Gerson, Jean. *Oeuvres complétes* III, ed. P. Glorieux. Paris, 1962.

Goch, John Pupper of. *De quatuor erroribus circa legem evangelicam exortis et de votis et religionibus factitiis dialogus*, ed. C. G. F. Walch. Monimenta medii aevi I.4, 74–239. Göttingen, 1760.

―――――. *De scholasticorum scriptis et religiosorum votis epistola apologetica*, ed. C. G. F. Walch. Monimenta medii aevi II.1. Göttingen, 1761.

―――. *De libertate Christiana*, ed. F. Pijper. Bibliotheca Reformatoria Neerlandica VI, 1–263. Hague, 1910.

―――. *Fragmenta*, ed. F. Pijper. Bibliotheca Reformatoria Neerlandica VI, 267–347. Hague, 1910.

Hesshusen, Tilemann. *De praesentia corporis Christi in coena Domini*. Magdeburg, 1561.

―――. *Verae et sanae confessionis: de praesentia corporis Christi in coena Domini*. Erfurt, 1583.

―――. *Grundliche Beweisung der waren Gegenwart des Leibs und Bluts Iesu Christi im heiligen Nachtmahl*. Helmstedt, 1586/87.

Hubmaier, Balthasar. *Schriften*, ed. G. Westin and T. Bergsten. Gütersloh, 1962.

Hunnius, Aegidius. *Calvinus Iudaizans*. Wittenberg, 1593.

Klebitz, Wilhelm. *Victoria veritatis ac ruina papatus Saxonici*. Freiburg, 1561.

Pareus, David. *Calvinus Orthodoxus*. Neustadt, 1595.

Ursinus, Zacharias. *Catecheticas Explicationes*. N.p., 1623.

Westphal, Joachim. *Apologia confessionis de coena Domini, contra corruptelas et calumnias Ioannis Calvini*. Oberursel, 1558.

GENERAL INDEX

SCRIPTURAL CITATIONS INDEX

Printed in the United States
6760